SALT YOUR THOUGHTS

The Secret for Living a Productive, Effective, Fulfilled Life

Billy C. Mullins II

Copyright © 2024 by Billy C. Mullins II

All rights reserved.

No portion of this book may be reproduced in any form without written permission from the publisher or author, except as permitted by U.S. copyright law.

This publication is designed to provide accurate and authoritative information in regard to the subject matter covered. It is sold with the understanding that neither the author nor the publisher is engaged in rendering legal, investment, accounting or other professional services. While the publisher and author have used their best efforts in preparing this book, they make no representations or warranties with respect to the accuracy or completeness of the contents of this book and specifically disclaim any implied warranties of merchantability or fitness for a particular purpose. No warranty may be created or extended by sales representatives or written sales materials. The advice and strategies contained herein may not be suitable for your situation. You should consult with a professional when appropriate. Neither the publisher nor the author shall be liable for any loss of profit or any other commercial damages, including but not limited to special, incidental, consequential, personal, or other damages.

First edition 2024

Introduction

IF YOU USE THIS book and the website as they are designed, they will become your own personal life coach — one that you will utilize for the rest of your life. The book will guide you through a process where you define and determine your life's desired outcomes, your dreams, and your goals, while the software will provide the tools you need to execute your plan.

The life principles and natural laws I share in this book did not originate with me. I have gathered them through my own life's journey and by reading and studying wisdom literature, including the Bible. I have organized these principles and natural laws in a specific pattern that I call **SALTing Your Thoughts**.

Salt enhances the flavor of any food. It sweetens the sour, enhances the sweet, and preserves what it touches for future use. Likewise, SALT — a **S**ystem to **A**lter Your **L**ife **T**houghts — does the exact same thing for your mind. It sweetens the sour, enhances the sweet, and preserves your mind for future use. I have SALTed My Thoughts for as long as I can remember.

I believe SALTing Your Thoughts is the true secret for living a productive, effective, and fulfilled life.

In Proverbs 23:7 (New American Standard Bible 2020), Solomon — the wisest man who ever lived — said, "For as he thinks within himself, so is he." This simple and yet profound proverb is the subject of this book.

This book is designed to challenge your mind and assist you in defining your purpose in life. To do that, I must challenge your worldview. I will endeavor to scientifically demonstrate to you that all energy is connected to a single source of Energy that emanates from God who created this universe and everything in it.

You must ultimately determine if you believe you are a random error in the great cosmos or an individual made by a Master Designer who created you for a specific purpose.

I choose to believe God longs for an intimate relationship with each of us. He continually reaches out to connect us with His Energy, His Spirit, and His Power.

I also believe you were uniquely designed to be a receptor for His Energy. This book provides you with a process you can use to connect with God and His Energy every morning. Aligning yourself with God's positive Energy every morning enables positive energy to flow through you all day. This engages the Reticular Activation System of your brain to prioritize the things you have identified as important in your life. SALTing Your Thoughts enables you to abide in Him 24/7.

The Speed of Information

Our world is happening at such a blistering pace. It brings challenge upon challenge to us as individuals, spouses, families, and as a society. We make knee-jerk decisions while rarely evaluating their implications. We have been programmed to react and not to think.

Professional marketers are paid large sums of money to identify and exploit fixed-action pattern stimuli that produce a "yes" response. These professional marketers are measured and compensated based on how much they can influence you, the buyer in the market. The desired outcome is to influence you to buy without thinking.

This is why it is so important to SALT Your Thoughts.

You are much more likely to be triggered into a fixed-action pattern response when you lack the time, energy, or cognitive resources to undertake a complete analysis of the situation. **When you are rushed, stressed, uncertain, indifferent, distracted, or fatigued, you tend to focus on less of the information available to you.** Unfortunately, most of us are rushed, stressed, uncertain, indifferent, distracted, or fatigued on a daily basis!

If you make decisions under these circumstances, you will most likely revert to the primitive single-piece-of-good-evidence approach that results in a fixed-action pattern response. Fixed-action patterns cause you to make stimulus/response decisions without thinking.

This book is designed to help you gain control of your life. It will teach you how to avoid a fixed-action pattern response. Most of all, this book will teach you how to **think**. Remember, you are what you think!

The Structure of This Book

I begin each chapter with a quote from a notable person that relates to the chapter's subject matter. Then I share what my friends and family refer to as a "Billy story," a tale from my own life that relates to the specific learning in that chapter. Then I present the primary learning material for the chapter, which concludes with an assignment.

When you have completed all the assignments of this book, you will have designed your **Master Vision Board for Your Life**. Each assignment builds on the previous one, so it is important to complete each one with sincere effort to ensure you have captured the essence of who you are with as much accuracy as possible.

This book is organized around the pattern of seven primary and fundamental principles that define the cognitive cause/effect relationship that begins with your **thought** and results in your **behavior**.

1. Your **thoughts** are the source and cause of your beliefs *(The Way You Think)*.

2. Your **beliefs** drive your attitudes *(The Way You Feel)*.

3. Your **attitudes** drive your needs *(The Way You Are Motivated)*.

4. Your **needs** drive your behaviors *(The Way You Act)*.

5. You can **choose** to use your self-awareness, your imagination, your conscience, and your independent will to plainly state to your subconscious mind exactly what you choose to think, believe, feel, need, and do!

6. Any lasting modification, change, or improvement of any behavior can only be achieved by changing it at its source — the **thought**.

7. Changing your behavior at its source (thoughts) is what I call **SALTing Your Thoughts**.

Beliefs

Are you making decisions today based on what is most important in your life? Have you ever taken the time to identify your own critical personal beliefs and values?

This book will help you identify your personal beliefs and the values associated with your beliefs. It will also provide you with a system to make decisions every day that are congruent with your beliefs. This is the primary antidote for stress and frustration.

The process to identify what is important to you begins by articulating your thoughts into the beliefs associated with them. But concentration and focus are hard. Concentration and focus do not come naturally to most of us. Yet they are essential habits to develop if you desire to be in control of your thoughts and your destiny. **A thought concentrated on a specific purpose is power**.

I cannot overemphasize how important it is to identify your core beliefs. I started my list when I was 12 years old. My mother had just been killed in an automobile accident on her way to work. I started my list to help me remember the principles she taught me from a young age.

As of the writing of this book, I have compiled a list of 78 core beliefs. Here are my top 25:

1. Everything happens for a reason. There are no coincidences.

2. MY behavior is a function of MY DECISIONS, not MY conditions.

3. It is better to focus on things within my control, rather than things I can do nothing about.

4. Great Success is often preceded by what others would call Failure.

5. The most effective mode of communication is Adult to Adult.

6. Everything that happens to me and mine is Father-filtered.

7. Decisions bring consequences. (Some good; some bad.)

8. Nothing that has ever happened to me, or will happen to me, will define me.

9. It is better to take responsibility for my decisions, than to blame others for it.

10. Nothing worthwhile in life comes easy.

11. Communication is one of the most important skills in life.

12. There are Natural Laws that govern human effectiveness.

13. Discipline is the bridge between goals and accomplishments.

14. My thoughts are the source of my beliefs.

15. My beliefs are the habits of my mind. *(The Way I Think)*

16. My beliefs have a cause-and-effect impact on my attitudes. *(The Way I Feel)*

17. Like attracts like.

18. Joy is not a response; it is a choice.

19. The secret of getting ahead is getting started.

20. There are NO quick fixes!

21. Natural Laws are deep fundamental truths that have universal application.

22. I am the salt of the earth.

23. I must find a job (profession) where I have both the INTEREST and the APTITUDE to be successful.

24. Never confuse MOTION with MOTIVATION. (Being BUSY does not equal being EFFECTIVE.)

25. Most things are better when it takes a little sweat to get it.

My Challenge to You

Most people live their whole life and do not identify what is truly important to them until their death bed. I do not want that to be your story.

I challenge you to set aside the time you need to identify:

- Your **Beliefs**: The way you choose to think

- Your **Attitudes**: The way you choose to feel

- Your **Needs**: The way you are motivated

- Your **Behaviors**: The way you choose to act

I challenge you to **choose** to use your self-awareness, your imagination, your conscience, and your independent will to plainly state to your subconscious mind exactly what you choose to think, believe, feel, need, and do!

When you identify behaviors in your life that you would like to modify or improve, remember: Any lasting modification, change, or improvement of any behavior can only be achieved by changing it at its source — the thought.

Finally, I will share with you the secret for living a productive, effective and fulfilled life and teach you how to **SALT Your Thoughts**.

This is your life, your plan — **NOW, GO MAKE IT HAPPEN!**

Acknowledgements

Everything happens for a reason. There are no coincidences. This work summarizes my own life's journey. It is the culmination of my experiences, education, study of wisdom literature and guidance from the Supreme Power in this universe – The Creator God.

For the development and production of this book I feel I must acknowledge some key contributors, because without them this book would not have happened!

- To God (my Lord) for being the "great I AM," and to the Holy Spirit for guiding me, inspiring my thoughts, and helping me write the principles of life that can positively impact the lives of the readers. And to Jesus for providing us a pathway back to God, for being the Savior of this universe.

- To Martha Hyde (my mother) for being my lighthouse and inspiration. The principles she taught me at an early age became my navigational aid to guide me through life! Even though she tragically died when I was 12, I wrote them down so I would never forget them! Her world view, her approach to life, her conviction, her example, her tenacity, her intelligence and the love she bestowed upon me everyday provided the foundation of who I am today!

- To Sandra (my wife) for her insights and the many hours she has spent word-smithing, listening to my every word and breath for this book, her constant encouragement to write my thoughts down believing in me, and believing my thoughts will make a difference in the lives of the readers around the world! She has been by my side constantly over the past 2 years that it has taken to complete this book. She inspires me to BE a better person every day. Sandra, You are my best friend! I love you with all my heart. Thank you for your contributions and the sacrifices you have made to make this book possible!

- To Isabella (my daughter) for being the catalyst to write this book in the first place! Thank you for contributing your artistic gifts to the cover of the book and to the beginning of each chapter. Isabella, I am so proud to be your stepdad and to be a part of your daily life! It is my desire that you, your generation, and for those to come to use this book as a life coach. Learn to SALT Your Thoughts every day! I love you and I am thankful for all of your contributions.

- To Trey (my son) for the many hours of encouragement and all the time he spent producing the audio version of this book! I am so blessed that my best "guy" friend is my son! Trey, thank you for the studio time, your love and encouragement. I love you and I value and appreciate our time together.

- To Jeana (my oldest daughter): I love you very much!

- To the late Stephen Covey for writing *The 7 Habits of Highly Effective People*! It has been a powerful piece of wisdom literature for me! I read it 1-4 times per year and have done so for the past 30 years!

- To the late Viktor Frankl for writing the book, *Man's Search for Meaning*. His premise is that between stimulus and response there is a space; in that space is our power to choose our response; and in our response lies our growth and our freedom. He illuminated the fact that humans have four unique attributes: 1) Self-Awareness, 2) Imagination, 3) Conscience and 4) Independent Will. I endeavor to utilize those attributes every day and encourage you to do the same!

- To Ryan Haddock for editing the book. Thank you for your patience through the many changes and edits.

- To Bujorel Tecu for taking my ideas and making them come to life through software! I believe this software will enable people all around the world to SALT Their Thoughts!

- To Bill Quick for providing his beautiful painting of Jesus' Feet!

Contents

Part 1
The Foundation

    1. Go Make It Happen!   3
    2. Sowing Seeds   23
    3. You Have The Power!   31
    4. What Are Thoughts?   37
    5. How Do I Start SALTing My Thoughts?   45
    6. How Do My Thoughts Affect Me?   55

Part 2
Your Beliefs: The Way You Choose to Think

    7. Your Beliefs Are Important   63
    8. Where Do You Come From?   69
    9. Remember Grateful Moments   81
    10. Find Your Joy   87
    11. Keep Your Finger On Your Triggers!   93
    12. What Do You DO?   99

Part 3
Your Attitudes/Needs: The Way You Choose to Feel

    13. I Finally Understand Me!   111

14.	Seek Pleasure & Avoid Pain	127

Part 4
Your Needs: The Way You Are Motivated

15.	What Do You Need?	139
16.	Push The Reset Button!	151

Part 5
Your Behaviors: The Way You Choose to Act

17.	What Is Success?	165
18.	Who Am I?	175
19.	Visualize That!	183
20.	Does It Really Matter?	191
21.	Your Vision Board	201

Part 6
The System: Execute Your Plan

22.	Execution	207
23.	Your New Morning SALT Ritual	213

Part 7
Tools for Measuring Your Progress

24.	What Gets Measured Gets Done!	233
25.	You Are Not A Victim!	241
26.	Everything In Its Place	247
27.	Are You Even Speaking The Same Language?	255
28.	How To Make Good Decisions	273
29.	Don't Forget To Think!	283

Assignments By Chapter	299
About the Author	305
Endnotes	307

PART 1

The Foundation

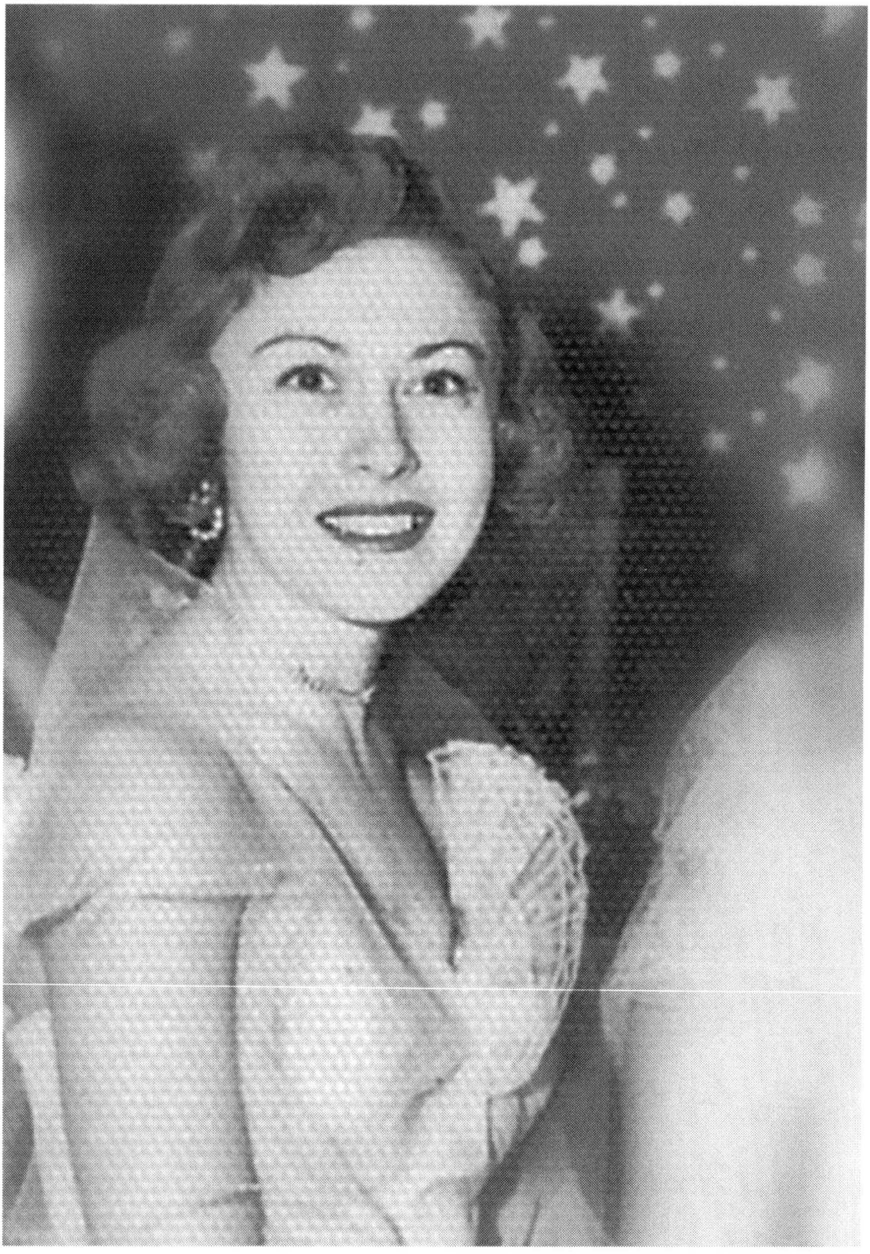

Chapter 1

GO MAKE IT HAPPEN!

"Our choices are shaped by what we believe is real and true, right and wrong, good and beautiful. Our choices are shaped by our worldview."
Chuck Colson

BOTH THIS BOOK AND the corresponding website were born from my desire to help my 15-year-old daughter Isabella identify her career path. I have assisted hundreds of people through this process in the past, but somehow this time was different.

I had sold my software company four years earlier, and I had been enjoying my retirement. But as I re-engaged my mind on this familiar task, I realized that it would be so much more impactful and effective for my daughter if I could somehow not just help her with career planning, but also *life* planning.

Many people have had tremendous professional success yet have lost any real connection with themselves. Their financial success has not resulted in real happiness. They find themselves living a duplicitous life, incongruent with who they intended to be. As I pondered the future for my daughter, I became compelled to teach her about human effectiveness and provide her with tools she could use for the rest of her life to stay connected with who she intends to be.

As I started to design a System to Alter her Life Thoughts (SALT), I realized the power of this system and became driven to share it with all who would take the time to listen. But, to better understand my motivation and my belief in the power of thought, I'd like to share my story.

I grew up on a working farm in Crossville, Alabama. We grew feed corn, soybeans, and pimento peppers. We got a penny a pound picking peppers, and if we complained, we got a penny a pound to pick cotton! (It takes a lot more cotton to make a pound than it does peppers!)

The Farm House

On October 27, 1973, my mother was killed in a car accident by a 17-year-old drunk driver. I was only twelve years old. She was a nurse. She hadn't been scheduled to work that night, but she was called in to help because the hospital was short staffed. My mother taught me that there is a Higher Power (whom I call God) who is connected to everything, and there is nothing that is not in His control.

She believed that *Everything Happens for a Reason* and that *There Are No Coincidences*. So, at the age of twelve, I chose to think and believe as my mother did — that God is in control. I remember with vivid detail my anger and rage, thinking, *If I don't let this go, it will hurt me the rest of my life.*

You can't live in the past. You must let the past go, or it will eat you alive! You must move forward!

The Pimento Pepper Field

The day of my mother's funeral, I was inspired to hug the 17-year-old who had killed her (we went to the same school) and tell him I forgave him. I told him that somehow this was all in God's plan.

I am grateful for the time I had with my mother. Many of the life principles I will share in this book came from the influence she had on my life. I think about them all the time!

I have two older sisters and a younger brother. After my mother was killed, my father decided the best thing for him to do was to send us all to a Christian boarding school. As the oldest boy, he told me that he was not going to be able to afford my tuition and that I would need to find jobs at the school to pay my own way.

As I signed up for my freshmen classes that year, I found out that the tuition fees were a flat rate. I thought, *Maybe I can take high school in three years instead of four and save a whole year of tuition!* So, I asked the registrar if that would be possible. She worked with me, and we planned a strategy to take four years of high school in three years. I worked three jobs during the school year and summers, but when I graduated in 1978, my tuition was paid in full!

During the fall of 1978, I enrolled in college. My father told me that since he had not paid for my high school, he would pay for my college as long as I didn't date. I made it two weeks and called to see if we could renegotiate, and he told me I was on my own.

My Mother, in the kitchen — the place where she taught me about life.

Easter Weekend, 1965

Being seventeen, the only jobs I could get were on campus, and campus jobs didn't pay very well. There was a food manufacturing company about a mile from the college that paid much better, so I set my sights to work there once I turned eighteen. My birthday is February 27th. In 1979, it fell on a Tuesday during the week of spring break. My roommate's family had a summer home in Destin, Florida, and they had invited me to join them for the week. I returned to college on Sunday, March 4th.

My father had called every week in February reminding me how important it was for me to get the job at the manufacturing company as soon as I turned 18. So, on Sunday March 4th, my father called once again and this time he asked, "Have you got that job yet?" I knew he would have been disappointed to know I went on spring break and didn't go apply on the day of my birthday. So, I said, "Yes, Dad. I start tomorrow". That's all he wanted to know, so he hung up.

On Monday morning, I thought about the long lines of applicants I had seen waiting to apply for jobs with this food manufacturing company. So I got up at 5:00 a.m. because I didn't have a car, and I knew I would have to walk to the company to apply for the job.

I arrived at the food manufacturer's door at 6:00 a.m. The doors opened at 8:00 a.m., and I was the first in line of about 300 people. I completed the employment application form and gave it to the receptionist. I applied for a full-time position on second shift. She very kindly thanked me for applying and told me I should hear something in the next 4-6 weeks. I quickly explained that I needed to start that day. She explained that it just didn't work that way. I thought, *What if someone doesn't show up for their interview? Maybe I could take their place!*

From the age of 14 onward, I was on my own.

I asked her if they had interviews scheduled for that day. She explained that they did, but that they were for people who had applied 4-6 weeks earlier. I asked her if I could sit in the lobby and see if anyone did not show up for their interview. She told me I could wait, but, even if someone didn't show up, there was no guarantee I could get an interview. I told her that I understood, but asked her to let the person interviewing know I was there and that I wanted to interview today. She said she would.

I sat there and watched from 8:00 a.m. until 5:00 p.m. It appeared to me that there were four interviewers (two men and two women). Each interviewer interviewed about four people every hour. I thought, *Wow! That is 128 people trying to get jobs just this day. I wonder how many days a week they*

First year of college at 17 — Ready to make it happen!

do this? It didn't look to me like there was anyone who was going to miss their interview. I thought and *believed* with all my heart that if I stayed there all day long someone would give me an interview. I *knew* if I could get an interview, I would get a job!

One of the interviewers seemed to notice that I was in the same seat all day long. At 5:00 p.m. he finally asked the receptionist, "Who is that guy? He has been sitting there all day." She explained that I had just turned in my application that morning and I was hoping to get an interview. He looked up at me and said, "Come on back, I will interview you."

My thoughts had become reality. At that moment I remembered what my mother always said: "Billy, if you want it, go make it happen!" So I jumped up with the biggest grin anyone could have ever had and went in for my interview.

My interview was pleasant. I was given a dexterity test to measure my hand-eye coordination. I knew my hand-eye coordination was good from working on the farm, as well as from the intramural sports I played in high school. Upon the completion of the test, he thanked me for staying all day and interviewing with him, and then he explained that I should hear something within the next two weeks.

I noticed that there was a book on his desk by his phone that looked like a ledger of some kind. I thought, *I bet he keeps the openings he is trying to fill in that book. I bet the worst job in that book is better than cleaning out the stalls on the farm. If I can help him by taking a job no one else wants, we both win.*

I pointed at the book and said, "Mister, I understand that you don't know me, but I grew up on a farm, and there is not a job in this plant that I am not willing to do. I know you have jobs in that book that will be hard for you to fill. Please, look in that book and find the worst job you have. I will take it if I can start tonight. I told my dad that I had a job starting tonight, and I don't want to be a liar!"

He looked at me and said, "Are you serious?"

And I said, "Yes sir, I am. I will take the worst job you have as long as I can start tonight."

He opened his book, thumbed through a few pages, and said, "How does 2:30 a.m. to 6:30 a.m. sound to you? It is the lowest paying job I have, and it is only part-time. I have been trying to fill this position for the last 2 weeks." I asked, "Can I start tonight?" He said with a big smile on his face, "Yes you can!"

I started that night! I called my dad the next day and told him about my new job. As I was going through the interviewing process, I thought to myself, *I would like to interview people like this guy someday. I bet if I work really hard, I can be doing a job like that within the next ten years!*

It was extremely hard to get up at 2:30 in the morning. I was told during orientation that three tardies in four months would result in my termination. I got one tardy the first week. So I thought, *I can't lose this job. I need to go in at 10:00 p.m.* (That was the beginning of the third shift). *I can do homework and sleep in the break room until my shift starts.* And that is exactly what I did. I went into work, sat in a break room chair and did my homework until I fell asleep in the chair until it was time to clock in for work.

It wasn't long until my supervisor realized I was there. He started using me to fill in for anyone who was absent. I thought to myself, *I need full-time work to pay for school. Since I am helping my supervisor out, I should tell him I want full-time and maybe he can help me get on full-time.* So, I did.

Within the first two weeks, I was able to go full time, but I was still in the lowest paid position. They also told me during orientation that I had to stay in that job for six months before I could transfer to a different position. So I thought, *If I'm going to be working full-time, I need to make the most money I can while I'm here. So, I need to find out what job pays the most money per hour.*

I found out quickly that the highest paid hourly job in the plant was a mixer. The mixer made the dough of cookies and cakes that were baked, wrapped, and shipped all over the United States.

At the time, I worked in the wrapping room. It was the final stage of preparation. The mixer was at the beginning of the manufacturing process. I thought, *The only person in management I see is my supervisor. I need to let him know I want to become a mixer.* So, I did. He smiled and explained that he had nothing to do with the jobs in that department. He said that after I had been in my job for six months I could go to HR and apply. I still asked him to keep me in mind if he heard of any openings.

Within the first three months, he came to me and said, "You are never going to believe this, but my plant manager just asked me if I had anyone who could lift a 100-pound bag of sugar or flour."

He explained to me that the bulk system that blew in flour and sugar to the mixing platform had broken down, and it might be several weeks before they could get it repaired. He explained that each mix contained several bags of flour and sugar, and they all came in 100-pound bags. He said they needed someone to pick up the bags of flour and sugar and carry them to the mixer making the dough. Then he said, "I know you worked on a farm, so you are probably stronger than you look. You mentioned your interest in becoming a mixer. Can you lift a 100-pound bag?"

"I can probably only pick up three at a time, is that enough?" I said.

He laughed. "You just have to pick up one at a time."

I told him I would love to do the job. He said, "Go on down there. They are waiting for you." He had already told them he had someone to fill the position.

The 100-pound bags reminded me of loading the picked bags of peppers into the bed of our pickup truck on the farm. I enjoyed the workout, but it also made me *think*. I saw a couple other fellows helping other mixers. When they got through lifting the bags for a mix, they would go to the break room and hang out with that mixer for 30-45 minutes until the next mix had to be made. I thought, *I need to learn how to make all the doughs. Then, when I apply to be a mixer, I will already be trained to do the job. I can see the supervisors over the mixers watching. So, they will know I can do it.*

I took advantage of my new position. I helped all the mixers and asked each of them to teach me how to mix. I didn't take breaks. I just moved down the platform to the next mixer that was making dough and helped him. Within just a few weeks I knew how to make all the doughs.

Four weeks later, a mixing position came open. I applied for the position and got the job. I was the most qualified applicant because I already knew how to do the job! In less than six months, I went from the lowest paid hourly job to the highest paid hourly job in the plant.

I won't bore you with all the details of my movements within the food manufacturing company. However, within a year of becoming a mixer, I became a production supervisor over the mixers.

Two years later, I became a shift superintendent. Two years after that, I became a plant manager. Two years after becoming a plant manager, I transferred into the human resource department and became the person doing the interviews and working with the guy that had hired me seven-and-a-half years earlier. I thought, *I bet the grin on my face is as big as the one the day I got interviewed!*

I made my ten-year goal in seven-and-a-half years. Two years later, I became the corporate human resource manager — the boss of the guy who hired me. I worked a total of eight years in the human resource department of that food manufacturing company. During my years in the plant, I had managed to complete my undergraduate degree in theology.

I have a passion to help people reach their fullest potential, but I needed further education in the field of human resources if I wanted to make a more significant impact.

First day as supervisor — Always be intentional even with smaller responsibilities; they give you the opportunity to receive bigger responsibilities!

I enrolled in graduate school and became an organizational psychologist. I thought about how difficult it is to do a short face-to-face interview and then predict whether that applicant will be able to do the job. So I focused my studies on statistics. I wanted to be able to gather information from an applicant that I did not know and *predict* their success in a position. I conducted job analysis and identified the knowledge, skills, and abilities for each job. I then created assessments to measure the knowledge, skills, and abilities of each applicant and benchmarked the applicant's data to the data collected from our top performers.

Using my methodology, the human resource team was able to reduce our new hire turnover from 55% to 8% in twelve months. I kept our new hire turnover at that rate for the eight years I managed the department.

In August 1994, I left the food manufacturing company to start my own software business. I *thought* and *believed* that I could take all that I had learned and apply it to other businesses to help them reduce their turnover as well. But, to do more with less, I had to create software that could, in essence, automate my consultative services. So I hired a team to help me accomplish that goal.

My company released its first software in early 1995. We had some small successes, but soon after the release I heard of a new software platform — you may have heard of it — called Windows. At that point, I hired a full-time software developer and tasked him to move everything I had developed in DOS to Windows, as well as the full Human Resource Software System I had in my mind.

By January 1996, the interviewing software was completed — but no sales. Everyone who saw my product loved it, but it was a little before its time. The whole "computer" thing was new. No one but me believed my software could predict performance and tenure better than a human.

Took 8 years to get my debt-free 4-year degree — it always takes grit and determination to finish!

The startup process for my company took longer than I expected. By December 1995, I had burned through all of my IRA I had set aside from my many years in manufacturing. I had employees to pay and the overhead of the office to cover. I went home one Friday in mid-January after paying payroll for everyone in the company but myself. I had $5.43 left in the business account and less than that in my personal account.

As I drove home that evening, doubt and despair began to overwhelm me. Then I thought about my mother. I remembered what she would say: "There's always something to be grateful for."

I started saying out loud all the things I was thankful for. I remembered her telling me that it is better to focus on things within my control rather than things I can do nothing about. But, at that moment, I couldn't think of anything that was in my control!

Then I remembered something she used to say to me quite often: "What matters most is how you choose to think. How you choose to think will give you the power to choose how you respond to what you experience in life."

So, I did what my mother taught me to do. I reached out to God, the Supreme Power in this universe. I had 25 acres of property at that time. It was raining cats and dogs, but I put on some rain gear and went into the woods and sat on a stump and started pleading with God.

I thanked Him for everything He had done for me. I told Him how I could see how He had led me all my life. I told Him that I thought I was on His Frequency. I thought I was right where He wanted me to be, but I was confused with the apparent result. I explained to God (as if He didn't know) that I was at a very low point in my life. I was weak!

In that moment, I needed to know my confidence in His leading me wasn't my own naivety. So, I asked God for a specific sign to let me know I was still on His *frequency*. I didn't ask Him what He was going to do. I just asked Him to confirm He was still in control!

I waited for His answer. He knew how desperate I was; after only 20 minutes of waiting, He answered my prayer. He gave me my specific sign that I requested! I received peace. I didn't know what was going to happen, but I knew everything was going to be OK.

Monday morning came, and I couldn't wait to see what was going to happen! I was watching to see what God was going to do!

My first phone call came about 8:00 a.m. from a prospect I had been working with for more than six months. He said he had been thinking about our product all weekend. He said he couldn't stop thinking about it, and he just needed to get started. He agreed to sign the contract that day for $100,000! I told him I needed half of the contract up front. I drove down to his plant to take him to lunch and talk about the implementation plan. He handed me the $50,000 check at lunch! I could feel the biggest lump in my throat as I swallowed. He had no idea the miracle that had taken place at that moment.

From 1996 to 2010, the company grew in several manufacturing businesses. Many of those businesses were purchased by one of our larger clients until I found myself in a situation where over 70 percent of our annual revenue came from a single client. That client tried to purchase us for pennies on the dollar or threatened to terminate our contracts. I refused their offer, and in August 2010 they terminated our contracts.

We went from 30 employees to six employees overnight. All of the employees I lost were directly associated with the manufacturing client. But they were also friends I had worked with for many years. 2010 was the worst business year of my life!

At that time, I had one client in the Senior Living space. I had conducted job analysis on 120 jobs at that company and created an assessment for each job. I remembered a few years earlier my Aunt Ruth (my mother's sister) grabbing me by the collar of my shirt and pleading with me to not let anyone put her in a nursing home; she was afraid they would kill her.

I became extremely passionate about this industry. I wanted my assessments to identify people with a passion for caring for our seniors and separate them from those who just needed a job. I came to think and believe that God's purpose for me and my company was to positively impact the senior living industry. And it was successful! We lowered turnover at each of our clients' facilities by more than 40 percent!

It was another life lesson for me: *When one door closes, usually another door opens.* From 2010 through 2017, my company was able to help hundreds of companies hire and promote the right people. I could tell you story after story of how I was able to think about what needed to come next; once I got the picture in my mind, my team was able to execute the plan.

Never give up on your dreams!

What I thought would be an overnight success took 23 years. But, in 2017, my company sold for *eight figures*!

I shared my personal story to demonstrate the power of your thoughts. I am a living example of how the power of your thoughts can help you achieve the American Dream!

SALT Your Thoughts is the system I created to teach Isabella — and YOU — how to alter your life thoughts. SALT Your Thoughts is the integration of my own experience and the many pieces of knowledge I have been exposed to in my life that can help you live a more effective life. If you choose to apply my SALT to your life, I believe with all my heart it will enhance the flavor of your life!

My Worldview

In the opening quote, Chuck Colson reminds us that our choices are shaped by what we believe is real and true, right and wrong, good and beautiful. That really means that our choices are shaped by our worldview. The choices I have made in my life were greatly influenced by my belief in a supreme power, the creator God revealed by the Word of God in the Bible.

I believe God is:

- Faithful (He is infinitely unchangingly true)

- Gracious (He is infinitely inclined to spare the guilty)

- Holy (He is infinitely unchangingly Holy)

- Immutable (He never changes)

- Infinite (He is self-existing, without origin)

- Just (He is infinitely, unchangeably right and perfect in all that He does)

- Loving (He is LOVE).

- Merciful (He is infinitely unchangingly compassionate and kind)

- Omnibenevolence (He is supremely good)

- Omnipotence (He is all-powerful)

- Omnipresent (He is always everywhere)

- Omniscience (He is all-knowing)

- Self-sufficient (He has no needs)

- Wise (He is full of perfect wisdom)

"The fear of the LORD is the beginning of wisdom, And the knowledge of the Holy One is understanding." (Proverbs 9:10, New King James Version)

"For the LORD gives wisdom From His mouth come knowledge and understanding." (Proverbs 2:6, NKJV)

"Wisdom is the principal thing; Therefore, get wisdom. And in all your getting, get understanding." (Proverbs 4:7, NKJV)

My calling is to be a *teacher* — not an evangelist. My intention in this book is to:

1. Teach you how to SALT Your Thoughts

2. Teach you the system for altering your thought process

3. Point you to and connect you to the only true source of energy in the universe: the creator God.

4. Help you become more effective by harnessing the power of your thoughts

I will spend the rest of this book sharing with you the secret for living a productive, effective and fulfilled life by teaching you how to utilize the **eight easy steps** to SALT Your Thoughts.

What Is Your Worldview?

The first step in any process improvement plan is to identify where you are today. As you read this book, you bring with you all your past experiences and your current thoughts and belief systems. Everyone has a worldview, but most of us spend more time picking out a pair of new shoes than we do thinking about our thought processes. One of my first goals in this book is to help you become *informed* and *intentional*. Being intentional means getting clear upfront about what you believe, then choosing to make decisions and take action on what's important to you. Your worldview determines how you live, make decisions, and define success.

Four Worldview Categories

Technically, a worldview is a conceptual scheme or intellectual framework by which a person organizes and interprets his/her experience. Less technically, a worldview is a way of looking at the world and one's place in it. It is a perspective on reality.

Every person has a worldview, but not every person has the same worldview. In fact, in preparation for this book I reviewed twenty-nine (29) of the most prominent worldviews. I then placed the twenty-nine worldviews into four (4) categories. The chart below is not intended to be comprehensive nor is it intended to be biased. The four worldview categories are: Naturalism; Pantheism; Polytheism; and Theism. I have attempted to look at these four categories of worldviews and differentiate them by seven features:

1. How they view God

2. What is the Ultimate Reality?

3. What is the Source of Knowledge?

4. What is the Origin of Humans?

5. Are There Absolute Moral Values?

6. What is the Problem?

7. What is the Solution?

Four Primary Worldviews Contrasted

Naturalism
Atheism, Agnosticism, Existentialism, Humanism, Marxism, Postmodernism

- **How Do They View God?** No God. The origin of the universe was a "Big Bang" or some other natural phenomenon.

- **What Is the Ultimate Reality?** All that exists is the physical, material universe. (Materialism)

- **What Is the Source of Knowledge?** The only source of knowledge is the scientific method. (Scientism)

- **What Is the Origin of Humans?** Humans result from the random process of evolution. Humans are purely physical beings only.

- **Are there Absolute Moral Values?** There are no absolute moral values. (Relativism)

- **What is the Problem?** This world is plagued with ignorance and superstition (mostly from religion).

- **What is the Solution?** Education and technology.

Pantheism

Buddhism, Hinduism, Taoism, New Age Consciousness

- **How Do They View God?** Everything is a god or part of a god.

- **What Is the Ultimate Reality?** All that exists is spirit, the physical world is an illusion. (Idealism)

- **What Is the Source of Knowledge?** The only source of knowledge is your own mystical experience. (Mysticism)

- **What Is the Origin of Humans?** Humans are inherently divine, but the physical aspect is the result of illusion.

- **Are there Absolute Moral Values?** There are no absolute moral values. (Relativism)

- **What is the Problem?** The world is an illusion, and reincarnation is a punishment.

- **What is the Solution?** Meditation and detachment from the physical world.

Polytheism

Spiritism, Animism

- **How Do They View God?** The world is populated by spirit beings (gods and demons) who govern what goes on.

- **What Is the Ultimate Reality?** Material things are real but have spirits associated with them and can therefore be interrupted.

- **What Is the Source of Knowledge?** Truth about the natural world is discovered through the shaman figure through visions.

- **What Is the Origin of Humans?** Humans were created by gods. Tribes or races have a special relationship with some gods who protect them and can punish them.

- **Are there Absolute Moral Values?** Moral values take the form of taboos, which are things that irritate or anger various spirits.

- **What is the Problem?** The gods are immortal, and humans are mortal.

- **What is the Solution?** To be favored and protected by a god.

Theism
Christianity, Judaism, Islam

- **How Do They View God?** An infinite, personal God exists. He created a perfect, finite, material world.

- **What Is the Ultimate Reality?** Reality is both material and spiritual and both were created by God. (Dualism)

- **What Is the Source of Knowledge?** Revelation from God is a source of knowledge as well as reason and science.

- **What Is the Origin of Humans?** Humans were created "by God, in the image of God," which means that we are personal, eternal, spiritual, and biological.

- **Are there Absolute Moral Values?** There are absolute moral values that are revealed by God.

- **What is the Problem?** Adam (the first man) sinned and brought sin to the world. Sin alienated man from God.

- **What is the Solution?** Salvation by God's grace through faith in God's atonement for man.

Every worldview can be analyzed by the way it answers three basic questions:

1. Where did we come from, and who are we (e.g. Creation versus Big Bang)?

2. What has gone wrong with the world (e.g. Sin versus Man's Ignorance and Superstition)?

3. What can we do to fix it (e.g. Redemption versus Education, Technology, and Meditation)?

Do you know what you believe? I have prepared a few quick surveys that will assist you in analyzing your own intellectual framework. When you are ready, complete them as this chapter's assignment:

Chapter 1 Assignment:

Complete the following surveys on **SaltYourThoughts.com**:

- *Worldview Part 1: ORIGINS (20 Questions)*
- *Worldview Part 2: THE NATURE OF MAN (10 Questions)*
- *Worldview Part 3: THE NATURE OF THE EARTH (10 Questions)*
- *Worldview Part 4: TRUTH (10 Questions)*
- *Worldview Part 5: HOPE (10 Questions)*
- *Worldview Part 6: WHAT IF? (12 Questions)*

SALT Summaries:
Chapter 1: Go Make It Happen

- This book and website were born from my desire to help my 15-year-old daughter Isabella identify her career path.

- **SALT Your Thoughts** is my chosen method for teaching Isabella — and YOU — how to alter your life thoughts.

- I will teach you how to live a productive, effective and fulfilled life by utilizing the **eight easy steps** to SALT Your Thoughts.

- SALT Your Thoughts is the integration of my own experience and the knowledge I have been exposed to that can help you live a more effective life.

- If you choose to apply SALT to your life, I believe with all my heart it will enhance the flavor of your life!

- My intention in this book is to:

    - Teach you how to SALT Your Thoughts

    - Teach you the system for altering your thought process

    - Point you to and connect you to the only true source of energy in the universe: the Creator God

    - Help you become more effective by harnessing the power of your thoughts

- Every worldview can be analyzed by the way it answers three basic questions:

    a. Where did we come from, and who are we? (e.g. Creation versus Big Bang)?

    b. What has gone wrong with the world? (e.g. Sin versus Man's Ignorance and Superstition)?

    c. What can we do to fix it? (e.g. Redemption versus Education, Technology, and Meditation)?

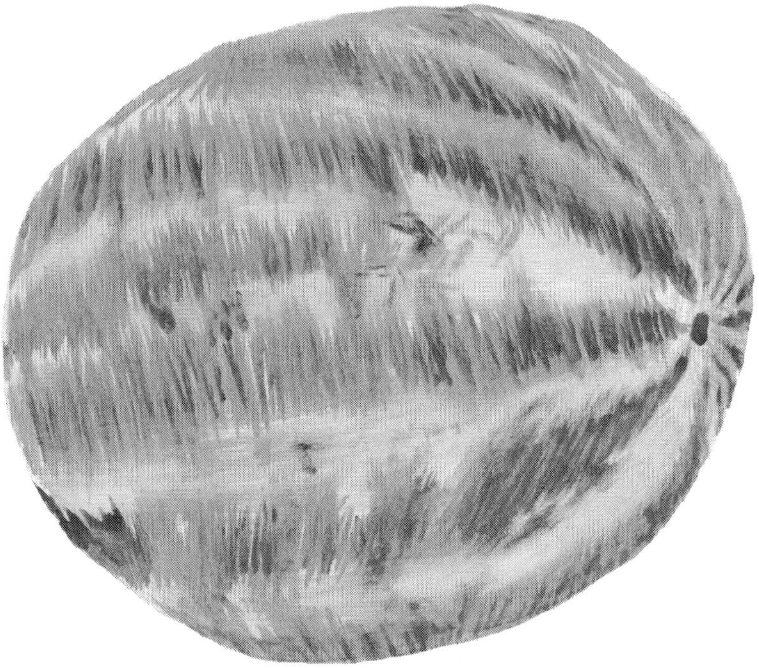

Chapter 2

SOWING SEEDS

"Opportunity is missed by most people because it is dressed in overalls and looks like work."
Thomas Edison

I WAS 8 YEARS old when I started my first business. Some of my friends had motorcycles. I wanted one so badly, I could hardly stand it! My dad decided he could use that desire to teach me a big lesson. "Son, let me tell you what I will do," he said. "I will give you two acres to grow whatever you want to grow. When it is time for harvest, you can sell what you grow, and buy whatever you want." So I thought, *What can I grow that would be easy to pick and sell?* Then I turned to my Dad and said, "Fantastic, Dad! I want to grow watermelons." And that is exactly what I did. I started visualizing myself riding my Honda motorcycle!

I planted 2 acres of watermelons. It seemed like forever until the seeds sprouted from out of the ground. But I hoed, watered, and fertilized them from early May to the end of June. I watched the little buds turn into little nubs that soon turned into small watermelons. By the end of June, the little watermelons had turned into big ripe watermelons. I set up a stand by the road with an old table we had in the garage, and I was in business. I would come home from school and go into the field and pick 15-20 watermelons. Then I would position them perfectly and wait for cars to stop and buy my melons. By the end of the summer, I was able to purchase my own Honda motorcycle!

Natural Laws

I learned about natural laws while working on the farm. **Natural laws are deep fundamental truths that have universal application.** The Seven Natural Laws of the Universe are easily found on the Internet and are most often attributed to William Walker Atkinson.[1] As part of his 1908 book, *The Kybalion*, he attempted to describe the workings of the universe in terms of a set of laws. According to Atkinson, the Seven Natural Laws are always working whether we believe or understand them. They are based on the quantum knowledge that *everything is energy*; everything in the universe, including us, is connected through a sea of energy. What we think, feel, say, and do are all forms of energy through which our realities are created.

These fundamental truths give us insight and direction into how everything works, including how to be better people. The Seven Natural Laws through which everyone and everything are governed are the Laws of:

1. Mentalism – "The All is Mind; the Universe is Mental."

2. Correspondence – "As above, so below; as below, so above."

3. Vibration – "Nothing rests; everything moves; everything vibrates."

4. Polarity – "Everything is dual; everything has poles."

5. Rhythm – "Everything flows, out and in; everything has tides; all things rise and fall."

6. Cause and Effect – "Every cause has its effect; every effect has its cause."

7. Gender – "Gender is in everything; everything has its masculine and feminine principles."

I could spend several chapters thoroughly describing each of these laws, but that is not the purpose of this book. As these laws impact our course of study, I will point them out.

For example, the Law of Growth and Gestation states that every seed has an incubation period. This law declares that there is a set incubation or gestation period for every seed (physical or spiritual) — a specific span of time that it needs to follow its blueprint to come into physical form. This law directly impacts our course of study and provides an extremely useful metaphor for understanding.

I believe that your thoughts are the seeds of your *conscious* mind. When you plant your *thought seeds* into your *subconscious* mind and cultivate them, they will sprout and grow. This book will teach you how to cultivate the thought seeds you choose to plant.

The Seven Principles of the Farm

The Seven Principles of the Farm are officially known as *The Seven Principles of the Natural Law of Growth and Gestation*. Most people have never heard of these, but they have seen evidence of these principles in their everyday life. The Seven Principles of the Farm are self-evident and irrefutable. The metaphor of sowing seeds directly applies to every dimension of our lives. Inwardly, it applies to your mental and spiritual self. Outwardly, it applies to your personal physical health, as well as the health of your social/emotional relationships.

The Seven Principles of the Farm:

1. We Reap Only What Has Been Sown.

2. We Reap The Same In Kind As We Sow.

3. We Reap In A Different Season Than We Sow.

4. We Reap More Than We Sow.

5. We Reap In Proportion To What We Sow.

6. We Reap The Full Harvest Only If We Hoe Out The Weeds.

7. We Can't Do Anything About Last Year's Harvest.

Let's take a moment and walk through each of these Principles.

Principle #1: We Reap Only What Has Been Sown.
Another way of saying this is that a seed NOT planted will NOT grow. Seeds must be planted to begin the process of germination. Step one in the process is to plant the seed!

Your thoughts are the seeds of your conscious mind. When you plant your thought seeds into your subconscious mind and cultivate them, they will sprout and grow.

Principle #2: We Reap The Same In Kind As We Sow.
This self-evident principle has somehow been forgotten in this day and age. Plainly stated, if you plant tomato seeds, you get tomato plants and, ultimately, tomatoes — not carrots, onions, or watermelons. This law also governs your thoughts. If you sow thoughts of courage, hope, enthusiasm, confidence, trust, faith, abundance, and harmony, you will reap courage, hope, enthusiasm, confidence, trust, faith, abundance, and harmony. If you sow thoughts of fear, worry, despair, anxiety, jealousy, and hatred, you will reap fear, worry, despair, anxiety, jealousy, and hatred. This law is immutable; your future is within your control. It is determined by the type of thought seeds you plant!

Principle #3: We Reap In A Different Season Than We Sow.
This principle declares that there is a set incubation or gestation period for every seed. Typically, you plant in the spring and harvest in the fall. Unfortunately, this law illuminates the fact that there are no shortcuts. You can't cram (like you may on an exam) on the farm. It just doesn't work that way. In the same manner, your thought seeds also need a gestation period. From a thought perspective, it takes time for them to be properly cultivated, nourished, watered, and fertilized.

Principle #4: We Reap More Than We Sow.
We know in the natural world that, depending on the type of seed, a seed will produce from ten to a hundred fold. In your mind world, this natural law is also evident. In fact, it is exponentiated because of another law called the *Law of Attraction*. The Law of Attraction simply means that *like attracts like*. We will discuss this further later. For now, understand that thought seeds of abundance attract more abundance. Thought seeds of fear attract more fear.

Principle #5: We Reap In Proportion To What We Sow.
Simply stated, if you sow a lot, you will reap a lot; if you sow a little, you will reap a little. In the farm world, you are limited on how much you can sow by how much property or acreage you have. In your mind world, *you* are your only limitation. In the statistical world, there is a law called Normal Distribution, otherwise known as the Bell Curve. This law allows statisticians to predict behaviors of populations in a variety of areas. The Bell Curve would imply that only 17% of the population are people who intentionally sow

thought seeds. It further implies that 83% of the population is entirely innocent of any deep thinking. The average person simply parrots the thoughts of people perceived to be *"influencers."* This passive attitude on the part of the average person is the target of this book. Creative thinking requires concentration. Developing the habit of concentration will increase the property or acreage in your mind world!

Principle #6: We Reap The Full Harvest Only If We Hoe Out The Weeds.
A weed is simply a plant in the wrong place. Weeds will choke the life out of your desired plants if they are not removed! In the farm world, if you *pull* the weed out, you take the chance of pulling up the roots of your desired plant. Hoeing or cutting out the weeds is the most effective way to reap your full harvest. In your mind world, weeds are unwanted thoughts. Just like the farm weed, they will choke the life out of your desired thoughts if you don't hoe them out.

Principle #7: We Can't Do Anything About Last Year's Harvest.
It has come and gone. You can't change the past. Living in the past is a great way to miss the opportunities of the present and ruin the future. You can't do anything about last year's harvest, but you can do something about next year's harvest! In your mind world, it is exactly the same. Your current life is a culmination of all of your past thoughts. Your past thoughts will only impact your future if you continue to think them. It is time now to think about and concentrate on only those things that YOU desire. It is time to take responsibility for your thoughts.

Your thought seeds are subject to the same Seven Principles of the Farm as regular seeds. So, it is imperative that you understand those seven principles so that you can grasp the *power* of your thoughts!

Chapter 2 Assignment:

When you plant your thought seeds into your subconscious mind and cultivate them, they will sprout and grow. Go to **SaltYourThoughts.com** and complete the **Reticular Activation System** survey.

SALT Summaries:
Chapter 2: Sowing Seeds

- Natural laws are deep fundamental truths that have universal application.

- The *Seven Natural Laws of the Universe* are:

    a. Mentalism: "The All is Mind; the Universe is Mental."

    b. Correspondence: "As above, so below; as below, so above."

    c. Vibration/Attraction: "Nothing rests; everything moves; everything vibrates."

    d. Polarity: "Everything is dual; everything has poles."

    e. Rhythm: "Everything flows, out and in; everything has tides; all things rise and fall."

    f. Cause and Effect: "Every cause has its effect; every effect has its cause."

    g. Gender: "Gender is in everything; everything has its masculine and feminine principles."

- The Seven Natural Laws are based on the quantum knowledge that *everything is energy*; everything in the universe, including us, is connected through this sea of energy.

    ○ What we think, feel, say and do are all forms of energy through which our realities are created.

- **The Law of Growth and Gestation** states that every seed has an incubation period.

    ○ This law declares that there is a set incubation or gestation period for every seed (physical or spiritual) — a specific span of time that it needs to follow its blueprint to come into physical form.

- This law directly impacts our course of study and provides an extremely useful metaphor for understanding.

- I believe that your thoughts are the seeds of your conscious mind.

- When you plant your thought seeds into your subconscious mind and cultivate them, they will sprout and grow.

- The Seven Principles of the Farm are officially known as the Seven Principles of the Natural Law of Growth and Gestation.

  - Principle #1 states that *We Reap Only What Has Been Sown*. Another way of saying this is that a seed NOT planted will NOT grow.

  - Principle #2 states that *We Reap the Same In Kind As We Sow*.

  - Principle #3 states that *We Reap In A Different Season Than We Sow*.

  - Principle #4 states that *We Reap More Than We Sow*.

  - Principle #5 states that *We Reap In Proportion To What We Sow*.

  - Principle #6 states that *We Reap The Full Harvest Only If We Hoe Out The Weeds*.

  - Principle #7 states that *We Can't Do Anything About Last Year's Harvest*.

I HAVE THE POWER TO MAKE MY CHOICES

STIMULUS

RESPONSE

SPACE

Chapter 3

YOU HAVE THE POWER!

"The price of greatness is responsibility."
Winston Churchill

IN THE SUMMER OF 1975, I was 14 years old. In the '70s, it was cool to have a perfectly combed, feathered back, middle parted mullet. I ALWAYS had a comb in my back pocket to keep every strand in place. Our family's traditional Fourth of July summer vacation was spent at the KOA Campground in Destin, Florida. On this particular trip, I was already tanned from working on the farm out in the sun, and I was ready to impress the KOA Campground girls with my perfect long hair and tan.

When I arrived at the pool with my best friend, the pool was already full of action. We decided the best viewpoint was on top of the building that housed the pool pump. We set up our lawn chairs and started taking in the view. I scanned the pool for the gorgeous girls I expected to see in Florida and noticed a young boy barely able to dog paddle along the side of the pool. About that time, an adult did a cannon ball right in front of the kid. The wave hit the kid just as he was taking in a big breath of air at the deep end of the pool. The wave bounced him away from the side of the pool so he could no longer touch it. He sucked in a deep breath of water and air. Gagged on the water. Stopped dog paddling. He had a look on his face of complete panic, and then he sank to the bottom of the pool. I stood up and yelled, "Somebody help that kid, he's on the bottom of the pool!" People looked at me like I was speaking another language. I looked at my buddy and said, "Looks like I'm the one that will have to MAKE IT HAPPEN!"

I need you to understand the context of this story. I had just completed my 8th grade year of middle school. Just a month later, I entered a Christian boarding school as a freshman in high school. I remember it well because at 4'10" tall and 85 pounds, I was the smallest kid in the whole school, including all the girls!

I climbed down from the pool pump building and jumped in. When I got to the bottom of the pool, the kid was face-down and not moving. I was able to get underneath him and press him above my head and use the side of the pool wall to help me balance him. I walked him down to the shallow end where I could basically roll him over the side of the pool.

When I pushed him over the side of the pool, his mother was there and grabbed him out of my arms. He was coughing up water from both his mouth and nose and heaving and gasping for air. Apparently, she thought I had caused the problem. She said, "What have you done to my son!?" My first thought was *I got my hair wet, and this lady is mad that I saved her kid!?*

Later that evening, the camp director came to our campsite and talked with my dad. He told my dad that the mother of the child had filed a complaint against me for attempting to drown her son. Fortunately, the camp director had investigated the situation and found several witnesses that testified I had saved the kid's life. He told my dad he should be proud.

My dad *was* proud. (It was worth getting my hair wet.) But then he told me that it wasn't my responsibility to save the kid. He said, "What if the camp director had just taken the word of the mother? You would have been in big trouble."

"If it wasn't my responsibility," I asked him, "whose responsibility was it?"

This story is like a lot of life situations. Sometimes, you must take *personal responsibility*. A quick decision can still affect your whole life or the life of someone else. Quick decisions should be made based on **your personal character**. In those cases, I believe what matters most is how you *respond* to what you experience in life. My long hair didn't matter, the fact that the water was cold didn't matter, and it didn't matter what anyone said about what I did. I knew the kid was going to drown if I didn't take action. So, I did. Bad things can happen to good people. How you respond to those bad things will make a difference in your quality of life.

Between Stimulus and Response, There is a Space

Before World War II, a Jewish man named Viktor Frankl worked in Vienna as a successful neurologist and psychiatrist. As a psychiatrist he was trained in the traditional Freudian view of Determinism. Determinism is the belief that whatever happens to you as a child shapes your character and personality and basically governs your whole life. During the Holocaust, he was imprisoned in the death camps of Nazi Germany. In 1945, within months of his liberation from a concentration camp, Frankl sat down to write a book. He was forty years old, and he wrote the manuscript in nine consecutive days. Although the book tells the story of the unfathomable horrors and suffering he endured as a prisoner at Auschwitz, Dachau and other camps, the primary purpose of the text is to explore the source of his will to survive. The book, titled *Man's Search for Meaning*, went on to sell over 16 million copies in 50 languages.

During his sufferings, Frankl discovered a fundamental principle about the nature of man: "Between stimulus and response there is a space. In that space is our power to choose our response. In our response lies our growth and our freedom."[2] In that space, humans have four unique attributes[3]:

1. **Self-Awareness** – The awareness of your own thoughts, feelings, and actions.

2. **Imagination** – The ability to visualize a new reality.

3. **Conscience** – The deep inner awareness of what is morally right or wrong.

4. **Independent Will** – The ability to choose to act based on our self-awareness.

These four unique human attributes cause us to be fundamentally different from any creature on this earth! There are some intelligent creatures, but they have no self-awareness for the need of training, nor do they have the imagination to create the training, nor do they have the independent will to do so. **Humans alone have the power and**

responsibility to choose! That choice, like everything else in life, begins with your thoughts!

Viktor Frankl took personal responsibility and made a lasting contribution to the world.

The fact that we are uniquely human gives us the *Power (and the Will) to Choose*. In other words, it is your responsibility to choose your thoughts. Failure to choose your thoughts will result in being reactive. We can choose to let the outside stimuluses of the world control us, or we can choose to control ourselves.

Your current reality, where you are in your life today, is the result of your past thoughts. If you like where you are today, keep thinking the same thoughts. But if you want better, or if you want more, you have the power to *choose your own* thoughts!

The power to choose your own thoughts is your greatest power! It means NO ONE, other than you, can determine your final outcome.

The first step of SALTing Your Thoughts is utilizing your God-given power to *choose your own thoughts*!

Everything you do begins with a thought. Every action, every word, every human creation began first with a thought.

Chapter 3 Assignment:

Who do you believe is *responsible*? Go to **SaltYourThoughts.com** and complete the **Locus of Control** survey.

SALT Summaries:
Chapter 3: You Have The Power!

- *"Between stimulus and response there is a space. In that space is our power to choose our response. In our response lies our growth and our freedom."*

- In that space humans have **four unique attributes**

  - **Self-Awareness** – The awareness of your own thoughts, feelings, and actions

  - **Imagination** – The ability to visualize a new reality

  - **Conscience** – The deep inner awareness of what is morally right or wrong

  - **Independent Will** – The ability to choose to act based on our self-awareness

- Humans alone have the power and responsibility to choose!

- The power to choose your own thoughts is one of your greatest powers!

- NO ONE, other than you, can determine your final outcome.

WHAT ARE THOUGHTS?

Chapter 4

WHAT ARE THOUGHTS?

"Thought is energy. Active thought is active energy. Concentrated thought is concentrated energy. Thought concentrated on a definite purpose becomes power."[4]
Charles Haanel

AS FAR BACK AS I can remember, when I would wake up and start my day, I would thank the Lord for giving me another day of life. After that, I would remind myself of five things I was thankful for. Then, I'd recall five beliefs my mother had taught me. Following that, I'd take a couple of minutes to think about the tasks I had planned for the day and imagine how I wanted things to go. Lastly, I would repeat to myself ten times, "I am ready! I am ready! I am ready!" After that, I would say a short prayer, asking God to guide my steps throughout the day. Once I completed this little ritual, I was ready for whatever the day might bring. I have always known this has given me an advantage. It wasn't until I did the research for this book that I understood how.

What Are Thoughts?

In an article titled, "What Actually Is a Thought? And How Is Information Physical?" for *Psychology Today*, Ralph Lewis, M.D. states that a thought is a representation of something. "A representation is a likeness—a thing that depicts another thing by having characteristics that correspond to that other thing," Lewis writes. "For example, a picture, image, imprint, or mold of an object is a representation of that object."

Dr. Lewis also used a map as another example of a representation:

> The mind is a kind of map. The brain — and its functional product, the mind — evolved as a map of the body's relation to its external environment. Fundamentally, our thoughts are maps representing and corresponding to things that our brains have either perceived with our senses, felt with our emotions, or formed as an action plan. ... All of these are electrochemically mediated processes. Thoughts may be fleeting, or they may later be consolidated as memories. Memory too is a physical process, encoded by structural molecular changes in neuronal connections.

Cognitive scientist Douglas Hofstadter and psychologist Emmanuel Sander suggest that all thoughts are built from analogy-making. They propose that categorization through analogy-making is "the driving force behind all thought." Your brain processes new information by first trying to relate the new information with something that has already been identified or established. This method of mental correlation provides a mental map associating the new with the old. This process allows you to create words that don't exist with concrete concepts that currently exist. Here is a sampling of some of the simpler analogies and metaphors from Hofstadter and Sander's elaborate collection: "the *legs* of a table; the *spine* of a book; the *tongue* spoken by the islanders; the *window* of opportunity for doing something; the *field* one studies."[5]

The human brain is composed of about 85-100 billion nerve cells (neurons) interconnected by trillions of connections called synapses. On average, each connection transmits about one signal per second. Some specialized connections send up to 1,000 signals per second. Thoughts emit measurable *frequencies*. The frequencies emit *brainwaves*. Our thought is the cause, the brainwave is the effect. Brainwaves are electrical impulses in the brain. All brainwaves are produced by thoughts, which are synchronized electrical pulses from masses of neurons communicating with each other. Our brainwaves occur at various frequencies. Some are fast, and some are slow. The classic names of these EEG bands are delta, theta, alpha, beta, and gamma. They are measured in cycles per second or hertz (Hz).

The point I am making here is that your thoughts emit a frequency. So, in essence, you are a human transmission tower.[6] We all use our radio/television. But I'm sure most of us don't really know how it works. Here is a simple way of explaining the process:

- The radio/television station's transmission tower broadcasts a specific frequency for each channel into the air.

- When we turn on the radio/television and tune our antenna into that frequency, we hear the music, information or weather that was transmitted on that frequency on our radio/television.

- By changing channels, we tune our antenna into other frequencies and hear different music, information or weather.

You are just like a radio/television station's transmission tower. You broadcast the frequency of your thoughts into the air.

At this point in our history, virtually all disciplines, religions, sciences, philosophy, quantum physics, etc. agree that this universe is completely made of energy and that this energy is somehow all connected.

The **Natural Law of Perpetual Transmutation of Energy** asserts that energy can neither be created nor destroyed. Still, it changes from one state to another. This means that the energy in the universe is always transmuting into and out of form. At no time will the energy be standing still. It simply moves from one form into another.[7]

The **Law of Vibration** states that everything moves, and nothing rests. This is a scientific principle at its core. We live in what many people call an "ocean of motion." Everything is built up of small molecules that are constantly vibrating. The law of attraction is a secondary law to the law of vibration.[8]

The **Law of Attraction** states that *like attracts like*. Vibrations of the same frequency resonate with each other, so like attracts like energy. *Like attracts like* means people attract energy like the energy they project. Positive people attract other positive people.

Negative people attract other negative people. The fact is that you attract people, ideas, and resources that are in harmony with your dominant thoughts.[9]

You — and only YOU — have the power to choose your own dominant thoughts. In other words, you have the responsibility and the power to be the author of your own narrative.

What you think about it is what you become! It is your responsibility to SALT Your Thoughts!

But how do we get from your *thoughts* to your *behaviors*? Let's look at the pyramid below:

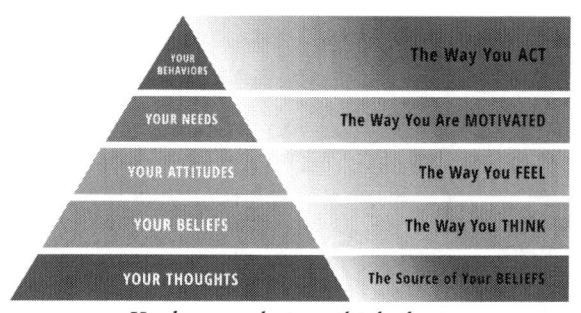

YOUR BEHAVIORS	The Way You ACT
YOUR NEEDS	The Way You Are MOTIVATED
YOUR ATTITUDES	The Way You FEEL
YOUR BELIEFS	The Way You THINK
YOUR THOUGHTS	The Source of Your BELIEFS

You become what you think about.

1. Your **thoughts** are the source of your beliefs (The Way You Think).

2. Your **beliefs** (The Way You Think) have a cause-and-effect impact on your attitudes (The Way You Feel).

3. Your **attitudes/values** (The Way You Feel) have a cause-and-effect impact on your needs (The Way You are Motivated).

4. Your **needs** (The Way You Are Motivated) have a cause-and-effect impact on your behaviors (The Way You Act).

You can choose to use your self-awareness, your imagination, your conscience, and your independent will to plainly state to your subconscious mind exactly what you choose to think, believe, feel, need, and do! Any lasting modification, change, or improvement of any behavior can only be achieved by changing it at its source – the **thought**. Changing your behavior at its source is what I call **SALTing Your Thoughts**.

Your life right now (as you read this book) reflects the habits of your past thoughts. All the great things you have done and all the not-so-great things you have done are a result of your past *thought habits*. When I look at my own life timeline my not-so-great things were done when I was not thinking, but reacting. We all make mistakes (and I have certainly made more than my share), but we make fewer mistakes when we are in control or at least aware of our thought habits. If you are like me, you want more of the great things and less of the not-so-great things!

Chapter 4 Assignment

I agree with Charles Haanel: "Thought concentrated on a definite purpose becomes power."

I believe that power is amplified IF you are "of the same mind" as the Creator of this universe. In other words, I believe when you sow thoughts of courage, hope, enthusiasm, confidence, trust, faith, abundance, and harmony, you will reap courage, hope, enthusiasm, confidence, trust, faith, abundance, and harmony because those thoughts are in alignment with the Creator.

Take 5 minutes to review your **Reticular Activation Report**.

SALT Summaries:
Chapter 4: What Are Thoughts?

- Thoughts are energy signals.

- Thoughts emit measurable frequencies, and the frequencies emit brainwaves.

  - Thought is the cause; the brainwave is the effect.

- The universe is completely made of energy, and this energy is somehow all connected.

  - The **Natural Law of Perpetual Transmutation of Energy** asserts that energy can neither be created nor destroyed.

  - The **Law of Vibration** states that everything moves and nothing rests.

  - The **Law of Attraction** states that *like attracts like*.

    - Vibrations of the same frequency resonate with each other, so like energy attracts like energy.

- *Like attracts like* means people attract energy like the energy they project.

  - You attract people, ideas, and resources that are in harmony with your dominant thoughts.

  - Think positive thoughts and you will attract positive results. What you think about is what you become!

- Your **thoughts** drive your beliefs (The Way You Think)

- Your **beliefs** (The Way You Think) drive your attitudes (The Way You Feel)

- Your **attitudes** (The Way You Feel) drive your needs (The Way You Are Motivated)

- Your **needs** (The Way You Are Motivated) drive your behaviors (The Way You Act)

- **Key Learning:** You can choose to use your self-awareness, your imagination, your conscience, and your independent will to plainly state to your subconscious mind exactly what you choose to think, believe, feel, need, and do!

- Your life right now (as you read this book) reflects your past thoughts.

- The key to any lasting modification of any behavior is to change it at the source: **to change the way you think.**

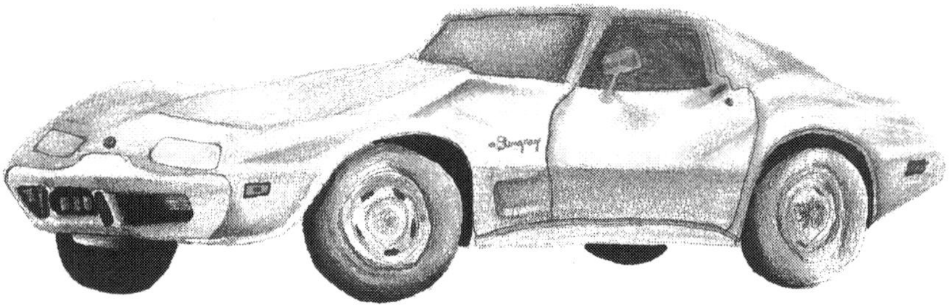

Chapter 5

HOW DO I START SALTING MY THOUGHTS?

"A man is but the product of his thoughts. What he thinks, he becomes."
Mahatma Gandhi

Waxing the Car

DURING THE FALL BREAK of 1976, I was a sophomore/junior in high school. (Remember, I completed high school in three years.) Both of my sisters were in college, and my younger brother was at a different school, so I was the only member of my family at my boarding school. This was before cell phones. So, it was difficult to make contact even with a pay phone. I thought, *I know my dad is at work, and there is no one else to pick me up. I don't really want to spend fall break at school. I am only 85 miles from home. I bet I can hitchhike home!* So, I explained to the boy's dean that my ride was picking me up early so there would be no concerns. I left at 6:00 a.m., and it took about an hour to walk the four miles to Highway 53.

When I got to Highway 53, I started walking toward Center, Alabama. Center, Alabama is where my dad moved after the death of my mother. It wasn't very long until I saw an old pickup truck going my direction, so I put out my thumb. A very nice old man (he was probably 60) stopped and asked where I was headed. I explained that I was on my way home for fall break, and that I lived in Center, Alabama. He smiled and explained he was traveling to Gadsden, and he would be happy to take me home. I thought, *Wow, this must be a divine appointment!* The old man and I talked the whole 90-minute drive. I told him about my mother being killed in a car wreck and how I ended up in Calhoun, GA at a Christian boarding school. He shared with me different events that had happened in his life and how he can look back now and see God's guiding hand on his life. I explained to him how I believe that God is in control and that there are no coincidences. He shared with me how important and valuable every person is to God. He told me that Jesus would have died on the cross just to save me alone — he told me to never forget that fact. He drove me all the way to my house! I thanked him and told him how much I appreciated the ride home. As I walked up to my house, I couldn't help but wonder if God had sent an Angel to drive me home that day. I remember thinking, "God either sent an Angel or used that man as an angel, either way, I was grateful to arrive home safely."

It was about 8:30 a.m. when I got home. My dad had already left to go to work. I knew my dad was still having a hard time over the loss of my mother so I thought, *I had better be as productive as I can be today before he gets home so he won't be mad that I showed up.* So, in an effort to make him glad I came home, I mowed the yard and washed his cars. He had recently purchased a Corvette to fit his new lifestyle. While I washed and waxed the car, I thought about my conversation with the old man in the truck all day.

At 3:30 that afternoon, I had just finished waxing the Corvette when my dad pulled in the driveway. He asked me why I was home and what I had done all day. I explained that it was fall break, and I was out until Sunday. Again, he asked me what I had done all day. I explained that I had mowed the yard, washed all his cars, and waxed his Corvette. He immediately went to inspect my wax job. I followed, realizing he was not in a good mood. He went to the garage and inspected the Corvette in excruciating detail. He found a tiny ball of wax between the S and the T in the car's *Stingray* plate. He turned to me at that moment and said what he had said to me many times before: "You aren't worth a s***, and you will never be worth a s***."

At fifteen years old, I finally told my dad that it was wrong for him to talk to me that way, and I wasn't going to put up with it anymore. I was empowered by the conversation I had with the old man in the truck! The fact that now I understood that Jesus would have died just for me made me realize just how important, valuable and treasured I am to God. It gave me "worth" from inside out! That day I chose to believe that I didn't have to listen to what anyone said about me. I chose to believe that what happened TO me did not define me. I choose to believe that God had a purpose for me and, with His help and guidance, I would become competent and successful in life.

My dad and I didn't talk much over the next five years. I called him one day and told him I was getting married, and I asked him to be my best man. From that point on, we became friends.

My dad had a very tough life. He wanted the best for me and wanted to make me a survivor. I know he loved me very much. He made a profound and positive impact on my life! He passed away July 4, 2001. But I know I will see him again!

Sometimes people you are very close to (your father, mother, sister, brother, etc.) can attempt to be the author of your own narrative. But it is **your responsibility** to choose to be the author of your own narrative.

Dad and I discussing business plans.

Remember Viktor Frankl

Let's remember what we learned from Viktor Frankl: "Between stimulus and response there is a space. In that space is our power to choose our response. In our response lies our growth and our freedom." In that space, humans have four unique attributes:

    1. **Self-Awareness** – The awareness of your own thoughts, feelings, and actions

    2. **Imagination** – The ability to visualize a new reality

    3. **Conscience** – The deep inner awareness of what is morally right or wrong

    4. **Independent Will** – The ability to choose to act based on our self-awareness.

The Difference between Conscious and Conscience

Sometimes there is confusion between the word "conscious" and the word "conscience." Though they sound very similar, they are in fact quite different.

Your **conscious** (Frankl's #1) is your awareness of yourself and the world around you. In the most general terms, it means being awake and aware. Some experts suggest that you are considered conscious of something if you are able to put it into words.

Your **conscious mind** (sometimes called your *objective mind*) deals with things outside of yourself. Perceiving and operating using the five physical senses (touch, taste, hearing, smelling, and seeing) the conscious mind deals with the impressions and objects of outward life. Your conscious mind has the ability to reason and explore cause and effect. Your conscious mind gathers information, identifies, defines, measures, compares and ultimately makes decisions on information that has been gathered. Your conscious mind is what Frankl called **self-awareness.**

Charles Haanel said that your conscious mind is your reasoning will. And your subconscious mind is your instinctive desire, the result of your *past* reasoning will.[10]

It is with your *conscious mind* that you influence others. Your *conscious mind* is also how you influence your *subconscious mind.* Your conscious mind is the gatekeeper, guardian, responsible ruler, and leader of your subconscious mind.[11]

Your **conscience** (Frankl's #3) is that deep moral awareness of right and wrong that keeps you from acting upon your most basic desires and urges. Your conscience is what produces guilt when you do something bad or unkind. Your conscience leads you to help others and to behave in a socially acceptable manner. **Your conscience is where your thought habits are stored.** Your conscience is stored in your subconscious mind.

The **subconscious mind** is a powerful secondary system. It controls everything in your life that is involuntary (Habits) — your respiration, heart rate, blinking, liver, spleen, stomach, etc.

In addition to "running" your body, your subconscious mind is the database for everything not in your conscious mind. It stores your conscience, your thought habits (beliefs), your values, your previous experience, your memories, and your skills. It stores everything that you have ever seen, done, or thought. It provides the record of who you are today.

It is also the source of your security system. It constantly monitors the information coming from the senses for dangers and opportunities. Your subconscious mind is the source of your fight-or-flight survival system.

The **solar plexus** is the organ of your subconscious mind.[12] The solar plexus is the home of your *sympathetic system*. Your *sympathetic system* provides oversight for all your subjective sensations like joy, fear, love, emotion, intuition, and imagination. It is the source of your "gut instinct". I believe that your subconscious mind is your link to the Creator God called your *soul*.

Unfortunately, your subconscious mind cannot reason, it cannot argue controversially. It depends on your conscious mind to be its gatekeeper. Your subconscious mind perceives information through intuition as a function of survival, thus "fight-or-flight."

During conditions of panic, anger, and excitement, the subconscious mind is unguarded and open to the suggestion of self-depreciation, fear, selfishness, hatred, greed, and other negative forces. These false suggestions embedded in the subconscious mind become the cause of fear, worry, disease, and poverty. The subconscious mind never sleeps, never rests, never takes a break. Which is the reason why our conscious mind needs to be on duty every waking hour of every day! The subconscious mind left unguarded leaves it susceptible to error and misinformation.

Your subconscious mind is the home of your habits, both good and bad. *Dictionary.com* defines a "habit" as, "an acquired behavior pattern regularly followed until it has become almost involuntary." Habits are behavior patterns that you have repeated enough that they are now controlled by your subconscious mind. Behavior patterns like riding a bicycle, typing on a keyboard, or playing the piano are repeated regularly enough that we do not have to think to perform them.

The communication between the subconscious mind and the conscious mind go both directions. Every time you have an idea, or an emotion, a memory, or an image from the past, this is the subconscious mind communicating to your conscious mind.

How Do I Change My Thought Habits?

You change your Thought Habits by utilizing your self-awareness (Frankl's #1), your imagination (Frankl's #2), your conscience (Frankl's #3), and your independent will (Frankl's #4) to plainly state to the subconscious mind exactly what we choose to think, believe, feel, need and do!

Thought is the cause of every effect. When we direct our thoughts consciously, systematically, and constructively, I believe we tune ourselves into the frequency of the universal Creative Power of the Universe (The Mind of God), which is the source of all energy and power. Our level of personal effectiveness is dependent upon how congruent we are with the Universal Laws the Creator utilizes to govern His creation. Being congruent and in harmony with the Mind of God means **we have direct access to the Energy of God!** Remember, thought is energy. Active thought is active energy. Concentrated thought is concentrated energy. Thought concentrated on a definite purpose becomes power.

Here is Step #1 of How to SALT Your Thoughts: Push the Reset Button: Focus your thoughts on positive energy.

Psalm 45:1 says, "My tongue is the pen of a ready writer. NKJV" How will you *pen* your life?

Another way to become aware of the dominant thoughts you are thinking is to listen to your own tongue. What is **your tongue** talking about?

Chapter 5 Assignment:

Take 5 minutes and complete the **What Does Your Tongue Talk About** survey on **SaltYourThoughts.com**.

SALT Summaries:
Chapter 5: How Do I Start SALTing My Thoughts?

- Your **conscious** (Frankl's #1) is your awareness of yourself and the world around you.

    - Your **c**onscious mind (sometimes called your *objective mind*) deals with things outside of yourself.

    - Your conscious mind gathers information, identifies, defines, measures, compares, and ultimately makes decisions on information that has been gathered.

    - Your conscious mind is what Frankl called **self-awareness**.

    - Your conscious mind is the gatekeeper, guardian, responsible ruler, and leader of your subconscious mind.

- The **subconscious mind** is a powerful secondary system.

    - It controls everything in your life that is involuntary (habits) — your respiration, heart rate, blinking, liver, spleen, stomach, etc.

    - Your subconscious mind is the database for everything not in your conscious mind.

        - It stores your conscience, your thought habits (beliefs), your values, your previous experience, your memories, and your skills.

        - It stores everything that you have ever seen, done, or thought.

- The **solar plexus** is the organ of your subconscious mind.

    - The solar plexus is the home of your sympathetic system.

    - Your sympathetic system provides oversight for all your subjective sensations like joy, fear, love, emotion, intuition, and imagination.

- It is the source of your "gut instinct."

- I believe that your subconscious mind is your link to the Creator God, called your *soul*.

  - The subconscious mind never sleeps, never rests, never takes a break.

    - Which is the reason why our conscious mind needs to be on duty every waking hour of every day!

    - The subconscious mind left unguarded leaves it susceptible to error and misinformation.

- Your subconscious mind is the home of your habits, both good and bad.

  - Habits are behavior patterns that you have repeated enough that they are now controlled by your subconscious mind.

- How do I change my thought habits?

  - You change your Thought Habits by utilizing your self-awareness (Frankl's #1), your imagination (Frankl's #2), your conscience (Frankl's #3), and your independent will (Frankl's #4) to plainly state to the subconscious mind exactly what we choose to think, believe, feel, motivate and do!

- Thought is the cause of every effect.

- Remember, thought is energy. Active thought is active energy. Concentrated thought is concentrated energy. Thought concentrated on a definite purpose becomes power.

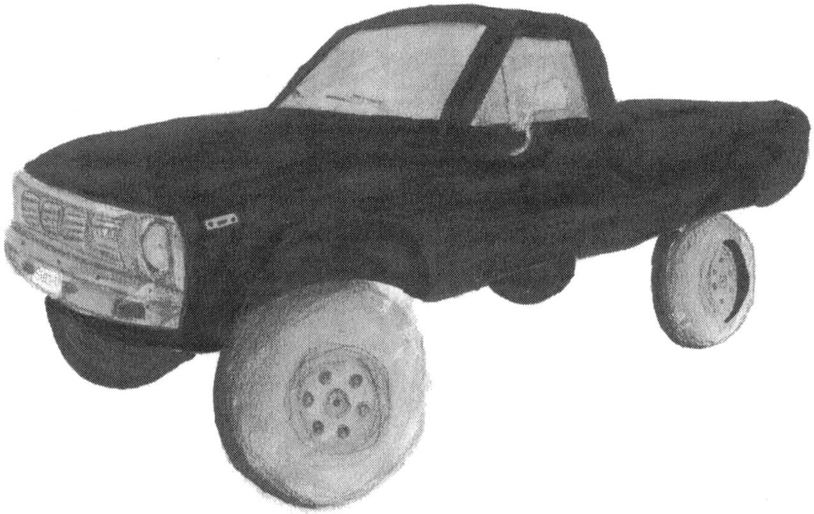

Chapter 6

How Do My Thoughts Affect Me?

"For as he thinks within himself, so he is."
Proverbs 23:7 NASB20

The Red Four-Wheel Drive Toyota Truck

MY FIRST CAR WAS a 1971 Tennessee Orange Volkswagen Beetle. It was originally one of my dad's cars, then he gave it to my oldest sister. When she got married and got another car, my dad got it back and sold it to me for $1,000 when I was 16.

The 1971 Tennessee Orange Volkswagen Beetle just was not the image I had for myself. But I drove that car for five years.

I think I was about 20 when I saw a beautiful red four-wheel drive Toyota truck driving on the interstate with a FOR SALE sign in the back window. I thought, *Now that looks more like me!* I quickly wrote the phone number down and placed it in my wallet. I had never seen a red one. I had seen gray and tan, but this was the only red four-wheel drive Toyota truck I had ever seen!

About six months later the old Volkswagen had over 200,000 miles on it, and it was nearly shot. It was finally time to get a more reliable vehicle. I thought, *I wonder if that red four-wheel drive Toyota truck is still for sale?*

I rummaged through my wallet and found the ragged piece of paper with the phone number. I called the owner and, to my surprise, it was still available. I made arrangements to meet the owner and take a test drive. He lived 45 minutes away. I did my test drive and ultimately purchased my dream vehicle, **the red four-wheel drive Toyota truck**!

Not my desired ride, but it got me to where I was going!

I left his house and got on the interstate to travel back home. I thought, *Finally, I have a vehicle that feels like me!* I had probably only been on the interstate for a few miles when I noticed *another* red four-wheel drive Toyota truck traveling the other direction on the interstate. I thought, *Well, I guess there is more than one.*

A few miles later, I exited the interstate. At the red light at the end of the interstate ramp, I saw another red four-wheel drive Toyota truck.

I was blown away! I got the truck because I really liked the truck, and I *thought* it was a unique color. By the time I finished my 45-minute ride home, I had seen several red four-wheel drive Toyota trucks just like mine!

What I did not know at the time is that each of us have a tiny piece of brain matter called the **reticular activation system**. This network of neurons is responsible for filtering the massive amounts of information your sensory organs are constantly throwing at it and selecting the ones that are most important for your Conscious Mind to pay attention to.

This was my desired ride!

My Reticular Activation System was now showing me all the red four-wheel drive Toyota trucks it had previously filtered out as "not important."

What Is the Reticular Activation System?

Your reticular activation system is a piece of the brain that starts close to the top of the spinal column and extends upwards around two inches. It has a diameter slightly larger than a pencil. All of your senses (except smell, which goes to our brain's emotional center) are wired directly to this bundle of neurons that's about the size of your little finger. The reticular activation system is like a filter or a nightclub bouncer that makes sure your brain doesn't have to deal with more information than it can handle.

The reticular activation system plays a big role in the sensory information you perceive daily. It's the gatekeeper of the information that is allowed into the Conscious Mind. Why do we need this little gatekeeper? Your senses are constantly feeding so much information to your brain that you can't possibly pay attention to all of it. The reticular activation system never gets a break!

Your reticular activation system decides what is important and what can be safely ignored. This doesn't just happen with sounds. Our skin is roughly 20 square feet that abounds with around a million nerve cells detecting pressure, pain, temperature, and location. And a human eye captures more than 300 megapixels of visual information every second!

Despite all this sensory information, it's estimated that the Conscious Mind can only handle slightly more than 100 pieces of information every second. There's a tremendous amount of paring down that needs to happen between your senses and your Conscious Mind. Your reticular activation system is the tool your brain uses to handle this excessive information problem. It is uniquely suited to distinguish between relevant and irrelevant pieces of information.

Your reticular activation system is the feedback loop between your Conscious Mind and your Subconscious Mind. Most people do not intentionally utilize their reticular activation system. Imagine what your reticular activation system can do if you intentionally tell it what is highly important!

There are certain types of information that always seem to get through the gates of the reticular activation system because it connects your Conscious Mind and your Subconscious Mind: for example, the sound of your name being called, or anything that threatens your safety or that of your loved ones. Our brains are literally wired to bring these things to the very top of our Conscious Mind because they're considered highly important.

A second — and the most commonly known — feedback loop for your thoughts are your **feelings**. If you are *feeling* happy, you are having happy *thoughts*. If you are *feeling* sad, you are having sad *thoughts*. Your feelings tell you what *frequency* you are thinking on. Using the farm metaphor, your thoughts are the seeds you sow. Your thoughts become things! And because you are different from any other creature on this earth, you have the power to change your thoughts!

Now that you are aware of the reticular activation system, you can develop the habit of using it intentionally. This critical feedback loop will inform you what you are really thinking. The next step is to exercise your self awareness!

Chapter 6 Assignment:

If it has been more than a week since you took the **Reticular Activation System** survey, take it again. If it hasn't been a week, review the report and identify whether you spent more thought time thinking **positive thoughts** or **negative thoughts**.

SALT Summaries:
Chapter 6: How Do My Thoughts Affect Me?

- The first feedback loop for your thoughts is your **reticular activation system**.
    - Your reticular activation system is a piece of the brain that starts close to the top of the spinal column and extends upwards around two inches.
    - Your reticular activation system is the gatekeeper of information that is let into your Conscious Mind.
    - Your reticular activation system decides what is important and what can be safely ignored.
    - Your reticular activation system is the feedback loop between your Conscious Mind and your Subconscious Mind.
    - Most people do not intentionally utilize their reticular activation system
    - Imagine what our reticular activation system can do for us if we intentionally tell it what is highly important!
- The second — and the most commonly known — feedback loop for your *thoughts* are your *feelings*.
    - If you are feeling happy, you are having happy thoughts.
    - If you are feeling sad, you are having sad thoughts.
    - Your feelings tell you what frequency you are thinking on.
- Using the farm metaphor, your thoughts are the *seeds* you *sow*.
    - Your **thoughts** become **things**!
- You have the power to change your thoughts!

PART 2

Your Beliefs: The Way You Choose to Think

you become what you think about.

- YOUR BEHAVIORS — The Way You "ACT"
- YOUR NEEDS — The Way You Are "MOTIVATED"
- YOUR ATTITUDES — The Way You FEEL
- YOUR BELIEFS — The Way You "THINK"
- YOUR THOUGHTS — The Source of your "BELIEFS"

Chapter 7

YOUR BELIEFS ARE IMPORTANT

"If you don't stand for something, you will fall for anything."
Gordon A. Eadie

My Beliefs — The Habits of My Mind

AS I MENTIONED IN the introduction, the death of my mother in 1973 had a major impact on my life. I suddenly had an enormous void in my life. My primary mentor, the person that gave my life clarity was now gone. I realized that I could sit around and feel sorry for myself, or I could do what my mother told me to do all the time: "Get up and make it happen." So, I did.

I started with a list my mother endeavored to teach me about the "Rules of My Universe." I wrote them down. They suddenly became very precious to me. I just remember that I felt like I was being overwhelmed with life, and I needed to find my own ground zero.

Through the years I have continued to add to my list. I have made a habit to contemplate my life events and look for the principle at work behind the scenes. At first, I didn't even name the list. Then, I felt like I needed to give my list a name. Over the years, I have called my list Life Lessons, Principles of Life, Axioms of Life, Key Principles of Life, Life Laws, and My Beliefs.

Now, I call my lists the Habits of My Mind, and I have divided them into four separate lists:

1. The Habits of My Mind - My Beliefs

2. The Habits of My Mind - My Beliefs about My Attitudes

3. The Habits of My Mind - My Beliefs about My Needs

4. The Habits of My Mind - My Beliefs about My Actions

The Freudian Trap

Most people never think about the way they think. They just think. They react to the world around them. They allow others outside of themselves to determine or define their narrative. Don't fall into the Freudian Trap of **Determinism**. Freud provides three excuses for your behavior:

1. Genetic Determinism — Your origins, your bloodline, your DNA all determine your behavior, which basically says your behavior is caused by what your grandparents did to you.

2. Psychic Determinism — Your childhood experiences and the way your parents raised you cause your tendencies. So, who you are is because of what your parents did to you.

3. Environmental Determinism — Something else outside of you (such as your socio-economic status, or your job, boss, or spouse) causes the way you behave.

All three of these theories of determinism provide excuses for your behavior and traps you into thinking you are stuck with the hand that "fate" dealt you.

You have learned that by using your self-awareness, your independent will, and your imagination, you can plainly state to your Subconscious Mind exactly what you choose to think, believe, feel, need, and do! The mental narrative (the thought) is the *cause*, the physical creation (the action) is the *effect*. You have learned that you can choose what thought seeds you want to plant and cultivate into thought habits (Beliefs).

Remember what you have learned:

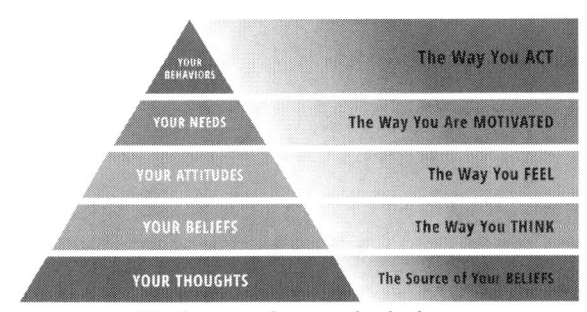

```
YOUR BEHAVIORS      The Way You ACT
YOUR NEEDS          The Way You Are MOTIVATED
YOUR ATTITUDES      The Way You FEEL
YOUR BELIEFS        The Way You THINK
YOUR THOUGHTS       The Source of Your BELIEFS
```

You become what you think about.

1. Your **thoughts** are the source of your beliefs *(The Way You Think)*.

2. Your **beliefs** (The Way You Think) have a cause-and-effect impact on your attitudes *(The Way You Feel)*.

3. Your **attitudes** (The Way You Feel) have a cause-and-effect impact on your needs *(The Way You are Motivated)*.

4. Your **needs** (The Way You are Motivated) have a cause-and-effect impact on your behaviors *(The Way You Act)*.

The Present: What Are Your Thoughts (Beliefs) About Yourself?

Each of us have our own little cocoon we live in called "My Universe." Knowingly or unknowingly, you take your life's experiences, successes, failures, victories, disappointments and categorize them into "The Rules of Your Universe." You have other influencers like parents, teachers, friends, and mentors. But all that outside information gets filtered by "The Rules of Your Universe."

Unfortunately, many people give away their right to lead and manage their own universe. The gravitational pull of another person's will can cause you to act contrary to your own

Rules. It is easy to fall into that trap if you aren't confident in your own thought habits (Beliefs).

You initiate a specific power to your beliefs, goals, and dreams when you write them down. Your universe is just a microcosm of the *actual* universe. Writing down your beliefs helps you reconcile your beliefs with the actual universe. It helps you put a stake in the ground so that you can manage new information and process it effectively. If you grow properly, you will always be adding new beliefs and getting rid of old ones that do not fit your universe any longer. Actually, you become 42 percent more likely to achieve your goals and dreams simply by writing them down on a regular basis. Your thoughts are the source of your beliefs (The Way You Think). It is time to get them written down!

Chapter 7 Assignment

I have developed four surveys to assist you in identifying your beliefs in four categories. Go to **SaltYourThoughts.com** and complete them:

- **THE HABITS OF YOUR MIND – 1 – YOUR BELIEFS** (Rank 25 Items)

- **THE HABITS OF YOUR MIND – 2 – BELIEFS ABOUT YOUR ATTITUDES** (Rank 15 Items)

- **THE HABITS OF YOUR MIND – 3 – BELIEFS ABOUT YOUR NEEDS** (Rank 10 Items)

- **THE HABITS OF YOUR MIND – 4 – BELIEFS ABOUT YOUR ACTIONS** (Rank 25 Items)

SALT Summaries:
Chapter 7: Your Beliefs Are Important

- Your beliefs are the way you think.

- Freud provides three excuses for your behavior.

    - Genetic Determinism: your origins, your bloodline, your DNA, which basically says your behavior is caused by what your grandparents did to you.

    - Psychic Determinism: which says your childhood experiences, the way your parents raised you cause your tendencies, so, who you are is because of what your parents did to you.

    - Environmental Determinism: says that something else outside of you, your socio-economic status, or your job, boss, or spouse causes the way you behave.

- All three of these theories of determinism provide excuses for your behavior and trap you into thinking you are stuck with the hand that fate dealt you.

- Each of us have our own little cocoon we live in called "My Universe."

- The gravitational pull of another person's will can cause you to act contrary to your own rules.

- Research shows you become 42 percent more likely to achieve your goals and dreams simply by writing them down on a regular basis.

- Writing down your beliefs helps you reconcile them with the actual universe.

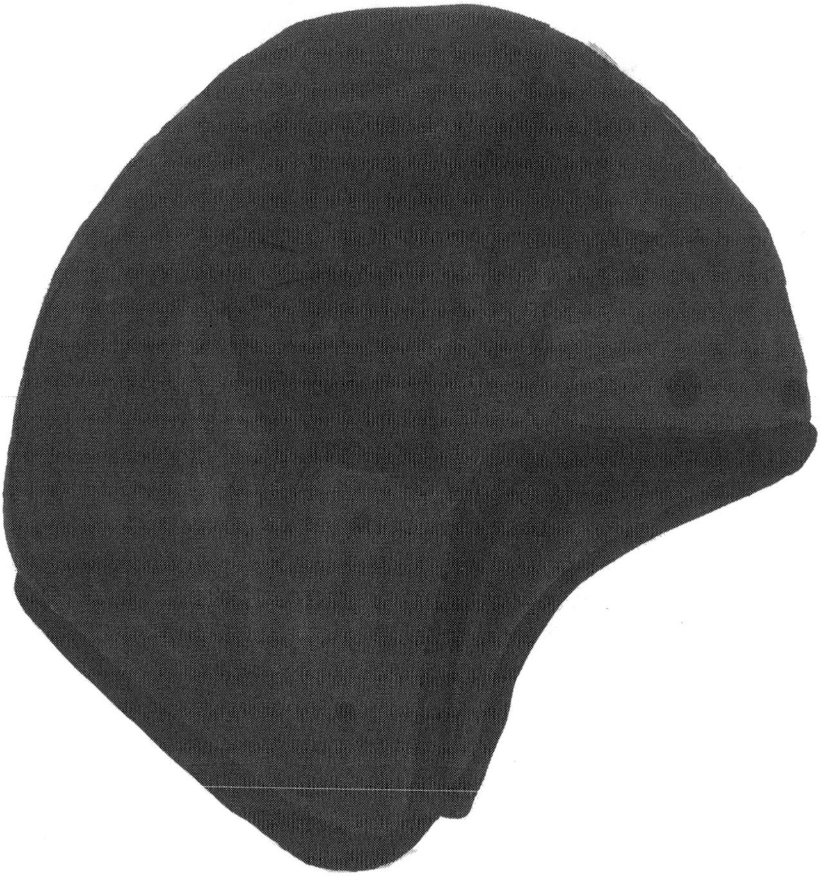

Chapter 8

WHERE DO YOU COME FROM?

"Insanity is doing the same thing over and over again and expecting different results."
Albert Einstein

When You Are in the Ditch

THE FALL OF 1972 yielded a good crop of watermelons! I was able to purchase a fairly new, but used, Honda QR50. I was 11 years old and proud of my new motorcycle! I rode it every chance I got! We lived about five miles from my grandparents and there was a dirt road that connected the two main roads from our house to theirs. Four of the five miles to their house was the dirt road. It was one of my most favorite places to ride because it was fun to make dust on the dirt road and it seemed like a long trip to me. Besides, there was always something wonderful to eat at my grandmother's house!

One day in the spring of 1973 I got home from school around 3:00 p.m. and decided to go to my grandparent's house. I had a great ride over and my grandparents were delighted to see me. Grandmother gave me a big piece of homemade blueberry pie (my favorite). It was now about 5:00 p.m. and I thought to myself, *I had better get home and find out what's for dinner!*

I went outside and was surprised that it had rained while I was inside. One of the reasons I got such a good deal on my motorcycle is that it was hard to start when it rained. I tried to kick start it a couple of times but had no success. I tried to push it off in the yard, but the grass was too wet and just made the back tire skid. I tried to push it down my grandmother's driveway, but still did not have success. So I went out to the road.

Now, you need to understand this asphalt country road didn't really go to any specific location. It was really just a connector to other small farms. There was very little traffic on this road and most of it was pickup trucks. Most of the roads connected to this road were dirt roads just like the one I used to get from my house to grandmother's house.

The Honda QR 50 — took a lot of watermelons to buy this baby!

Normally, I would push the motorcycle off without my helmet on because it was hard to do with a helmet on. But this time, for some reason I heard my mother's voice in my head say, "Put your helmet on!" So, I did.

I pushed the motorcycle down the road toward home trying to get enough speed to jump on and pop it in gear and get it started, but the back tire just kept on sliding on the wet asphalt. I tried pushing toward my house twice, but I could not get it started. I turned around and started pushing it back toward grandmother's house, thinking I might need another piece of pie if this thing doesn't start soon! Finally, I caught enough friction to turn the back tire and it started. I pulled over to the shoulder of the road to catch my breath with the motor still running.

Suddenly, I hear tires squealing, metal bending, and turn around just in time to see a car coming toward me out of control, swerving all over the road.

I don't remember ever seeing a car on this road, much less one going that fast! The car went nose first into the opposite ditch, then the rear end went into the ditch, then it popped out of the ditch and headed straight for me. I thought to myself, *I'm not even on the road and that car is going to hit me.* And it did. Before I could reach the throttle on the handlebar to get out of the way, I felt the impact.

The car that hit me was a 1973 light blue Ford Maverick. Fortunately, the bumper of the car hit my seat, and it threw me up in the air. My back hit the windshield. My helmet hit the roof as I did a backflip over the car. I landed in a seated position on the pavement which gave me a significant road rash. I continued to tumble and skid leaving much of my skin and half of my helmet on the pavement.

There wasn't much left of my cutoff blue jeans when I woke up in the opposite ditch. My first thought was how bad my whipping was going to hurt because I barely had any skin left on my butt! My fear of my daddy's belt was more intense than my injuries. I could feel the bone sticking out of my left elbow. I could tell my ribs were broken because it was very difficult to get a breath of air. My legs were covered with blood. I wondered if my legs would even move.

I always got into trouble for anything that didn't go according to plan, and this event was certainly not according to the plan!

As I opened my eyes, it looked like I was in the bottom of a well looking up. I could barely make out the sky. I figured my dad would blame me for the accident because I was on the side of the road even though this lady was driving really fast on wet asphalt. At that point the pain of my injuries became more intense. For a moment I just wanted to stay in the ditch! As my eyes came into focus, I realized I could hear the voice of my grandfather screaming, "Get this car off my boy!"

Then, I realized no one knew I was in the ditch. This increased the temptation to stay in the ditch. As long as I stayed there, it delayed me having to deal with what happened.

I got my thoughts together and overcame the temptation to stay in the ditch. I sustained several fractured ribs and vertebrae, and about half of my body was covered in road rash (it was summer, and I did not have a shirt on). Getting out of the ditch was one of the hardest things I had ever done. But I was glad to be alive! Even in my 12-year-old mind, I knew it was better to be alive and deal with the consequences than to stay in the ditch.

The Power of Your Thoughts

You can use your unique human characteristic of self-awareness to identify where your thoughts have taken you up to this point in your life. Then you can determine if you like your current situation or if you would like to choose some different results. If you want different results, you must change your thoughts. **You must get out of the ditch!**

You can use the unique human characteristic of imagination to think different thoughts. Using your imagination, you can visualize different results. You can change the frequency of your thoughts. Remember, each thought transmits a frequency. Sustained thoughts create the patterns of the frequencies for your life.

I believe it is time to harness those thoughts and ensure they are working for you and not against you! It is critical to think more on what you *want*, and less about what you *don't want*.

Research reveals you have about 60,000 thoughts a day. Can you imagine trying to control all your thoughts?

Fortunately, the creator of the universe gave you at least two short cuts. The first shortcut is your reticular activation system (explained in Chapter 6). The second one is your feelings (also explained in Chapter 6). Your feelings tell you what you are thinking. Your thoughts are the *cause*, and your feelings are the *effect*. Your *feelings* (positive or negative) intensify the strength of your *frequency*.

The Natural Law of Attraction states, "Like attracts like." When the frequencies of your thoughts are intensified (by feelings), they attract more of the same back to you. We see many manifestations of the Law of Attraction in nature: for example, "birds of a feather flock together."

The frequencies you transmit will be brought back to you through your feelings and your reticular activation system.

The Three Tenses of Life

Life as we know it is composed of the past, the present, and the future. Using your self-awareness, you can utilize these three tenses to consider **your life's timeline**.

The **past** is anything that has happened before this moment. It is a result of your previous thoughts, beliefs, attitudes, and behaviors. It is where your experience was developed. It also holds your memories, both positive and negative. The past is something to learn from — NOT to live in.

The **present** is now, this moment — your thoughts, beliefs, attitudes, and behaviors. It is being who you are, making decisions on what to think, believe, feel, need, and do today. The present is where you want to *act* rather than be *acted upon*.

The **future** begins with the next moment. The next moment is where todays are created. The next moment is where you can exchange old habits for new and better ones. You can choose to become who you desire to be rather than just react to what has happened to you. The next moment is full of possibilities only limited by your own imagination.

What is the Purpose of Your Memories? (Where Have You Been?)

Your memories provide an exercise for your self-awareness. They provide a sense of self as you move through time. They provide an important record of who you were — the result of your past thoughts and decisions. Your memories may also provide you with potential solutions to current problems.

Your memories should give you confidence. When you remember what you've been through it can give you confidence that you will get through whatever you are going through now!

You don't need to live in the past, but I hope a quick glance in the rear view mirror will spark an attitude of gratefulness, both for the highs that you have had, as well as making it through the lows in your past.

"Insanity is doing the same thing over and over and expecting different results."

In the opening quote for this chapter, Einstein reminds us that doing what we've always done will result in what we've always gotten. Expecting different results without any change is truly insanity.

It is time to get out of the ditch! If you want different *results,* you must think different *thoughts*.

Creating Your Life's Timeline

The easiest way I know to help you begin the process of discovering the way you think is to ask the question, **"What is your life's timeline?"** You need to take a few moments and consider your past.

If you were to plan a summer vacation for you and your family, you must begin with two things: First: Where are you now? What is the location of your starting point? Second: What is the location of your destination?

Your first step in uncovering your current belief system is to identify the location of your starting point. The best way I know to slowly and deliberately identify your starting place is to complete your life's timeline.

Creating your timeline takes about 30 minutes. Find a place where there are minimal distractions. Some people find it easier to plot life events on a graph, while others prefer spreadsheets. I have provided both. Begin by writing the month/day/year of your birth, below the word "Birth" on the graph or spreadsheet. Then write today's date month/day/year, below the words "Present Day." Now we have defined a specific amount of time to consider.

Next, consider your experiences and choose five events in your life that you consider to be highs or positive events. Grade the event to be either a High Point, a Moderately High Point, or an Extremely High Point. Don't get overwhelmed by detail; you can come back and refine at any time. Obviously if you are under 20 years old, it may be difficult to identify five major events. But if you are 60 years old, it may be easy to come up with 20 or more events. The key here is to consider and plot those events that have made a positive difference in your life — the events that may have helped you define the world you live in.

Next, consider your experiences and choose five events in your life that you consider to be lows or negative events. Grade the event to be either a Low Point, a Moderately Low Point, or an Extremely Low Point. Again, don't get overwhelmed by detail; you can come back and refine at any time. There is no magic to the number 5 either. You can define more if you need to or less if you need to. Again, the key is to identify those negative events that have influenced your life view.

These events may include choices, successes, or failures in education, career, relationships, finance, and family: births, deaths, marriages, divorces, graduations, promotions, demotions, accidents, and miracles. The more honest you can be with yourself the better! Now expand the list until you feel confident you have captured the most important events in your life. Don't rush this process. Take as much time as you need to feel you have identified your Key Life Events. You are engaging your memories that are stored in your subconscious mind.

Chapter 8 Assignment:

Using the template below and the chart on the following page, complete your life's timeline.

EXTREMELY HIGH POINT			SALT Your Thoughts	Life's Timeline: Birth to Present
HIGH POINT			
MODERATELY HIGH POINT			
BIRTH			PRESENT DAY
MODERATELY LOW POINT			
LOW POINT			
EXTREMELY LOW POINT			

SALT Your Thoughts | My Life's Timeline: Birth to Present

MY LIFE'S TIMELINE				
DATE	AGE	EVENT	Extremely High / High / Moderately High / Moderately Low / Low / Extremely Low	NOTES
	0	Birth	High	

SALT Summaries:
Chapter 8: Where Do You Come From?

- If you want different *results*, you must think *different* thoughts.

- Sustained thoughts create the patterns of the frequencies for your life.

- It is critical to think *more* on what you *want*, and *less* about what you *don't want*.

- When the frequencies of your thoughts are intensified (by feelings), they attract more of the same back to you.

- The Three Tenses of Life

    - The **past** is anything that has happened before this moment.

        - It is a result of your previous thoughts, beliefs, attitudes, and behaviors.

        - The past is something to learn from — NOT live in.

    - The **present** is now - this moment.

        - Your thoughts, beliefs, attitudes, and behaviors.

        - It is being who you are, making decisions on what to be, do, and say today.

        - The present is where you want to *act* rather than be *acted upon*.

    - The **future** begins with the next moment.

        - *The next moment is full of possibilities only limited by your own imagination.*

- **What is the Purpose of Your Memories? (Where Have You Been?)**

    - Your memories provide an exercise for your self-awareness.

    - They provide a sense of self as you move through time.

- They provide an important record of who you are.

- Your memories may provide you with potential solutions to current problems.

- When you remember what you've been through it can give you confidence that you will get through whatever you are going through now!

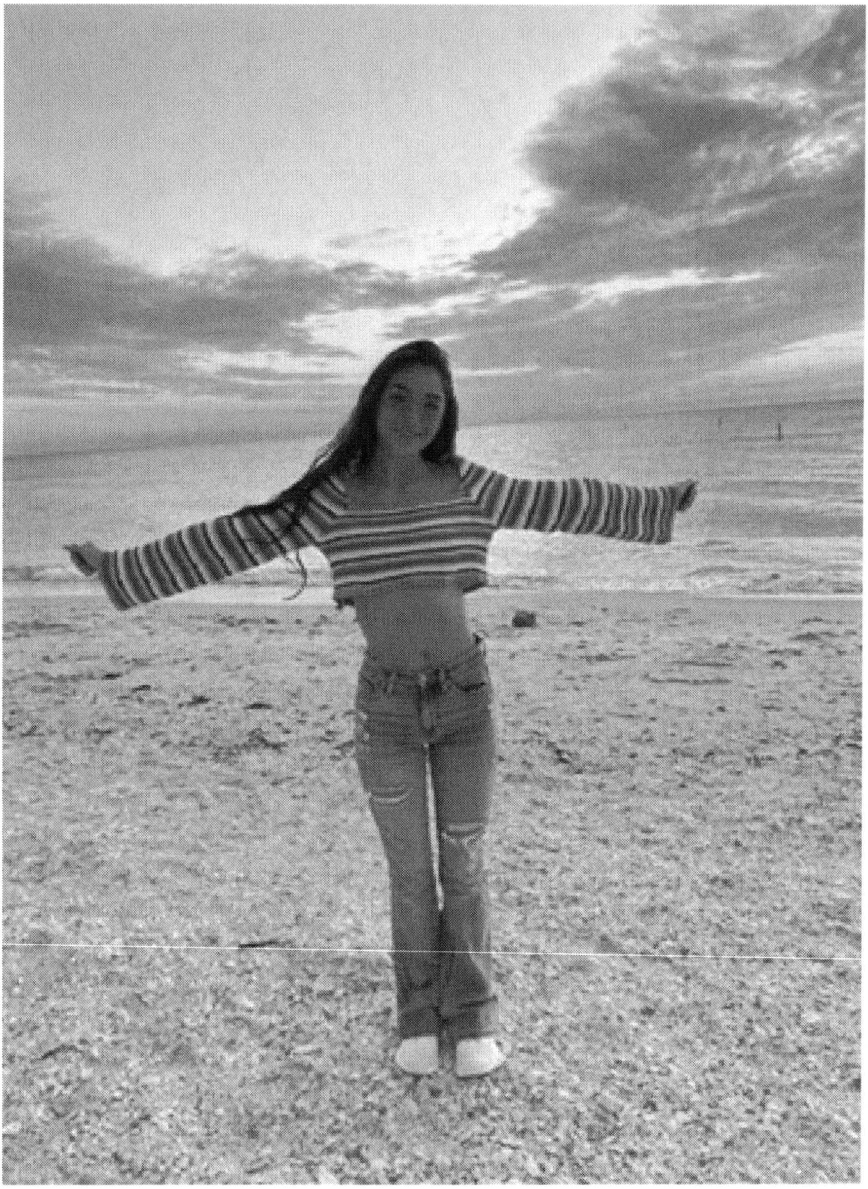

Chapter 9

REMEMBER GRATEFUL MOMENTS

"Gratitude: the state of being grateful; thankfulness."
Merriam-Webster Dictionary

My Own Life's Timeline

I GIVE MORE THAN 100% to everything I do. But I have learned that living life with that level of intensity can also have some negative consequences. I have sustained several concussions and broken many bones giving everything I must to win at whatever sport I was playing at the time. I have had several near death experiences which makes me even more grateful to be alive. It is easy to see how God has watched over me my whole life. I am very grateful that I have had the opportunity to write this book. It will not surprise me to find out one of my primary purposes in life was to write this book.

What Are You Grateful For?

The "State of Being Grateful" can easily be categorized into three separate experiences of gratitude:

1. **The Experience of Gratitude as an Emotion:** This immediate and sometimes intense feeling of gratitude is most closely associated with a specific event or act. An example might be when someone returns your lost wallet with all its contents. There is immediate relief and immediate appreciation for the person who returned your wallet. You may even offer a reward out of your appreciation. But the emotion of gratefulness is brief. You get busy with your next task and your thoughts move on.

2. **The Experience of Gratitude as a Mood:** This feeling of gratitude is experienced over a period of time. In most cases where the mood of gratitude is present, it has resulted from a significant gain or loss in an individual's life. A significant gain could be a particular accomplishment like a graduation, a marriage, a birth, or a promotion. Because of the significance of the life event, the mood of gratitude may last for several days, weeks, or months. But as the individual's life continues and gets busy, the feeling of gratitude ultimately diminishes and gets lost in the hustle and bustle of life.

3. **The Experience of Gratitude as a Character Trait:** This feeling of gratitude is experienced by an individual who chooses to develop the habit of gratitude. This individual doesn't wait on something from outside of their control to experience gratitude. They choose to have a general attitude of gratitude. They take time every day to be grateful.

In the introduction of this book, I shared with you about a time I came home from work with only a few dollars left in both my business and personal bank accounts, and how I desperately reached out to the Supreme Power of this universe. When I look back at that memory, I am filled with gratitude. Whenever I am discouraged or challenged or need encouragement, I remember how the Creator has led me and provided for me in the past. It puts me in the "state of being grateful."

To SALT Your Thoughts, you must learn to be grateful in any circumstance. Remember the first step to SALT Your Thoughts involves pushing the reset button, then focusing your thoughts on positive energy. Purposefully choosing to be grateful brings your thoughts into focus on positive energy.

The System: SALT Your Thoughts:

Step #1: Push the Reset Button: Focus your thoughts on positive energy.

- Reset - Yesterday is behind you; Focus on Today and Tomorrow (Chapter 16)

- Focus on your Gratitude List (Chapter 9)

One of the best gifts you will ever give yourself is to develop the habit of gratitude. You need to start every morning in the state of being grateful. Starting each morning in the state of being grateful aligns and calibrates the way you think, what you believe, the way you feel, what you need, and the way you act for that day. This state of being tells your Reticular Activation System to find things for which to be grateful. Regardless of what happens to you that day, you are looking for ways to be grateful. This habit sets you up for a much more enjoyable life!

Chapter 9: Assignment

Go to **SaltYourThoughts.com** and complete the "Your Gratitude List" survey.

SALT Summaries:
Chapter 9: Remember Grateful Moments

- The **State of Being Grateful** can easily be categorized into three separate experiences of gratitude:
  - An Emotion
  - A Mood
  - A Character Trait
- One of the best gifts you will ever give yourself is to develop the habit of gratitude
- Starting each morning in the state of being grateful aligns and calibrates the way you think, the way you feel and the way you act, for that day.

Share the Salt

Chapter 10

Find Your Joy

"Joy: the feeling of great pleasure and happiness."
Merriam-Webster Dictionary

Making a Difference

A FEW MONTHS AGO, my wife Sandra and I went to the mall to pick up a birthday present for one of our grandchildren. I saw a man out of the corner of my eye watching us. We continued shopping and turned a corner and there he was.

He looked at me straight in my eyes and put out his hand and said, "Billy Mullins — I'm sure you don't remember me, but I am Pastor John. I came to your church almost 20 years ago asking for money to start my inner city school ministry and church."

"Yes, Pastor John, now I remember you," I said. "How have you been doing?"

Pastor John replied, "Billy, I was just thinking about you the other day. The seed money you gave me 20 years ago gave our ministry a start. This year we have 80 students enrolled in our inner schools programs, and our church has about 250 members, and we have changed hundreds of lives due to our ministry! I was hoping one day I could see you and tell you how much I appreciated the difference you have made in so many lives!"

"Pastor John," I said, "I am filled with joy to know that the seeds we planted 20 years ago have been fruitful and multiplied!"

We talked for a few more minutes and then said our goodbyes. I turned to Sandra after he had gone and said, "One of my greatest desires in life is to have a positive influence in the lives of my family and to others. What I did not realize is how much joy it gives me to actually see the fruits of those efforts!"

What Is the Difference Between Joy and Happiness?

I believe joy and happiness are very different. I think they aren't mutually exclusive, meaning you can have one without the other. It is fantastic when you have them both, but they are different.

Joy is a choice. It is one of the *Gifts of the Spirit* (Galatians 5:22-23). It seems to me that joy is something that is *inside* (or internal). Joy comes from your spirit. The energy that is held within our spirit. When your energy is connected to the Supreme Energy in the Universe, your *energy* has an endless supply.

Joy is bigger than an event. Joy is a lifestyle. When you are *connected to* and have *confidence in* the Supreme Power in the Universe, you can lose a loved one and experience joy and sadness at the same time. Joy because you know it is all a part of His plan, and sadness because you will miss them. Joy is deliberate and intentional. Joy is a smaller word but a much bigger concept than happiness.

Happiness seems to depend on *outside* circumstances. Therefore, happiness is something *outside* (or external). For example, my wife Sandra experiences happiness when she eats a piece of chocolate. Happiness is most often associated with an emotional response. That emotional response can be just for a moment in time. But it doesn't have endurance. Happiness seems to me to be more personal. Meaning, happiness is really for you, while joy is bigger. It's for everyone! People may seek happiness, but *joy* is the real reward!

To *SALT Your Thoughts*, you must also learn what brings real joy to you. Remember the first step to SALT Your Thoughts involves pushing the reset button, then focusing your thoughts on positive energy. Purposefully choosing to be grateful brings your thoughts into focus on positive energy. Purposefully choosing to focus on what brings you joy further enhances your efforts to focus your thoughts on p*ositive energy*.

The System: SALT Your Thoughts:

Step #1: **Push the Reset Button:** Focus your thoughts on positive energy.

    1. *Reset - Yesterday* is behind you; *Focus* on *Today* and *Tomorrow* (Chapter 16)

    2. *Focus* on your *Gratitude List* (Chapter 9)

    3. *Focus* on your *Joy List* (Chapter 10)

Chapter 10: Assignment

"This is the day the LORD has made; I WILL Rejoice and be GLAD in it!" Go to **SaltYourThoughts.com** and complete the **What Is Joy to You** survey.

SALT Summaries:
Chapter 10: Find Your Joy

- Joy and happiness are very different, and they are also mutually exclusive.
- Joy is a choice.
    - It is one of the Gifts of the Spirit (Galatians 5:22-23).
- Joy comes from your spirit.
- Joy is a lifestyle.
- Joy is deliberate and intentional.
- Joy is a smaller word but a much bigger concept than happiness.
- Happiness seems to depend on outside circumstances.
- Happiness can be just for a moment in time, but it doesn't have endurance.
- Happiness is really for you, while joy is bigger; it's for everyone!
- People may seek happiness, but joy is the real reward!

Find your Triggers

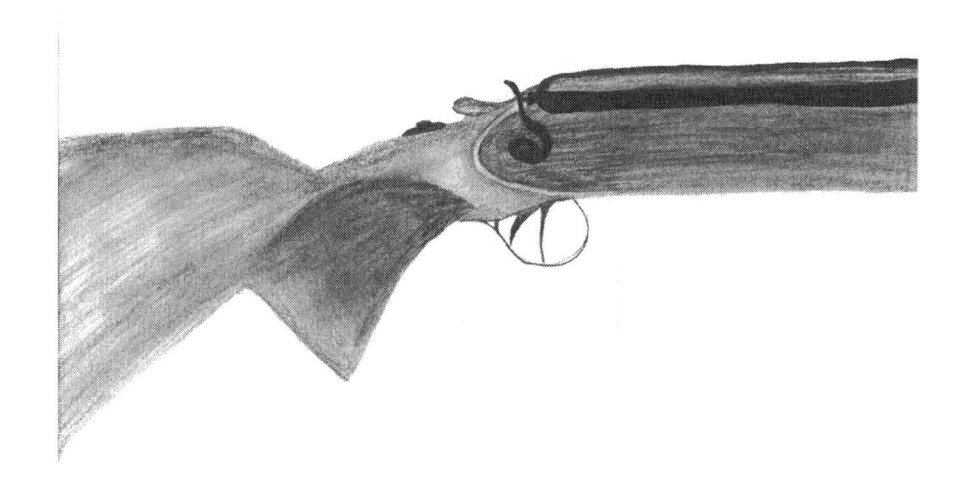

Chapter 11

KEEP YOUR FINGER ON YOUR TRIGGERS!

"Happiness depends on ourselves."
Aristotle

Triggers

ONE DAY, MY DAD sent me out hunting after a particular pest that was eating our crops. I was 10 years old. My gun was a single shot Stevens 22 cal./410 shotgun over and under. He felt I needed a bigger gun, so he let me use his double-barreled 12-gauge shotgun. The gun had two triggers; the trigger in the front shot the barrel on the right, and the trigger in the back shot the barrel on the left. My dad's double-barreled 12-gauge did not have a safety on it. If you are not familiar with guns, most guns have a button or switch that you can press that will not allow you to pull the trigger. (That is why it is called a safety!) Because this gun didn't have one, my dad gave specific instructions: "Don't run with your fingers on the triggers!"

You probably already know what happened. I spied my target, but it was moving, so I had to move quickly! I took a few steps (with my fingers on the triggers) and then jumped over an old log to get the perfect shot. I must have tightened my grip on the gun when

I jumped (I didn't want to drop my dad's gun) and, in mid-air, my fingers tightened on the trigger and pulled them both at the same time! I believe it was the first time I ever performed a gainer. (A *gainer* is the acrobatic trick of performing a backwards somersault while still moving forward.) Well, I guess mine was more of a half gainer, because I landed face down. I didn't hit my target, but I learned that my triggers are my responsibility!

Your Triggers Are Your Responsibility

There is another definition of a trigger. As a verb, **trigger** means "to cause (an event or situation) to happen or exist," according to the Cambridge English Dictionary.

People, things, or events that trigger or cause your behavior are *your responsibility*. You may find that it is important — if not necessary — to install a safety on some of them!

You learned in Chapter 6 about the Reticular Activation System. It is much more important to focus your Reticular Activation System on people, things, or events that trigger a positive change in your mood.

I call these triggers your **Positive Mood Triggers** — thoughts or actions that immediately trigger a shift in your mood.

What Are Your Positive Mood Triggers?

Positive Mood Triggers are those thoughts or actions that immediately change or shift your mood in a *positive* direction. It could be looking at a picture of a loved one, or a fun moment in time, or listening to your favorite song, or thinking about the beach, the mountains, the stars, your favorite food, or place. You will utilize your Positive Mood Triggers in the future. Your Reticular Activation System and your feelings tell you what you are thinking. If your thoughts are causing you to feel sad, frustrated, or angry, *change your thoughts*! Your list of Positive Mood Triggers are a quick way to help you change your thoughts!

To *SALT Your Thoughts*, you must identify your Positive Mood Triggers. Remember the first step to SALT Your Thoughts involves pushing the reset button, then focusing your thoughts on positive energy. Purposefully choosing to be grateful brings your thoughts into focus on positive energy. Purposefully choosing to focus on what brings you joy further enhances your efforts to focus your thoughts on positive energy. Identifying your Positive Mood Triggers provides you a shortcut to positive energy.

The System: SALT Your Thoughts:

Step #1: **Push the Reset Button**: Focus your thoughts on positive energy.

    1. *Reset - Yesterday* is behind you; *Focus* on *Today* and *Tomorrow* (Chapter 16)

    2. *Focus* on your *Gratitude List* (Chapter 9)

    3. *Focus* on your *Joy List* (Chapter 10)

    4. *Focus* on your Positive Mood Triggers (Chapter 11)

Chapter 11: Assignment

Go to **SaltYourThoughts.com** and complete the **What Are Your Positive Mood Triggers** survey.

SALT Summaries:
Chapter 11: Keep Your Finger On The Triggers!

- Your triggers are your responsibility.

    - Trigger means: *"to cause (an event or situation) to happen or exist."*

    - People, things, or events that trigger or cause *your* behavior are *your* responsibility.

- **Positive Mood Triggers** are those thoughts or actions that immediately change or shift your mood in a *positive* Direction.

    - You will utilize your Positive Mood Triggers in the future.

- Your Reticular Activation System and your feelings tell you what you are thinking.

- If your thoughts are causing you to feel sad, frustrated, or angry, use your list and *change your thoughts*!

- Your list of Positive Mood Triggers is a quick way to help you change your thoughts!

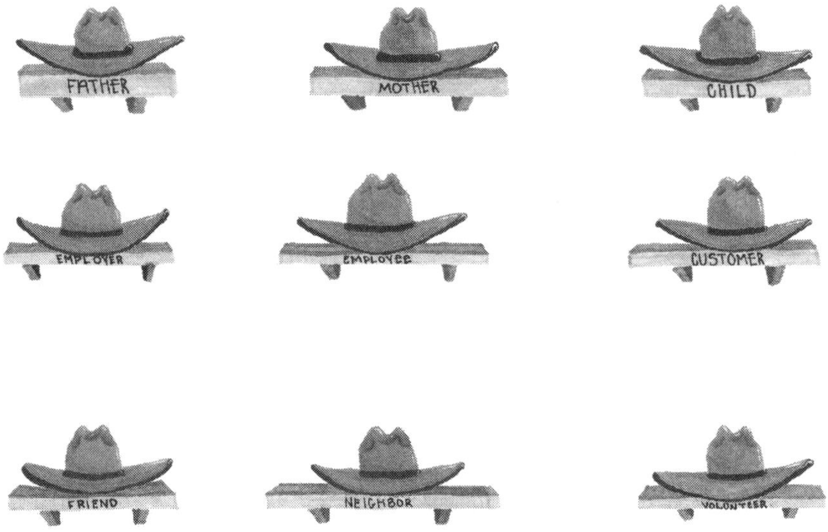
FATHER
MOTHER
CHILD
EMPLOYER
EMPLOYEE
CUSTOMER
FRIEND
NEIGHBOR
VOLUNTEER

Chapter 12

WHAT DO YOU DO?

"Role (noun): the position or purpose that someone or something has in a situation, organization, society, or relationship."
Cambridge Dictionary

What Hat Am I Wearing Now?

JUST LIKE EVERY ENTREPRENEUR, I had to "wear every hat" when I started my company. I had to wear "hats" like CEO (Chief Executive Officer), COO (Chief Operation Officer), CIO (Chief Information Officer), CFO (Chief Financial Officer), CSO (Chief Sales Officer), CMO (Chief Marketing Officer), CPD (Chief Product Development), CPE (Chief Product Engineering), HR Director, and Facilities Director (which meant I was the person everyone called when the toilet was clogged). The early days at my company were chaotic to say the least.

I finally realized I needed to ask myself, *What hat am I wearing now?* Clarifying my **roles** helped me become more effective in making decisions on a day-to-day basis. As the company grew and I started hiring more people, I was specifically looking for each new hire to take one of my roles. I wanted the person responsible to wear that hat so I could reduce the number of hats I was still having to wear.

Identifying *your* hats will clarify your focus. Understanding the roles you are responsible for on a day-to-day basis can turn a life of chaos into a life of structure and order.

What Are Your Current Roles?

The simplest way I know to identify where you are now is to look at your **current roles**. Some people have never taken the time to consider the different roles in which they function on a day-to-day basis. Becoming aware of your roles gives you the opportunity to define and refine them.

To get started in this process, consider your everyday life and the current roles you inhabit. Start with the big picture, and then "chunk it down." I will help you get started.

The first set of roles you should consider are your roles as an *individual*. To be healthy and stay healthy as an individual, you must create balance in the four roles of your individual health:

1. Your Physical Health

2. Your Spiritual Health

3. Your Mental Health

4. Your Social/Emotional Health

What would your individual health *roles include?*

The second set of roles you should consider are your roles as an *immediate family member*. Immediate family roles are typically categorized by these four family dimensions:

1. Husband/Wife

2. Father/Mother

3. Son/Daughter

4. Brother/Sister

What would your immediate family member *roles include?*

The third set of roles you should consider are your roles at your *work*.

"Work" is a very prominent role for most people. So, I asked myself the following two questions:

- How much time does the average person spend at work?
- How much discretionary time do we each have?

If you work for your complete adult life, from age 18 to 65, that is a total of 47 years of paid employment.

If you consider the average full-time hours worked per week (40 hours), multiplied by 50 weeks per year, that equals 2,000 hours per year. Multiply 2,000 hours per year by 47 years, and you will work a total of **94,000 hours** over the course of your working life.

40 hours per week spent working is:

- 13% of your total time over the course of an 80-year lifespan (with an average projected life expectancy of 80)
- 23% of your total time during the course of a 47-year work-life period.
- 20% of your total waking hours over an 80-year lifespan, assuming 8 hours of sleep a night.
- 34% of your total waking hours over a 47-year working-life period, assuming 8 hours of sleep a night
- 50% of your total waking hours of your work week.

Your work life IS a significant part of your life, but it is not the whole of your life.

If you look at your job description, your roles are most likely at least vaguely defined. If you do not have access to your job description, these categories may help you: Employee/Employer; Leader/Manager; Planning; Inspecting Inputs; Executing a Process; Measuring the Outputs.

What would your work *roles include?*

The fourth set of roles you should consider are your roles in your *community*. Your roles in your community would include roles like: Being a Friend; Volunteering in Your Church; Volunteering in Your Neighborhood; Volunteering in Your Political Party, and so on.

What would your community *roles include?*

Work/Life Balance

Effective living involves balancing other life responsibilities with your work. Think broadly, what are your other life responsibilities? Did you include personal exercise and renewal? My suggestion is to keep your list between seven and twelve roles. More than twelve becomes very difficult to manage and measure.

For example, I have identified seven roles for myself. Each role includes several aspects, but to list each aspect as a role itself would be too difficult to manage:

1. Personal Renewal & Exercise (Spiritually, Physically, Mentally, and Socially. Includes personal devotion, study, teaching, modeling, mentoring, learning, and exercising)

2. Husband (includes providing, leading, learning, listening, companionship, loving)

3. Father (includes providing, leading, learning, listening, companionship, loving each child)

4. Leader (includes my businesses, writing, coaching, teaching, modeling, mentoring, learning)

5. Investor (includes the complete portfolio)

6. Family Member (includes leading, learning, listening, loving each extended family member)

7. Community (includes leading, learning, listening to my friends, my small group at church, and the groups for which I volunteer)

Chapter 12 Assignment:

Now, consider the table below and identify *your* specific roles. You don't have to get it perfect — just get a good start. You will have plenty of time to edit as we move forward.

It's time now to go to **SaltYourThoughts.com** Life Tools and complete the **My Roles** worksheet.

SALT Your Thoughts | My Roles — Worksheet

General Roles	*My Roles*
Individual: Physical	
Individual: Spiritual	
Individual: Mental	
Individual: Social/Emotional	
Family: Husband/Wife	
Family: Father/Mother	
Family: Son/Daughter	
Family: Brother/Sister	
Work/School Role #1	
Work/School Role #2	
Friend Role #1	
Friend Role #2	
Community Service Role #1	
Community Service Role #2	

Who Is the Customer of Each Role?

Once you have identified your current roles, think about who the customer of that role is. In business, the word "customer" is typically defined as a person who purchases goods or services from another.

The definition of "customer" for this book is: *the person who receives any service, product, idea, or affection obtained from you via your relationship with that person.*

For example, you are the customer of your own health. But your family is also a customer of your own health. If you are not well, it affects your whole family as well as your friends. If you are a husband or wife, then your spouse (put their name in the customer box!) is the customer. If you are a father or mother, then write your children's names in the box, and so on.

SALT Your Thoughts | My Roles — Worksheet

My Roles	Customer

Go back to **SaltYourThoughts.com**, find **Life Tools**, and complete the **CUSTOMER** of each of your roles.

Creating a Positive Affirmation Statement for Each Role

When you profess a strong, positive affirmation in the form of a **belief** and **commitment** statement about each of your roles, it enables you to identify and visualize what your desired actions are as an end goal for each role. A positive affirmation statement is a fantastic tool to overcome negative thoughts that can sometimes take over and make you doubt yourself.

Examples of Positive Affirmation Statements

In the table below in the column labeled "General Roles," the first row of that column is labeled "Individual: Physical." In the column labeled "My Roles" on the first row, I would write "My Physical Health." In the next column labeled "Customer", on the same row, I would write "Me."

In the next column labeled "Positive Affirmation Statement," I would write the following:

I will exercise for a minimum of 30 minutes each day.

One of my Very Important roles is being the husband of my wife, Sandra. So, in the table below in the column labeled "My Roles" on the fifth row down where it says "Family: Husband/Wife," I would write "Husband." In the next column labeled "Customer" on the same row, I would write my wife's name "Sandra."

In the next column labeled "Positive Affirmation Statement," I would write the following:

My wife Sandra is my soulmate. She is the most important person in my life. I have and will display the utmost love, respect, integrity, affection, encouragement, communication, and understanding at all times to my best and dearest friend and lover.

Go back to **SaltYourThoughts.com**, **Life Tools** and complete your **Positive Affirmation Statement** for each of your roles:

My Goals

You have a column for a **weekly goal**, a **quarterly goal**, and an **annual goal**.

Weekly Goal: To continue with my example of "My Physical Health," remember in the column labeled "Positive Affirmation Statement," I wrote, "I will exercise for a minimum of 30 minutes each day." So, now in the column labeled "Weekly Goal," I would write "(2 miles/day) (7 days/week) = 14 miles/week."

Quarterly Goal: To continue with my example of "My Physical Health," there are 13 weeks in a quarter. So, 14 miles/week multiplied by 13 weeks = 182 miles/quarter. So, now in the column labeled "Quarterly Goal," I would write "(14 miles/week) (13 weeks) = 182 miles/quarter."

Annual Goal: To continue with my example of "My Physical Health," there are 4 quarters in a year. So, 182 miles/quarter multiplied by 4 quarters = 728 miles/year. So, now in the column labeled "Annual Goal," I would write "(182 miles/quarter) (4 quarters) = 728 miles/year."

Sometimes it is easiest to define a weekly goal and then calculate the numbers going forward. Other times, it may be easier to define the annual goal and then divide it into quarterly and weekly goals. For example, let's say you identify a book that you want to read this year. Let's say the book consists of 1300 pages. Your annual goal would be to read 1300 pages. Your quarterly goal would be (1300 pages/year) divided by (4 quarters in a year) = 325 pages/quarter. Your weekly goal would be (325 pages/quarter divided by 13 weeks/quarter) = 25 pages/week.

The fact that your goals are connected to your roles means that the goals that you are setting are, by definition, important to you. **You are the person in control.**

Using your self-awareness to identify your current roles in life clarifies the starting point of our journey together!

> Go back to **SaltYourThoughts.com**, **Life Tools** and complete the **Weekly Goal, Quarterly Goal**, and **Annual Goal** for your roles.

SALT Summaries:
Chapter 12: What Do You DO?

- Understanding the roles that you are responsible for on a day-to-day basis can transform a life of chaos into a life of structure and order. What are your current roles? What are your current responsibilities?

- The **first set of roles** I would suggest you consider are your roles as an individual. To be and stay healthy as an individual, you must create balance in the four roles of your individual health:

  - Your Physical Health

  - Your Spiritual Health

  - Your Mental Health

  - Your Social/Emotional Health

- The **second set of roles** I would suggest you consider are your roles as an immediate family member. Immediate family roles are typically categorized into these four family dimensions:

  - Husband/Wife

  - Father/Mother

  - Son/Daughter

  - Brother/Sister

- "Work" is a very prominent role for most people. Spending 40 hours per week working constitutes 50% of your total waking hours in a work week.

- The **third set of roles** I would suggest you consider are your roles at work. If you look at your job description, your roles are most likely at least vaguely defined.

- The **fourth set of roles** I would suggest you consider are your roles in your community. Your roles in the community may include being a friend, volunteering in your church, volunteering in your neighborhood, volunteering in your political party, and so on.

- Keep your list of roles between seven and twelve. Having more than 12 becomes very difficult to manage and measure.

- Who is the **customer** of each role?

    o The definition of a customer for this book is the person who receives any service, product, idea, or affection obtained from you through your relationship with that person.

- What is a **positive affirmation statement**? A positive affirmation statement is a phrase you can say to express your belief and commitment about each of your roles.

- **My Goals:** You have a column for a weekly goal, a quarterly goal, and an annual goal.

PART 3

Your Attitudes/Needs: The Way You Choose to Feel

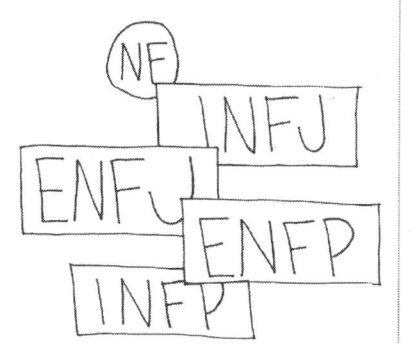

NT

ENTJ INTP
INTJ ENTP

SP

ESTP ESFP
ISFP ISTP

SJ

ESTJ ISTJ
ESFJ ISFJ

NF

INFJ
ENFJ ENFP
INFP

Chapter 13

I Finally Understand Me!

"The really valuable thing in the pageant of human life seems to me not the State but the creative, sentient individual, the personality; it alone creates the noble and the sublime, while the herd as such remains dull in thought and dull in feeling."
Albert Einstein

Understanding Yourself

I WAS INTRODUCED TO the Myers/Briggs Type Indicator (MBTI) in 1986 when I was a part of a management team. We all took the assessment, and I discovered that I am an ENTJ. These results provided me with tremendous insight into understanding myself. Sometimes, our minds need to label something to gain a better understanding of it.

The MBTI results also gave me valuable insights into the management of the company for which I worked. All the company officers shared the same MBTI Type, and 85% of the management team were of the same MBTI Type as the officers. However, I did not belong to that type. I understood that as the reason they needed me, which allowed me to flourish in that company and make a positive impact.

I was so impressed with the MBTI as a communication tool that I became certified by the Association for Psychological Type to administer the assessment. I firmly believe that MBTI is a fantastic tool for enhancing understanding in communication between individuals, team members, corporations, and employees. For over 30 years, I have taught the principles of MBTI to corporations, churches, schools, employees, customers, friends, and anyone willing to listen! I consider it a tool you can use to SALT Your Thoughts.

What Is Your MBTI 4-Letter Type?

The MBTI is a self-report questionnaire designed to make the psychologist Carl Jung's theory of psychological types understandable and applicable in everyday life. The results identify valuable differences between normal, healthy people — differences that can often be the source of much misunderstanding and miscommunication. It also provides a useful method for understanding people by examining eight personality preferences that everyone employs at different times. These eight preferences are organized into four opposite pairs. When an individual takes the indicator, the four preferences (one from each pair, identified as being most like you) are combined to form what is called a "personality type."

The four pairs of preferences, known as dichotomies, describe four key activities:

1. How we gain energy:

    - Extraversion (drawing energy from people and external stimuli) or

    - Introversion (recharging by reflecting inwardly)

2. How we perceive information:

    - Sensing (using our five senses to gather information) or

    - Intuition (relying on intuition and the "sixth sense")

3. How we make decisions based on information:

    - Thinking (making decisions based on objective analysis) or

    - Feeling (making decisions based on subjective values and emotions)

4. Our general attitude towards life:

- Judging (preferring structure, control, and order) or

- Perceiving (preferring flexibility and adapting to the flow)

The official MBTI Assessment Form M consists of 96 questions. However, for your convenience, I have created a simplified version with only 40 questions. In the appendix of this book and the accompanying software, you will find a "portrait" of each 4-letter type. If you prefer to take the official version, I have provided the contact information in the appendix as well.

Take a few minutes to complete the SALT Type Indicator. Take your time and avoid overthinking your responses. It's important to consider how you function in your home environment. Generally, the workplace can be characterized as ESTJ. If you are an ESTJ, your behavior at home mirrors your behavior at work. However, if you are not an ESTJ, you can learn the necessary skills to function effectively in the workplace. Our goal here is to help you identify your true self outside of work.

I firmly believe that your MBTI and Temperament represent your natural wiring across the four dimensions of energy, information gathering, decision-making, and lifestyle preferences. These represent your innate inclinations in each dimension. It's crucial to understand that this serves as your *starting point*, not your final destination. You have the ability to acquire the skills and abilities of any other dimension should you choose to do so.

Chapter 13 Assignment:

Go to **SaltYourThoughts.com**, and take the **SALT Type Indicator** assessment.

Personality Type Percentages

Many people are curious about the prevalence of different personality types and where their own type falls on that scale. The following population distribution data is sourced from personalitymax.com:

- Extroverted: 49.3%

- Introverted: 50.7%

- Sensing: 73.3%

- Intuition: 26.7%

- Thinking: 40.2%

- Feeling: 59.8%

- Judging: 54.1%

- Perceiving: 45.9%

Understanding and Measuring Your Temperament: The Four Temperaments

Some of the most important work in the field of Personality Typing has been conducted by David Keirsey, who developed the theory of temperament associated with type. This approach takes the 16 MBTI types and groups them into four categories called Temperaments. Each temperament consists of four MBTI types and carries a specific label, while each MBTI type is associated with a title.

The four temperaments and their corresponding MBTI types are as follows:

1. SJ – "The Guardians"

    - ESTJ – "The Supervisors"

    - ISTJ – "The Inspectors"

    - ESFJ – "The Providers"

    - ISFJ – "The Protectors"

2. SP – "The Artisans"

- ESTP – "The Promoters"
- ISTP – "The Crafters"
- ESFP – "The Performers"
- ISFP – "The Composers"

3. NT – "The Rationals"

- ENTJ – "The Executives"
- INTJ – "The Masterminds"
- ENTP – "The Inventors"
- INTP – "The Architects"

4. NF – "The Idealists"

- ENFJ – "The Teachers"
- INFJ – "The Counselors"
- ENFP – "The Champions"
- INFP – "The Healers"

Each temperament is associated with a set of personal values, which prove valuable in understanding yourself and interacting with others on a daily basis. These personal values, or attitudes, can greatly assist you in identifying your natural motivators and finding your comfort zone in the world. When you feel comfortable with yourself, it becomes easier to comprehend and appreciate the diverse temperaments of others.

On the following pages, you will find additional information on each temperament, including the percentage of the population represented by each temperament and its corresponding MBTI types, as well as a summary of the temperament and potential career paths.

SJ – The Guardians

The SJ group's primary objective is "Security Seeking." The SJ grouping includes the following types:

- ESTJ – "The Supervisors" – 8.7% of the population in the United States
- ISTJ – "The Inspectors" – 11.6% of the population in the United States
- ESFJ – "The Providers" – 12.0% of the population in the United States
- ISFJ – "The Protectors" – 13.8% of the population in the United States
- **Total: 46.1% of the population**

SJs' personal values include:

- Responsibility
- Duty
- Conservative Values
- Respect for Authority
- Service
- Tradition
- Hard Work

SJs are concrete in their communication and cooperative in implementing goals. They tend to excel in logistics and often engage in supervising and inspecting (SJT administering) or supplying and protecting (SJF conserving). They are reliable in action, perform good deeds, and command respect. Seeking security, they place their trust in legitimate power and desire membership. They usually adopt a stoic attitude toward the present, pessimistic outlook on the future, and fatalistic view of the past. Their preferred time and place is the past.

In terms of education, they lean towards commerce, and vocationally, they gravitate towards regulations and material work. As parents, they focus on enculturating their children. As spouses, they act as helpmates, and as children, they tend to be conformity-oriented. SJs make up 46.1% of the population.

Work that aligns with these values involves a stable and predictable environment, clear reporting hierarchy, and significant responsibility. The more structure and clarity provided, the better. SJs appreciate being evaluated and rewarded for their hard work and ability to accomplish tasks in an efficient and organized way. They prefer minimal change and value co-workers who share a similar sense of responsibility.

Example occupations include: accountants and financial officers, administrative assistants, business executives, computer programmers, judges, medical doctors, dentists, counselors, police officers, sales representatives, and teachers.

Presidents George Washington, Harry S Truman, and William Howard Taft are examples of Guardians.

SP – The Artisans

The SP group's primary objective is "Sensation Seeking." The SP grouping includes the following types:

- ESTP – "The Promoters" – 4.3% of the population in the United States
- ISTP – "The Crafters" – 5.4% of the population in the United States
- ESFP – "The Performers" – 8.5% of the population in the United States
- ISFP – "The Composers" – 8.8% of the population in the United States
- **Total: 27.0% of the population in the United States**

SPs' personal values Include:

- Freedom
- Fun

- Action and Variety

- Autonomy

- Excitement

- Skill

SPs are concrete in their communication and utilitarian in implementing goals. They can become highly skilled in tactical variation and often engage in promoting and operating (SPT expediting) or displaying and composing (SPF improvising). Artisans are graceful in action, daring, and adaptable. Seeking sensation, they trust in spontaneity and crave an impact on others. They typically have a hedonic perspective on the present, an optimistic outlook on the future, and a cynical view of the past. Their preferred time and place is the here and now.

In terms of education, they lean towards arts and crafts. Vocationally, they gravitate towards techniques and operations work. As parents, they tend to be permissive. As spouses, they act as playmates. And as children, they are play-oriented. SP-Artisans make up 27.0% of the population.

Work that aligns with these values includes jobs with a great deal of variety and change, where each day is different from the one before. SPs enjoy flexible and relaxed environments without excessive bureaucracy. They prefer to be evaluated based on their skillfulness and ability to independently complete their work. They excel when working with tangible objects, often demonstrating their talent with tools, crafts, or artistic endeavors.

Example occupations include: athletes, artists, performers, actors, carpenters, marketers, interior decorators, musicians, photographers, and fashion designers.

Ernest Hemingway, Franklin Delano Roosevelt, and Bob Dylan are examples of Artisans.

NT – *The Rationals*

The NT group's primary objective is "Knowledge Seeking." The NT grouping includes the following types:

- ENTJ – "The Executives" – 1.8% of the population in the United States

- INTJ – "The Masterminds" – 2.1% of the population in the United States
- ENTP – "The Inventors" – 3.2% of the population in the United States
- INTP – "The Architects" – 3.3% of the population in the United States
- **Total: 10.4% of the population in the United States**

NTs' personal values include:

- Intelligence
- Mastery and Constant New Learning
- Creativity and Ingenuity
- Logic
- Competence
- Independence
- Excellence

NTs are abstract in their communication and utilitarian in implementing goals. They excel in strategic analysis and often engage in marshaling and planning (NTJ organizing) or inventing and configuring (NTP engineering) as their most practiced and developed intelligent operations. They are competent in action, autonomous, and strong-willed. NTs are always in pursuit of knowledge, placing their trust in reason and having a hunger for achievement. They tend to be pragmatic about the present, skeptical about the future, and solipsistic about the past. Their preferred time and place are the interval and the intersection.

In terms of education, they lean towards the sciences, and vocationally, they gravitate towards technology and systems work. Rationals tend to be individualizing as parents, mind mates as spouses, and learning-oriented as children. Rationals are relatively rare, comprising only 10.4% of the population.

Work that aligns with these values includes an environment focused on high intellectual pursuits and achievements. NTs enjoy mastering new technologies and using creativity to solve complex and theoretical problems. They thrive when working with individuals they respect, particularly if they report to that person. NTs require constant challenges and numerous opportunities to work on new and original projects, as opposed to repetitive tasks. They excel at perfecting flawed systems and can exhibit ingenuity in problem-solving.

Example occupations include: business administrators, systems analysts, engineers, entrepreneurs, mathematicians, scientists, technical writers, and university professors.

Albert Einstein is the iconic example of a Rational.

NF – *The Idealists*

The NF group's primary objective is "Identity Seeking." The NF grouping includes the following types:

- ENFJ – "The Teachers" – 2.5% of the population in the United States
- INFJ – "The Counselors" – 1.5% of the population in the United States
- ENFP – "The Champions" – 8.1% of the population in the United States
- INFP – "The Healers" – 4.4% of the population in the United States
- **Total: 16.5% of the population in the United States**

NFs' personal values include:

- Harmonious Relationships
- Integrity
- Personal Expression
- Personal Growth
- Originality and Creativity
- Meaning and Possibilities

NFs are abstract in their communication and cooperative in implementing goals. They excel in diplomatic integration and often engage in teaching and counseling (NFJ mentoring) or conferring and tutoring (NFP advocating) as their most practiced and developed intelligent operations. Idealists have an instinct for interpersonal integration, display an increasing zeal for learning ethics, sometimes assume diplomatic leadership roles, and often speak interpretively and metaphorically about the abstract world of their imagination. NFs are empathic in action, benevolent, and authentic. Idealist types actively search for their unique identity, yearn for deep and meaningful relationships, seek a touch of romance in their daily lives, place implicit trust in their intuitive feelings, and aspire for profound experiences. They tend to be credulous about the future, mystical about the past, and their preferred time and place are the future and the pathway.

Educationally, they lean towards the humanities. Vocationally, they gravitate towards ethics and personnel work. In family interactions, they strive for mutuality, provide spiritual intimacy for their partners, foster opportunities for fantasy for their children, and engage in continuous self-renewal. Idealists are also relatively rare, comprising approximately 16.5% of the population.

Work that aligns with these values includes any work that NFs find personally meaningful and rewarding. NFs need to believe in the significance of their work and see the positive impact it has on others. They prefer a low-tension work environment where they can collaborate with caring individuals who appreciate and like them. Solving global problems in creative ways is particularly enjoyable for NFs, as is work that allows them and others to reach their greatest individual potential.

Example occupations include: early childhood teachers, clergy and religious workers, event coordinators, human resources personnel, politicians, psychiatrists, reporters, and writers.

Mohandas (Mahatma) Gandhi and Eleanor Roosevelt are examples of Idealists.

Your Temperament

What is your temperament? When I identified my temperament as "NT," it was my first real glimpse into how I am wired. It gave me comfort to know that there are others like me and helped me understand that the majority of people are not like me. When I saw the list of personal values associated with my temperament, I became excited! Finally, the values that I hold dear were written down for me to see.

Remember, it is critical to understand that your temperament is just the starting point in the journey of life. Each temperament has its own strengths and weaknesses. If there are aspects you would like to change, you can choose to learn new skills. For example, if you discover that your temperament is SP, as an SP, you enjoy flexible and relaxed environments without a lot of bureaucracy. However, you may have a job that is highly structured and organized. In that case, you may realize that you could be more effective if you were a little more "J." So, you decide to learn a couple of "J" skills like organization and planning. This will make your job easier to handle.

SALT Summaries:
Chapter 13: I Finally Understand Me!

- The MBTI is a self-report questionnaire designed to make Carl Jung's theory of psychological types understandable and applicable in everyday life.

- Its results help identify valuable differences between normal, healthy individuals, which often serve as the root cause of misunderstandings and miscommunications.

- Moreover, it provides a practical framework for understanding people based on eight personality preferences that everyone utilizes at different times.

- These preferences, organized into four pairs or dichotomies, describe four distinct activities:

  - How we derive energy:

    - Extraversion: Drawing energy from people and things outside ourselves.

    - Introversion: Re-energizing by turning inward and reflecting on oneself.

  - How we gather information:

    - Sensing: Reliance on what we can observe through our senses—sight, hearing, smell, touch, and taste.

    - Intuition: Utilizing a sixth sense or instinctual understanding beyond tangible stimuli.

  - How we make decisions based on gathered information:

    - Thinking: Employing an objective approach to decision-making.

    - Feeling: Applying subjective considerations and personal values in decision-making.

  - Our overall attitude toward life:

- Judging: Preferring structure and order, seeking control.

- Perceiving: Embracing flexibility, adapting to circumstances.

* Have you discovered your 4-Letter Type yet? Additionally, what percentage of the population shares your temperament and MBTI type? Explore the personal values, summary, and career options associated with your temperament.

Personal Values

Personal Needs

THE OTHER END OF THE STICK

Chapter 14

Seek Pleasure & Avoid Pain

"If you can't explain it simply, you don't understand it well enough."
Albert Einstein

The Difference Between Personal Values and Character

I BELIEVE THAT PERSONAL values are attitudes or qualities that reflect individual needs and drive one's actions. Personal values serve as a guiding force in decision-making and can be compared to picking up a stick — when you pick up one end, you also pick up the corresponding need on the other end. Personal values, therefore, shape attitudes and are intrinsic to oneself. They serve as an internal measure of oneself.

For instance, individuals with the SJ temperament, known as "The Guardians," primarily seek security. They find security in values such as responsibility and hard work, which in turn generate corresponding needs. The value of responsibility creates an inner need to be responsible, while the value of hard work creates a need to actively avoid laziness.

On the other hand, character traits are how others perceive and describe you from an outside perspective. When reading a book, the author uses character traits to help readers understand and connect with the characters. Character traits can describe physical attributes like height or clothing choices, but they mainly focus on behavioral aspects. Descriptive adjectives such as patient, faithful, or jealous are often used to portray character traits.

Personal values form internal definitions of who you are or aspire to be, providing a framework for your emotions and feelings. Character, on the other hand, represents how others describe your behavior and actions.

Personal Values

I conducted a directed study called "Personal Values" in 1993, involving about 3,500 people. What I found was that many people struggled to articulate the difference between a personal value and a character trait. As I further developed the study, I became convinced that personal values define our attitudes, which refer to the way we feel. To establish a common understanding, let's refer to the ABC Model of Attitudes,[13] also known as the tri-component model, which described attitudes in terms of three components:

1. **Affective Component:** This involves a person's feelings and emotions about the attitude object. For example: "I am scared of spiders."

2. **Behavioral Component:** It pertains to how our attitudes influence our actions or behaviors. For example: "I will avoid spiders and scream if I see one."

3. **Cognitive Component:** This refers to a person's beliefs or knowledge about the attitude object. For example: "I believe spiders are dangerous."

The ABC Model effectively defined attitude attributes in 1934. However, I suggest modifying the flow of the definition to CAB: Cognitive (Your Beliefs), Affective (Your Values/Attitudes), and Behavioral (Your Actions).

Now let's integrate several separate pieces of learning that have been useful in my experience to form an integrated whole.

The Cognitive Component (Your Beliefs): You have discovered that your thought habits are the source of your beliefs (the way you think). Your beliefs (the way you think) have a cause-and-effect impact on your attitudes (the way you feel). Relating this concept back to what you have learned in Chapter 5, your consciousness is your awareness of yourself and the world around you. Your conscious mind, or sometimes called your objective mind, deals with things from outside of yourself. It perceives and operates using the five physical senses (touch, taste, hearing, smelling, and seeing). The conscious mind deals with the impressions and objects of outward life. Your conscious mind has the ability to reason and explore cause and effect. It gathers information, identifies, defines, measures, compares, and ultimately makes decisions based on the gathered information. Your conscious mind is what Frankl called self-awareness. It is the cognitive component (your beliefs). Your beliefs (the way you think - your conscious mind; the cognitive component) precede the affective component (feeling). Your conscious mind is your reasoning will. Your subconscious mind is your instinctive desire, the result of past reasoning will. Your conscious mind is how you influence your subconscious mind. It is the gatekeeper, guardian, responsible ruler, and leader of your subconscious mind.

The Affective Component (Your Attitudes or Personal Values/Needs): I believe it is helpful to divide the affective component into two components:

- **Your Attitudes or Personal Values (The Way You Feel)** — At the core of being human, your attitudes or personal values relate to moving toward pleasure and/or away from pain. I believe it is most effective to label these attitudes, feelings as personal values. Relating this concept back to what you have learned in Chapter 5, your conscience is that deep moral awareness of right and wrong that keeps you from acting upon your most basic desires and urges. Your conscience produces guilt when you do something bad or unkind. Your conscience leads you to help others and to behave in a socially acceptable manner. Your conscience is where your thought habits are stored, and it is stored in your subconscious mind. Your subconscious mind controls everything in your life that is involuntary (habits) — your respiration, heart rate, blinking, liver, spleen, stomach, etc. Your subconscious mind is also the source of your security system. It constantly monitors the information coming from the senses for dangers and opportunities. It is the source of your "fight-or-flight" survival system. Your subconscious mind is the database for everything not in your conscious mind. It stores your thought habits (beliefs), your values, your previous experience, your memories, and your skills. It stores everything that you have ever seen, done, or thought. It provides the record of who you are today. Your values are stored in your subconscious mind, but you choose what values to have in your conscious mind. You did not choose your temperament. Your temperament is the source of your most basic desires and urges. If you do not like those basic desires and urges, you can choose to change them. You can choose to change the values you move toward and the values you choose to move away from.

- **Your Needs (The Way You Are Motivated)** — Your personal values create your core needs. Your needs are the other end of the stick. This subject is big enough to merit its own chapter, so I will discuss your needs in Chapter 15.

The Behavioral Component (Your Actions): Your behaviors are caused or influenced by your core needs (your motivators). Most of the time, the easiest thing to measure is your behaviors because they are easy to see. They are external to your mind. They are tangible. Your beliefs, attitudes, and needs are internal to your mind. Your personal values create your core needs. For example, if one of your personal values is "achievement," then it creates a need to achieve that must be fulfilled to be congruent with your personal value. You move toward "achievement" and away from "failure." It is only when we meet our core needs that we are energized and most effective. If your core needs are not met, the failure to meet your core needs will cause stress or even dysfunctional behavior. This cause-and-effect relationship between your personal values and your core needs sets up the opportunity for chronic stress. Personal values create core needs; unmet core needs are the cause of chronic stress. Anytime you find yourself demonstrating behaviors that are incongruent with your personal values, it causes chronic stress. You must remember that the key to any lasting behavioral modification is to change it at the source: **your thoughts**. *Thought* is the *cause* of every *effect*.

Now that we are aligned on the flow, let's discuss a real-life example. Amy is an ISFJ (Protector) freshman college student. Her values are responsibility, duty, conservative values, respect of authority, service, tradition, and hard work. Her core needs are membership or belonging and responsibility and duty. But her professor puts her as the team leader of a semester-long project. She is now managing six team members to complete the project. Her natural desire is to "protect" her team members, but her leadership role demands that she both inspect and supervise each member's productivity. This new role causes her a lot of stress. Amy believes managing her time effectively will improve her GPA and give her peace of mind. But because of her stress level, she spends hours on social media to calm her nerves.

In general, I believe that people are rational and strive to behave rationally. They desire their behaviors to align with their personal values. However, much of the time, we act in ways that are incongruent with our personal values, leading to chronic stress.

Let's break down Amy's components:

1. The Cognitive Component (Amy's Thoughts/Beliefs – The Way She Thinks): Managing her time effectively will improve her GPA and give her peace of mind."

2. The Affective Component Part A (Amy's Attitude/Personal Value – The Way She Feels): She wants to have a greater than average GPA and to feel good about herself.

3. The Affective Component Part B (Amy's Needs – Her Motivators): She wants to avoid conflict and stress while seeking pleasure.

4. The Behavioral Component (Amy's Behaviors – The Way She Acts): Because of her stress level, she spends hours on social media to calm her nerves.

It is easy to see the incongruence when you write it out on paper. But how do you fix it? It is most likely that Amy has other conflicting beliefs like: "The best stress relief is watching videos on social media until I forget about my stress." She is not aware that some of her beliefs are incongruent with her other beliefs. Most people will move toward pleasure and avoid pain. In her case, moving toward the pleasure of relieving stress by watching videos on social media became more important than the pain she associated with having a lower GPA.

This is why it is crucial for you to create your list and identify any incongruities. We often underestimate the power of the brain. As humans, we have the ability to define what constitutes pain and pleasure for ourselves. The key to any lasting behavioral modification is to change it at the source: the Thought!

Do You Have the Power to Change Your Attitude?

Remember, the traditional Freudian narrative is determinism, the doctrine that all events, including human actions, are ultimately determined by causes external to the will. Determinism implies that individual human beings have no free will and cannot be held morally responsible for their actions.

The postmodernist narrative argues that there is no known or absolute truth. Truth is defined only at the individual level. The postmodernist narrative challenges the concepts of natural laws, logic, and reason, reducing them to subjective constructs that hold validity only if an individual deems them so.

SALT Your Thoughts is based on the absolute *opposite* narrative!

1. Your Thoughts are the source of your Beliefs (The Way You Think).

2. Your Beliefs (The Way You Think) have a cause-and-effect impact on your Attitudes (The Way You Feel).

3. Your Attitudes (The Way You Feel) have a cause-and-effect impact on your Needs (The Way You Are Motivated).

4. Your Needs (The Way You Are Motivated) have a cause-and-effect impact on your Behaviors (The Way You Act).

5. You can choose to use your self-awareness, your imagination, your conscience, and your independent will to clearly state to your subconscious mind exactly what you choose to think, be, feel, and do!

Spanish philosopher George Santayana is credited with the old adage: "Those who cannot remember the past are condemned to repeat it." Failing to acknowledge natural laws and how they impact our lives on a daily basis is an irresponsible way to live. When a nation is unwilling to take responsibility for its choices, it is a signal that the nation is on the path to bondage.

Scottish philosopher Alexander Tyler of the University of Edinburgh noted eight stages that describe the rise and fall of the world's great civilizations:

1. From bondage to spiritual growth

2. From spiritual growth to great courage

3. From courage to liberty

4. From liberty to abundance

5. From abundance to complacency

6. From complacency to apathy

7. From apathy to dependence

8. From dependence back to bondage

I believe Alexander Tyler's model for nations may also apply to us as individuals. Where do you stand on this spectrum? Wouldn't you prefer to spend as much time as possible in Stage 4: From Liberty to Abundance? That appears to be the most effective stage to me. However, we must not allow our abundance to lead to complacency. I agree with Tyler's observation on the rise and fall of nations. However, it is individuals like you and me who make up "nations." And I believe that as individuals, we have the power and responsibility to choose our response!

Values That You Move Toward

A personal value is an attitude of personal quality that causes a need that a person moves towards. Personal values define your home base for which you make decisions. They fulfill your core needs as mentioned in Chapter 13.

Character Traits You Move Away From

Your character traits are how people would describe you from the outside. Character traits you move away from are character traits you would prefer not to be used to describe you. Most of the time, they are the opposite side of your extremely important values. The character traits that you move away from are typically the trigger points for stress. It is important to identify the values you move away from so that you can manage your own stress level.

The first time my 15-year-old daughter made her list, her top three Moving Towards values were leadership, independence, and freedom. Her top Moving Away From character trait was conflict. When I saw her list, I asked her if she saw any problems with it. She gave me the cutest little grin and said, "People in leadership have to deal with conflict all the time?" And I said, "You are absolutely correct! So, now what do we do?" She said, "So, can you help me change my attitude about conflict?" I said, "I absolutely can!" I am so proud of her!

You must do the same thing. Look at your Moving Away From list and see if there are any obvious conflicts. If there are, the most effective resolution is to redefine your pain so that you no longer need to move away from that situation.

Chapter 14 Assignment:

It is time to go to **SaltYourThoughts.com** and complete the following assessments:

- **Personal Values I Move Towards** (Rank 24 Items)
- **Character Traits I Move Away From** (Rank 24 Items)

SALT Summaries:
Chapter 14: Seek Pleasure & Avoid Pain

- Your personal values are on the inside.

- Your character traits are how people would describe you from the outside.

- Your personal values are your internal definitions of who you are or want to be and provide you a framework for how you feel.

- Your character is how others describe your behavior or how you act.

- **The Cognitive Component (Your Beliefs):**

  - You have discovered that your thought habits are the source of your beliefs (the way you think).

  - Your beliefs (the way you think) have a cause-and-effect impact on your attitudes (the way you feel).

  - Your conscious mind is what Frankl called self-awareness.

  - Your conscious mind is the cognitive component (your beliefs).

- **The Affective Component (Your Values (Attitudes)/Needs)** should be divided into two components:

  - Your attitudes (the way you feel).

    - At the human core, your attitudes relate to moving toward pleasure and/or away from pain.

    - It is most effective to label these attitudes, feelings as personal values.

    - Your conscience is that deep moral awareness of right and wrong that keeps you from acting upon your most basic desires and urges.

    - Your conscience is stored in your subconscious mind.

- Your subconscious mind controls everything in your life that is involuntary (habits) - your respiration, heart rate, blinking, liver, spleen, stomach, etc.

- Your values are stored in your subconscious mind, but you choose what values to have in your conscious mind.

- You can choose to change the values you move toward and what values you move away from.

  o Your needs: the way you are motivated.

  - Your personal values create your core needs.

- **The Behavioral Component (Your Actions):**

  o Your behaviors (the way you act — the behavioral component) are caused/influenced by your core needs (your motivators).

  o Your beliefs, attitudes, and needs are internal to your mind.

  o Your personal values create your core needs.

  o If your core needs are not met, it is the cause of stress or even dysfunctional behavior.

  o Personal values create core needs; unmet core needs are a source of chronic stress.

  o Thought is the cause of every effect.

- Our needs are what actually motivate us.

PART 4

Your Needs: The Way You Are Motivated

WHAT DO YOU NEED ?

Chapter 15

WHAT DO YOU NEED?

"Start where you are. Use what you have. Do what you can."
Arthur Ashe

What Motivates You?

I HAD JUST BEEN promoted to the Plant Manager level over the Environmental Services Department at the food manufacturing company I mentioned in the introduction. Although I felt confident in my leadership and management skills at that point in my career, I lacked confidence in my knowledge of Environmental Services.

Coincidentally, my first shift supervisor (the experienced person) was on vacation during my first week on the job. So, on Monday, I filled in for my supervisor while focusing on efficiency and effectiveness since most employees were familiar with their usual assignments.

Three employees were assigned to clean three of the "ovens." These ovens were each approximately 300 feet in length and contained a continuous oven band. Positioned about 15 feet above the ground, the employees needed to climb ladders to access the work area. This task was performed weekly by the same employees.

Prior to my supervisor's absence, he left me a note describing one of the employees, whom we will refer to as "Cindy," as a problem employee. He explained that Cindy's coworkers, whom we will call Rachel and Lea, continuously complained that Cindy didn't do her job and they had to do it for her. Rachel and Lea had both been with the company in the same job for 30 years, while Cindy was around 20 years old. Expecting challenges on my first day, I closely observed the situation.

The oven that most urgently needed cleaning was assigned to Cindy due to her lower seniority. Rachel was assigned to oven #1, Cindy to oven #2, and Lea to oven #3. Cleaning each oven required a full 8-hour shift. The shift began at 6:30 a.m. with a break at 8:30 a.m., followed by lunch at 10:30 a.m., and another break at 12:30 p.m. During the employees' breaks, I went to the oven area to assess the progress.

At oven #1, I found Rachel's ladder properly placed next to her oven. From the floor, I could see that her bucket and cleaning materials were about 1/4 of the way down the oven, which was in line with my expectations by the first break. I then proceeded to oven #2, where it seemed that Cindy hadn't even started. There was no ladder or cleaning materials to be found. Disappointed, I thought to myself, *I really didn't want to have to issue a disciplinary action on my first day with the department, but it seems like I'll have to.* Next, I checked oven #3 and found Lea's ladder correctly positioned. From the floor, I could see that her bucket and cleaning materials were about 1/4 of the way down the oven. At least two of them were performing their duties properly.

During the lunch break at 10:30 a.m., I returned to oven #1. Rachel's ladder was appropriately placed beside her oven, and her bucket and cleaning materials were about halfway down the oven. I then proceeded to oven #2, where it still appeared that Cindy hadn't started at all. There was still no ladder or cleaning materials. Finally, I checked oven #3 and found Lea's ladder correctly positioned, with her bucket and cleaning materials about halfway down the oven.

As I walked toward my office, I spotted Cindy chatting with her friends in the mixing area. At that moment, I decided to prepare the necessary documentation to address her performance. Just as I was about to do so, I received a page requesting my presence in another area.

I returned to the ovens at 12:30 p.m. with only 2 hours remaining in the shift. As expected, from the floor, I could see that Rachel and Lea were about 3/4 done with their tasks. Surprisingly, I noticed that Cindy had set up a ladder next to oven #2. Curiosity got the better of me, and I climbed up the ladder to inspect her progress. Unfortunately, I was dismayed to find that she hadn't even started the cleaning. I couldn't help but wonder if I was being set up to test my reaction. The more I thought about it, the more irritated I became. I immediately went to my office and prepared the necessary paperwork.

At 2:00 p.m., I returned to the ovens. Rachel had finished her work and was on top of her oven. I climbed up the ladder to inspect the quality of her job. The top of the ovens was made of polished stainless steel, and there was no dust present. However, it seemed that Rachel had used a wet rag to wipe away the dust, leaving a circular residue on the oven top. It reminded me of how our kitchen counter would look when I "helped" my mother clean up flour after she made biscuits. I asked Rachel if this was the method she had been instructed to use, and she confirmed that she had been doing it that way for 30 years. Since there was no ladder at oven #2, I proceeded to oven #3 and found Lea cleaning up for the end of the shift. As I climbed up her ladder and inspected the top of her oven, I discovered the same circular residue that I had noticed on Rachel's oven.

I looked around, but Cindy was nowhere to be found. I borrowed Lea's ladder and climbed up to oven #2. Stepping off the ladder, I found a spotless, beautiful stainless steel oven. I could even see my reflection in it. I was stunned!

That was the moment I realized that *movement does not always indicate motivation*.

Rachel and Lea were content with their traditional approach of using a bucket and a rag, a method they had followed for 30 years. However, Cindy utilized a vacuum backpack. It took Cindy only 2 hours to complete the job that Rachel and Lea took the whole day to do, and she did it better. Cindy's driving need was *social interaction*, which motivated her to complete the task as quickly as possible. She knew exactly how much time it would take her.

The following week, the job was assigned to take 2 hours, and all employees were provided with vacuum backpacks to accomplish the task.

Your needs drive your motivation as well. This is a good time to briefly summarize Maslow's Hierarchy of Needs. This classic theory of motivation provides insight into how needs influence behavior.

Maslow's Hierarchy of Needs

Maslow's hierarchy of needs is a psychological concept presented by Abraham Maslow in his 1943 paper titled "A Theory of Human Motivation."[14] The hierarchy is often depicted as a pyramid, with the most fundamental needs at the bottom and the need for self-actualization at the top. According to Maslow, individuals must have their basic needs met before they are motivated to pursue higher-level needs.

MASLOW'S HIERARCHY OF NEEDS

- **SELF-ACTUALIZATION**: achieving one's full potential, including creative activities
- **ESTEEM NEEDS**: prestige, feeling of accomplishment
- **BELONGINGNESS & LOVE NEEDS**: intimate relationships, friends
- **SAFETY NEEDS**: security, safety
- **PHYSIOLOGICAL NEEDS**: food, water, warmth, rest

While this may initially seem uninteresting, bear with me. The goal is to use this knowledge as a framework to understand your own needs and self-motivation.

Maslow referred to physical, security, love and friendship, and esteem needs as "Deficiency Needs." He argued that if these needs are not met, individuals will experience anxiety and tension. He also believed that deprivation drives the motivation to fulfill unmet needs.

According to his model, the "Deficiency Needs" must be fulfilled before a strong desire for higher-level needs arises. Initially, Maslow suggested that lower deficiency needs must be completely satisfied before progressing to higher growth needs. However, he later clarified that the satisfaction of needs itself can be a progression.

The Basic Needs encompass Physiological Needs and Safety Needs, while the Psychological Needs include Love and Social Belonging Needs and Esteem Needs. The highest level of needs is Self-Fulfillment Needs or Self-Actualization.

Let's break it down into smaller pieces of information for better understanding.

Basic Needs #1: Physiological Needs
Physiological needs serve as the foundation of the hierarchy (the bottom of the pyramid). These needs are the biological requirements for human survival. According to Maslow, individuals must satisfy physiological needs first in order to pursue higher levels of intrinsic or natural satisfaction. Physiological needs include air, water, food, sleep, clothing, and shelter.

Basic Needs #2: Safety Needs
Once an individual's physiological needs are met, safety needs become dominant. For adults, safety needs typically include health, financial security, personal security, and emotional security.

Psychological Needs #1: Love and Social Belonging Needs
After physiological and safety needs are satisfied, the third level of human need revolves around interpersonal connections and a sense of belongingness. Maslow posited that humans have an inherent need for acceptance and belonging among social groups. Meeting love and social belonging needs results in the individual receiving acceptance, respect, and love. Social belonging needs encompass family, friendship, intimacy, trust, acceptance, and both giving and receiving love and affection.

Psychological Needs #2: Esteem Needs
Maslow identified two types of esteem needs. The "lower" type is the need for respect from others, which may encompass a desire for status, recognition, fame, prestige, and attention. The "higher" type is the need for self-respect, which includes a need for strength, competence, mastery, self-confidence, independence, and freedom.

Self-Fulfillment Needs #1: Self-Actualization
According to Maslow, every individual possesses an innate need to realize their full potential. He famously stated, "What a man can be, he must be." Self-actualization or growth refers to the realization and fulfillment of one's talents, potentialities, and reaching one's full potential. Maslow emphasized that to comprehend this level of need, a person must not only succeed in the previous needs but also master them. Self-actualization needs encompass acquiring a partner, parenting, utilizing and developing talents and abilities, and pursuing personal goals.

Application of Maslow's Model

There have been thousands of papers and books written on motivation theory. While I am not attempting to comprehensively cover the subject, I do believe that approaching motivation based on the concept of needs is a very practical method you can use to become more self-aware and, therefore, more effective.

Don't forget Cindy in the opening story. Her driving need was social interaction, which motivated her to get her job done as quickly as possible.

Let's apply this to your life. I would expect that for most of you reading this book, your physical, security, love and friendship, and esteem needs, which Maslow called "deficiency needs," are fulfilled at least to some level. It is critical to understand that your motivation decreases as deficiency needs are met.

For example, if you suddenly found yourself in a room that was deprived of oxygen, you would immediately be **motivated** to find a way to get some air. However, once that intense need is met, it only takes moments to forget that you are breathing because normal breathing is involuntary.

Now, remember a time when you stretched yourself financially to purchase a car or a house, which motivated you to make a little more money and seek another job, promotion, or raise. But once you reached the level of being able to pay all your bills, money ceased to truly motivate you. Unless of course you found something else you wanted to purchase!

I remember a time in my own life when I would say things like, "I will be happy when I get a new job" or "I will be happy when I get a new car" or "I will be happy when I get a new house." What is interesting is that when I achieved those things, I still was not satisfied, and I was still saying, "I will be happy when..."

My own experience led me to believe that physical, security, love and friendship, and esteem needs, which Maslow called "deficiency needs," I would re-label as **dissatisfiers**. By that, I mean you are dissatisfied if you don't have them, but once you get them, you are no longer dissatisfied, but you are not really satisfied either. You are not satisfied because all of these things come from outside of you. That is why you see people who apparently "have it all" and are still not happy.

I believe happiness and satisfaction come from somewhere else.

At the top of Maslow's pyramid are Self-Actualization Needs or Growth Needs. These growth needs do not come from lacking something; they come from inside you. They come from the desire to become or be the best you can be.

What is fascinating to me is that ***motivation increases as growth needs are met***. In other words, the more you grow, the more you want to grow. You are designed to become, and you become what you think about.

> "We must be before we can do, and we can do only to the extent which we are, and what we are depends upon what we think."
> **Charles Haanel**[15]

Conclusion about Motivation

This brings us full circle to the reality that you are the only person who can truly motivate yourself. You are responsible. Just like Cindy at the beginning of the chapter, your needs drive your motivation. But you — and only you — define your needs.

You have discovered your personality type, your temperament, and your personal values (your attitudes/needs). Now, you can choose which needs will drive your motivation, resulting in your behaviors (your actions).

Chapter 15 Assignment:

Visit **SaltYourThoughts.com** and complete the **Core Needs/Motivators** assessment.

SALT Summaries:
Chapter 15: What Do You Need?

- Maslow's Hierarchy of Needs is a classic theory of motivation that provides some insight into how needs drive behavior.

    - **Basic Needs #1: Physiological Needs** — These needs are the biological requirements for human survival.

    - **Basic Needs #2: Safety Needs** — For adults, these safety needs typically include health, financial security, personal security, and emotional security.

    - **Psychological Needs #1: Love and Social Belonging Needs** — Social belonging needs encompass family, friendship, intimacy, trust, acceptance, and receiving and giving love and affection.

    - **Psychological Needs #2: Esteem Needs** — Maslow defined two types of esteem needs. The "lower" type of esteem is the need for respect from others, which may include a need for status, recognition, fame, prestige, and attention. The "higher" type of esteem is the need for self-respect, which can include a need for strength, competence, mastery, self-confidence, independence, and freedom.

    - **Self-fulfillment Needs #1: Self-Actualization** — Self-actualization needs include partner acquisition, parenting, utilizing and developing talents and abilities, and pursuing goals.

- Application of Maslow's Model

    - My own experience led me to believe that physical, security, love and friendship, and esteem needs, which Maslow called "Deficiency Needs," could be re-labeled as *dissatisfiers*.

        - By that, I mean you are dissatisfied if you don't have them, but once you obtain them, you are no longer dissatisfied, though you may not be truly satisfied either. This lack of satisfaction stems from the fact that all of these things come from outside of you. That is why you see people who seemingly "have it all" but are not happy. Happiness and satisfaction come from somewhere else.

- At the top of Maslow's pyramid are Self-Actualization Needs or Growth Needs. These growth needs come from "inside" you, reflecting the desire to become or be the best you can be. What is fascinating is that motivation increases as growth needs are met. You are designed to become, and you become what you think about.

*"We must **be** before we can **do**, and we can **do** only to the extent which we **are**, and what we **are** depends upon what we **think**."* - Charles Haanel

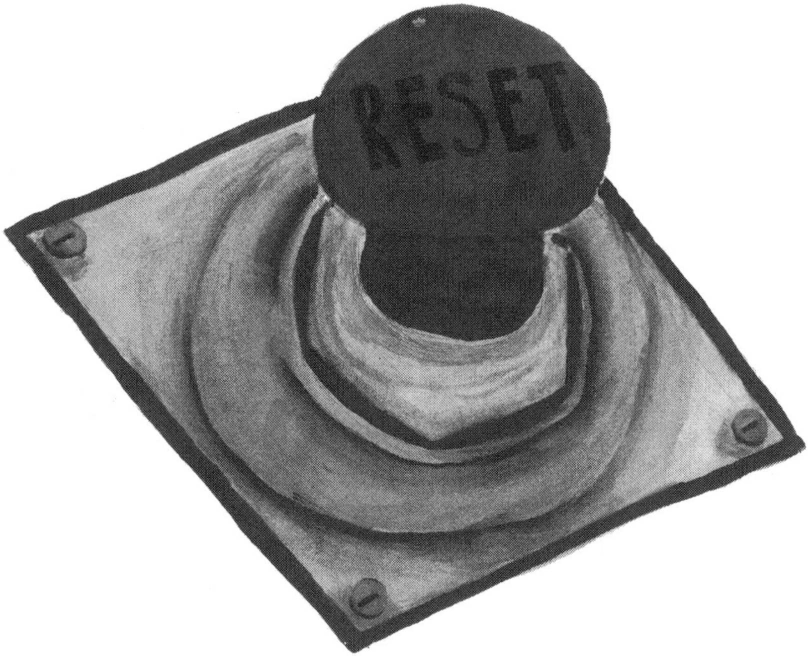
RESET

Chapter 16

Push The Reset Button!

"The greatest weapon against stress is our ability to choose one thought over another."
William James

2010

IN THE INTRODUCTION OF this book, I shared with you how 2010 was the worst year of my business life. In the early years of my company, we were very successful in helping the carpet manufacturing industry hire the right employees. From 1996 to 2010, there was quite a bit of consolidation happening in the carpet manufacturing industry. Seeing that trend, we were both glad to see our client base growing but, on the other hand, concerned that they were accounting for a significant percentage of our total revenue. So, we started looking for other business sectors to diversify into.

However, by 2010, one of our clients in the carpet manufacturing industry purchased all the other smaller clients. I found myself in a situation where over 70% of our annual revenue came from a single client. This client made an offer to purchase my company for pennies on the dollar or threatened to terminate our contracts. I refused their offer.

In August of 2010, they terminated our contracts, and overnight my company went from 30 employees to six. All the employees we lost were directly associated with the manufacturing client, but they were also friends whom I had worked with for many years. My son, Trey, had just graduated from college and decided to work for the company instead of pursuing other opportunities in New York. Now, I was concerned that he might have made the wrong decision. My daughter, Jeana, had just been accepted into the Orthotics and Prosthetics medical school at Loma Linda, California. Now, how could I help her make it happen?

What I did not share in the introduction is that, at the exact same time I was dealing with these business challenges, I found out that my wife of 29 years was having an affair. My entire world — my family and my business — was crumbling in front of my eyes!

I went through the same grieving process I did when I lost my mother. Then, I was only 12 and didn't have any responsibilities, so this felt much bigger. I must admit, I felt a little like Job in the Bible. This was the most intense stress I had ever had to deal with. I did what many people do under that level of stress: I began a downward spiral of self-deprecation.

One night, while I was alone in my home, I happened to see a gimmick someone had given to me at a trade show. It was a big red "RESET" button. It wasn't really connected to anything; it was just a fake reset button. But I pushed it anyway. Nothing happened. I pushed it again and again and again.

I recognized the deep pit of despair I was in. I had been there before, so I reminded myself of my own beliefs:

- Everything happens for a reason. There are no coincidences.

- Everything that happens to me and mine is Father-filtered.

- My response to everything that happens to me (and mine) is my response-ability.

- What matters most is how I respond to what I experience in life.

- There is always something to be grateful for.

- I can change the way I feel at any moment by changing my thoughts.

So, I really pushed my own personal reset button. I used my independent will and chose to engage my Reticular Activation System and focus my mind on those things for which I was grateful. I remembered how God had led me in the past, which gave me confidence that He will lead me in the future. I used my positive mood triggers, and I chose to change my state of mind.

I chose to **SALT My Thoughts**.

From a business standpoint: Once I SALTed my thoughts, the company began to sell more and more to the senior living industry. We were able to replace the revenue we lost from the manufacturing company within 12 months. In 2012, my company grew new sales at 50% of the previous year's total revenue! From 2013 to 2017, we grew new sales compared to total revenue at 50% to 60% each year. By 2017, our software was in over 3,600 companies in 46 states! As I reflect on the accomplishments of those six years of the company's history, I can only give God the glory for this amazing turnaround. Over 24 companies reached out, showing an interest in purchasing the company in 2017. We narrowed that list down to 5 and had onsite meetings. We received 3 offers and chose the offer that allowed all of our employees to keep their jobs. My company sold for eight figures! Look at the opportunity I would have missed if I had stayed in the ditch. Instead, I chose to SALT My Thoughts.

From a personal standpoint: If any of you have ever gone through a divorce, you can understand how difficult it feels to move forward. But again, I realized I needed to SALT My Thought**s**, so I did. I reminded myself that everything happens for a reason and there are no coincidences. I chose to believe I could find happiness again. I knew that if I found the right woman, I could even get married again. Then, on June 28, 2013, I was set up on a blind date with a woman named Sandra. We quickly became friends. In September of 2013, we started dating and fell in love. We got married on February 14, 2014! We are best friends! We have each other's back!

My Positive Mood Trigger!

I have never been happier in my whole life! Being married to Sandra gives me both joy and happiness! Again, look at the opportunity I would have missed if I had not SALTed My Thoughts!

If I had not chosen to SALT My Thoughts, I am not sure where I would be today.

How Do You Handle Stress?

Many of you deal with chronic stress. Chronic stress is linked to six leading causes of death, including heart disease, cancer, lung ailments, accidents, cirrhosis of the liver, and suicide, according to the American Psychological Association. It is important to take steps to manage chronic stress to ensure that your body is functioning as it should and for your overall health and well-being. This chapter will help you put an end to your chronic stress.

If your needs are not met, it is a cause of stress or even dysfunctional behavior. This cause-and-effect relationship between your personal values and your needs sets up the opportunity for chronic stress. Unmet needs are a source of chronic stress.

Stress and Temperament

It is critical to understand that your temperament is just the starting point in the journey of life. Each temperament has its own set of primary values, needs, and stressors. The key here is that you are not stuck with your temperament; you can choose to learn new skills.

GUARDIAN (SJ):
CORE VALUES include:

- Responsibility
- Diligence
- Respect for Authority
- Service
- Traditional Ways
- Hard Work

CORE NEEDS include the NEED to:

- Be Accountable

- Display effort and accomplishment
- Hold in esteem those who hold positions of authority
- Help others
- Follow vetted customs
- Exert physical effort to accomplish a task

CORE STRESSORS include being considered as or being:

- Irresponsible
- Unable to display effort to accomplish a goal
- Disrespectful of Authority
- Selfish
- Subjected to new ways of doing old things
- Lazy

ARTISAN (SP):
CORE VALUES include:

- Freedom
- Fun
- Action and Variety
- Autonomy
- Excitement
- Skill

CORE NEEDS include the NEED:

- To act, speak, or think as one desires without external restraints

- For lighthearted pleasure

- To be active and doing different things

- To be in control of your own affairs

- For the feeling of excitement

- To do something well

CORE STRESSORS include being considered as or being:

- Restrained from doing, speaking, or thinking on your own

- Subjected to boring activities

- Inactive and bored

- Placed under the authority of someone

- Being subjected to doing, speaking, or thinking dull activities

- Unable to learn a new skill

RATIONAL (NT):
CORE VALUES include:

- Intelligence

- Ingenuity

- Logic

- Competence

- Independence

- Excellence

CORE NEEDS include the NEED:

- For knowledge and skill

- To be clever or inventive
- To distinguish good reasoning from bad reasoning
- To perform successfully and effectively
- To be free from another's authority
- To do better than anyone else

CORE STRESSORS include Being considered as or:

- Being without skill or the aptitude to acquire a skill
- Being unable to reason cause & effect
- Being illogical
- Being incompetent
- Being dependent on others
- Having sub quality performance results

IDEALIST (NF):
CORE VALUES include:

- Harmonious Relationships
- Integrity
- Personal Expression
- Personal Growth
- Originality
- Potentiality

CORE NEEDS include the NEED:

- For agreement and lack of conflict

- To live in accordance with moral and ethical principles

- To be heard or seen by others

- To improve personally

- To be seen as different

- To find the possibilities

CORE STRESSORS include being considered as or:

- Being around (Seeing, Hearing, Participating) Conflict

- Being deceitful or unethical

- Being considered "just one of the group"

- Being personally stagnate

- Being considered the same as everyone else

- Unable to identify any possibilities

Stress is a normal psychological and physical reaction to the demands of life. A small amount of stress can be good, motivating you to perform well. But multiple challenges daily can push you beyond your ability to cope. Remember, your brain comes hard-wired with an alarm system for your protection: your Subconscious Mind. Your subconscious mind cannot reason, it cannot argue controversially. It depends on your conscious mind to be its gatekeeper. Your subconscious mind perceives information through intuition as a function of survival, thus triggering the "fight-or-flight" response.

During conditions of stress, panic, anger, and excitement, the subconscious mind is unguarded and open to suggestions of self-depreciation, fear, selfishness, hatred, greed, and other negative forces. These false suggestions embedded in the subconscious mind become the cause of stress, fear, worry, disease, and poverty. The subconscious mind never sleeps, never rests, never takes a break. That's why our conscious mind needs to be "on duty" every waking hour of every day. Leaving the subconscious mind unguarded makes it susceptible to errors and misinformation.[16] When your subconscious mind perceives a threat, it signals your body to release a burst of hormones that increase your heart rate and raise your blood pressure. This "fight-or-flight" response helps you deal with the threat.

Once the threat is gone, your body is meant to return to a normal, relaxed state. Unfortunately, the nonstop complications of modern life mean that some people's alarm systems rarely shut off. This puts your subconscious mind at risk! Understanding your temperament, your core needs, and your stressors enables you to choose the antidote for stress: to SALT Your Thoughts and choose to change your state of mind!

When you SALT Your Thoughts, you enable your conscious mind to reset the alarm system of your subconscious mind. Without this reset, your subconscious mind will always be on high alert, burning up your adrenals and causing the electrical system, the frequencies the brain uses to communicate with the organs of your body, to malfunction. Being on high alert all the time is what causes disease, including cancer, lung ailments, accidents, cirrhosis of the liver, and suicide, according to the American Psychological Association.

This book isn't really about stress management. However, you can choose to change your state of mind by choosing to SALT Your Thoughts! Chapter 23 will provide the process and purpose behind what it means to SALT Your Thoughts. I suggest that it becomes your new morning ritual, but for now, review the eight steps to SALT Your Thoughts.

Chapter 16: Assignment

Review the **8 Easy Steps to SALT Your Thoughts**, found below:

Step #1 - Push the reset button: Align your thoughts (the source of your beliefs) with the positive energy of God every morning. (Chapter 4-5)

   1. Let go of the past! Choose to control your state of mind!

   2. Focus on your gratitude list.

   3. Focus on your joy list.

   4. Focus on your positive mood triggers.

Step #2 - Review your beliefs (the way you think), so that your decisions are congruent with your beliefs. (Chapter 7)

    1. Review Your Mission - Core Beliefs (Chapter 18).

Step #3 - Choose to engage your four human attributes (Chapter 3):

    1. Self-awareness: Your awareness of your own thoughts, feelings, and actions

    2. Imagination: Your ability to visualize a new reality

    3. Conscience: Your awareness of what is morally right or wrong

    4. Independent will: Your ability to choose to act based on self-awareness

Step #4 - Engage your reticular activation system — you find what you seek. (Chapter 6)

Step #5 - Review your attitudes/personal values (the way you choose to feel) that define your home base for which you make decisions. (Chapter 13-14)

    1. Review Your Mission - Core Attitudes/Values (Chapter 18).

Step #6 - Review your needs (the way you are motivated) because your needs drive your behaviors. (Chapter 15)

    1. Review Your Mission - Core Needs (Chapter 18).

Step #7 - Align your behaviors (the way you choose to act) with their source - the thought. (Chapter 17)

    1. Review Your Mission - Core Behaviors (Chapter 18).

Step #8 - Visualize today's end goal: Ask, believe, and receive. (Chapter 18)

    1. Look at your weekly plan, then look at your schedule for today.

    2. Respond to any unanticipated events, relationships, prioritizing activities as needed.

SALT Summaries:
Chapter 16: How Do You SALT Your Thoughts?

- Unmet needs are a source of chronic stress.

- When you SALT Your Thoughts, you enable your conscious mind to reset the alarm system of your subconscious mind.

  - Without this reset, your subconscious mind will always be on high alert.

    - Being on high alert all the time is what causes heart disease, cancer, lung ailments, accidents, cirrhosis of the liver, and suicide, according to the American Psychological Association.

- Stress is a normal psychological and physical reaction to the demands of life.

- Your brain comes hard-wired with an alarm system for your protection: your subconscious mind.

  - Your subconscious mind cannot reason; it cannot argue controversially.

  - During conditions of stress, panic, anger, and excitement, the subconscious mind is unguarded and open to the suggestion of self-deprecation, fear, selfishness, hatred, greed, and other negative forces.

    - These false suggestions embedded in the subconscious mind become the cause of stress, fear, worry, disease, and poverty.

  - When your subconscious mind perceives a threat, it signals your body to release a burst of hormones that increase your heart rate and raise your blood pressure.

    - Once the threat is gone, your body is meant to return to a normal, relaxed state.

    - Unfortunately, the nonstop complications of modern life mean that some people's alarm systems rarely shut off.

- Understanding your temperament, your core needs, and your stressors enables you to choose the antidote for stress – to SALT Your Thoughts.

PART 5

Your Behaviors: The Way You Choose to Act

PEER PRESSURE

Try it! No one is looking.

What are you worried about? Everyone else does it.

Do less work, you're making us look bad.

If it bothers your conscience try not to think about it.

Chapter 17

What Is Success?

"Success is getting what you want. Happiness is wanting what you get."
Dale Carnegie

Peer Pressure

YOU MAY BE READING this book, like my 15-year-old daughter, just beginning life as an adult and learning the cause-and-effect relationship between your choices and their consequences. Or you may be a person about to get married or a person in mid-career considering a job change. You could also be an "empty nester" trying to figure out what comes next. Wherever you find yourself at this point in your life, it is critical for you to understand the negative influence of peer pressure.

> ***Peer Pressure (noun):*** *a feeling that one must do the same things as other people of one's age and social group in order to be liked or respected by them."*
> *(Merriam-Webster Dictionary)*

Do you remember the story of the food manufacturing company from the opening chapter of this book? I was hired for a job that required me to work from 2:30 A.M.

to 6:30 A.M. My job as a "Palletizer" involved two workstations. The first workstation required placing a shipping case over 16 cartons of product, folding the shipping case closed, and pushing it into a tape machine that sealed it. The second workstation involved taking the taped shipping case and arranging it in a specific configuration on a shipping pallet.

After about three weeks, I was able to go full-time, and the company hired someone else to work from 2:30 A.M. to 6:30 A.M. Everything went smoothly for a couple of weeks until, one day, the person who worked from 10:30 P.M. to 2:30 A.M. left the workstation at the end of their shift, but the replacement never showed up. If you've ever seen the classic *I Love Lucy* television series and the episode where she is working on a chocolate factory production line and struggles to figure out where to put all the candy that keeps coming, that's the situation I found myself in. The cartons just kept on coming!

I had to work quickly and handle both workstations until they found a replacement. I rearranged workstation #1 to also stack the shipping cases coming out of the tape machine, completing the task of workstation #2. It took me a few minutes to adjust to the new pace of the product flow, but I was able to keep up easily.

Two hours later, a break person came over to give me a break and realized I was doing both jobs simultaneously. She refused to do the work of both workstations and called my supervisor. He came over and apologized for not being aware of my situation. He informed me that there was no one available to help and asked if I could continue for the rest of the shift. I told him that I was fine and actually enjoying the challenge. So, he did the job of one workstation and the break person did the job of the other workstation and together they gave me a 10-minute break.

During my break in the breakroom, the palletizers from the other three lines approached me and told me I needed to stop showing off or management would make everyone do what I was doing. I was very confused. I thought I was being helpful, but everyone else on the team was upset that I was achieving above-average results.

Let's take a moment from my story to define two words:

- **Accomplishment:** doing something that benefits others and the world outside of oneself. (An example of an accomplishment could be being a good father/mother or selling your company.)

- **Achievement:** doing something that primarily benefits only oneself. (An example of an achievement could be choosing to train for and run a marathon or becoming the top salesperson at your company.)

My **accomplishment** was keeping the production line flowing smoothly so that the other employees on the line could experience a nice, uninterrupted workflow.

My **achievement** was demonstrating, as an individual performer, that I could handle pressure and perform well when most others would struggle.

Two Critical Life Principles:

1. Look for opportunities to perform where you accomplish something for others AND that accomplishment also earns you recognition as an individual performer.

2. Look for opportunities to perform where most other people fail.

    - This minimizes the impact of your potential failure (if you fail, it isn't bad because everyone else has also failed).

    - This maximizes your opportunity for success (when you succeed where most others fail, it is like getting bonus points)

Back to my story. The other palletizers told me they would sabotage my line if I tried to finish out the shift. And sure enough, they spent the rest of the shift jamming the tape machine, jamming the carton machine, and doing anything else they could think of to disrupt the product flow. Much to their dismay, I was able to finish the shift.

Peer pressure attempts to influence you to perform at a lower level so that low performers do not stick out, and neither do you!

The Bell Curve

You are more familiar with the Bell Curve than you may think. If you have ever heard the saying "20% of the people do 80% of the work," that refers to the top 20% (on the right) of the Bell Curve.

Another related statement is "20% of the people cause 80% of the problems," which represents the bottom 20% (on the left) of the Bell Curve.

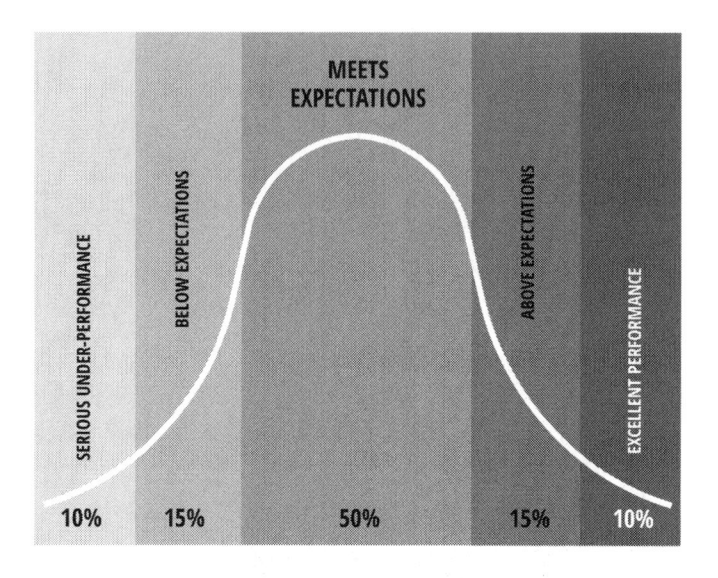

```
SERIOUS UNDER-PERFORMANCE | BELOW EXPECTATIONS | MEETS EXPECTATIONS | ABOVE EXPECTATIONS | EXCELLENT PERFORMANCE
10% | 15% | 50% | 15% | 10%
```

People who perform "Below Expectations" do not want you to perform "Above Expectations." I was fortunate to be rewarded for my consistent Above Expectation performance by being promoted to a supervisor at the age of 20. I worked for a company that valued such performance. Consider the cause and effect principles at play here. In my case, Above Expectation performance led to promotion. However, if Above Expectation performance is never rewarded, the lack of recognition will convey that it is not valued, and in most cases, it will stop. *The goal of peer pressure is to eliminate Above Expectation performance.*

The American Dream is founded on the principle that Above Expectation performance leads to Above Expectation rewards!

How Do You Define Success?

Statistically speaking, the probabilities would imply that if you are reading this book, you are most likely in the top 40% on the Bell Curve, which means you expect top performance from yourself! Your expectation ignites a burning desire within you to achieve both accomplishments and personal growth.

Throughout my professional career, I have conducted numerous career planning sessions. Regardless of age, I always begin with the question, "What do you want to be when you grow up?" More often than not, the response is, "I don't know, that's why I'm meeting with you!" The problem lies in the magnitude of the question. So, let's break it down.

For the purpose of this book, let's define the stages of life as follows:

1. Infant: 0 to 1 year

2. Toddler: 2 to 4 years

3. Child: 5 to 12 years

4. Teen: 13 to 19 years

5. Adult: 20 to 39 years

6. Middle-Aged Adult: 40 to 59 years

7. Senior Adult: 60 and above

As a reader of this book, you are most likely in stages 4-7. Regardless of which stage you are in, it is now time to define your end goal. This is an important task that requires some dedicated time for reflection.

Chapter 17: Assignment

Go to **SaltYourThoughts.com** and complete the assessments found in the questions below:

1. What character traits do you desire to demonstrate as a successful person? Complete the following assessment: **How Do You Define Success, Part 1: Character Traits (Rank 12 Items)**

2. What skills should you empower your family with that will leave a lasting positive impact? Complete the following assessment: **How Do You Define Success, Part 2: Your Family (Rank 12 Items)**

3. What do you want to be known for at work? Complete the following assessment: **How Do You Define Success, Part 3: Your Work (Rank 12 Items)**

4. What are your individual needs? Complete the following assessment: **How Do You Define Success, Part 4: Your Needs (Rank 12 Items)**

5. What traits do you desire most to demonstrate to your spouse? Complete the following assessment: **How Do You Define Success, Part 5: As A Spouse (Rank 12 Items)**

6. How do you want your children to remember you? Complete the following assessment: **How Do You Define Success, Part 6: As A Parent (Rank 16 Items)**

7. What aspects of your health are most important to you? Complete the following assessment: **How Do You Define Success, Part 7: Your Health (Rank 18 Items)**

8. What character traits do you desire to demonstrate as a friend? Complete the following assessment: **How Do You Define Success, Part 8: As A Friend (Rank 16 Items)**

9. What is your legacy? Complete the following assessment: **How Do You Define Success, Part 9: Your Legacy (6 Questions)**

SALT Summaries:
Chapter 17: What Is Success?

- Peer pressure: a feeling that one must do the same things as other people of one's age and social group in order to be liked or respected by them.

- An "Accomplishment" is defined as doing something that benefits others and the world outside them. Examples of accomplishments include being a good father/mother or selling your company.

- An "Achievement" is defined as doing something that principally benefits only yourself. Examples of achievements include choosing to train and run a marathon or becoming the top salesperson at your company.

- Two critical life principles:
    - Look for opportunities to perform where you accomplish something for others and that accomplishment achieves recognition as an individual performer.
    - Look for opportunities to perform where most other people fail. This minimizes the impact of your failure (if you fail, it isn't bad because all others have failed as well) and maximizes your opportunity for success (when you succeed where most others fail, it is like getting bonus points!).

- The Bell Curve:
    - "20% of the people do 80% of the work" comes from the top 20% (on the right) of the Bell Curve.
    - "20% of the people cause 80% of the problem" refers to the bottom 20% (on the left) of the Bell Curve.

- The goal of peer pressure is to eliminate "above expectation" performance.

- The American Dream is built on the principle that above expectation performance results in above expectation reward!

- How do you define success?
  - Regardless of which stage of life you are in, it is time to define the end goal.

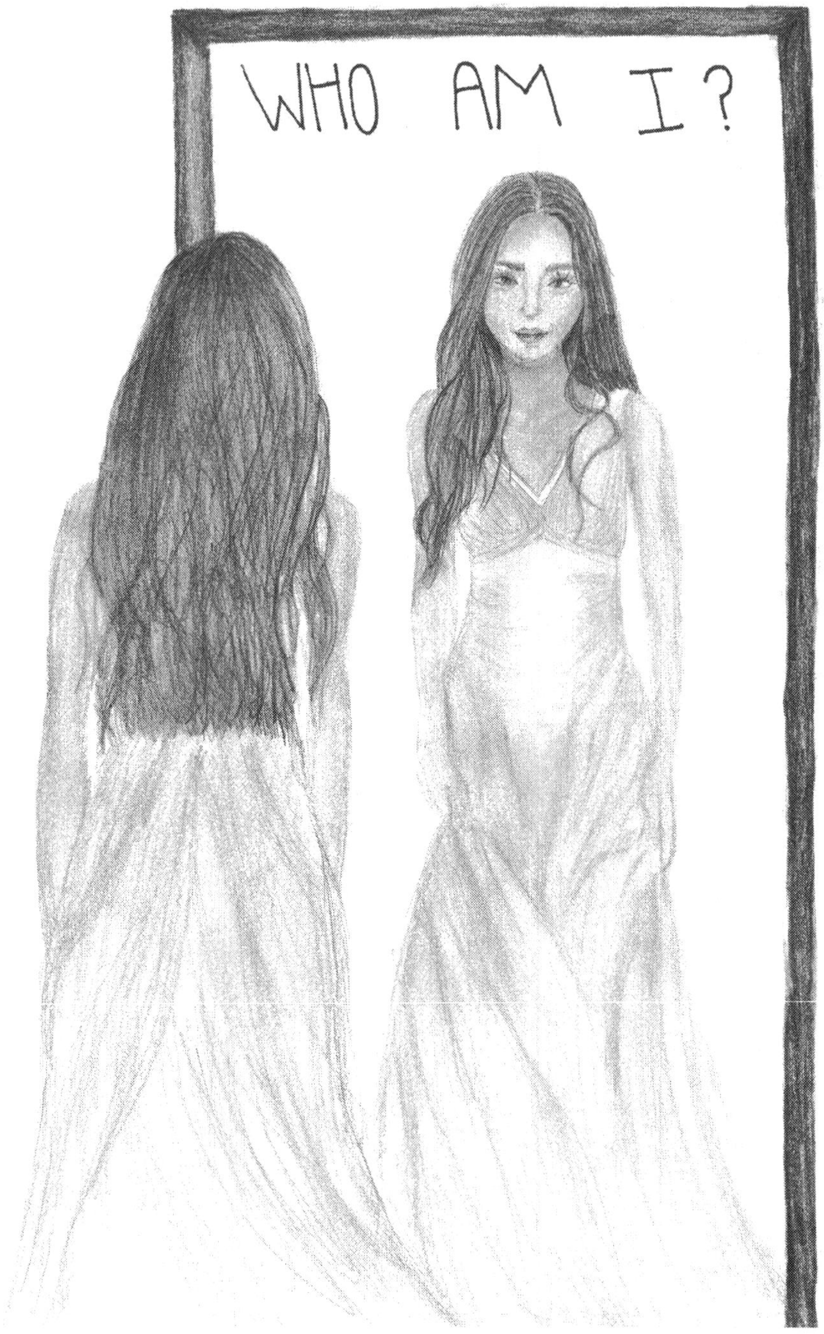
WHO AM I?

Chapter 18

WHO AM I?

"Your mission statement becomes your constitution, the solid expression of your vision and values. It becomes the criterion by which you measure everything else in your life."
Stephen Covey

Who Am I Going To Be?

MY UNDERGRADUATE DEGREE IS in Theology. My mother instilled a passion in me for studying the Bible, so I thought becoming a pastor would be a good use of my knowledge and skills.

During my high school years, I didn't have any desire to go home in the summers, so I worked at a Christian Summer Camp in Alabama from 1975 to 1978. Working at the summer camp provided me with excellent experience (knowledge, skills, and abilities) and exposure to the Alabama Conference officials. The denomination I belonged to at that time hired pastors through a Conference that mainly covered two states. In my case, it was the Alabama/Mississippi Conference.

At the end of my fourth summer (1978) working at the summer camp, the leadership of the Alabama/Mississippi Conference offered me a pastoral position upon my college graduation based on my performance as the leader of the waterfront area at the camp and my relationship with the conference leadership.

I had taken several classes during my senior year of high school that earned me college credit, so when I graduated in 1978, I was almost a sophomore. By the spring of 1981 (the end of my second year), I was already a junior in college. I spent most of my weekends preaching, teaching, or singing at various churches in the Southeast. However, as mentioned in Chapter 1, I was also working full-time at a food manufacturing company.

One weekend in March of 1981, I was preaching at a small church in Gadsden, Alabama. I delivered a Spirit-filled message. After the sermon, as I stood at the front door shaking hands with the church members, I noticed the Conference "Hiring Manager" in line to greet me. He asked me to meet him in the pastor's office after everyone had left.

Once everyone had left, I went to the pastor's office. The hiring manager informed me that the Conference President who had hired me had been promoted to the General Conference. The new president didn't know me and had several concerns. First of all, they didn't think a pastor should drive a red 4-wheel drive pickup truck. Instead, they believed I should be driving a black 4-door sedan. Secondly, they felt that I hadn't spent enough time in the Theology department. I explained that I had a full-time job and was quite busy, but my explanation didn't seem to matter to him. He also mentioned that I needed to wear looser-fitting clothes as mine were too tight. He explained that if I complied with all the requested changes, I would be considered on "probation," and they might extend an offer after I graduated.

I was devastated! What was I going to do? I had dreamed of being a pastor for so long. But now it seemed that just because the president who knew me had been promoted, my job was in jeopardy because I didn't have a connection with the new person. I had a terrible knot in the pit of my stomach. I knew in my gut (my solar plexus) that being a pastor in this denomination was more about who you knew than your relationship with the Lord.

When I went home, I asked myself, "If I'm not going to be a pastor, who am I going to be?" I struggled with God all night, praying for a clear answer.

The next day, I went to work at 1:30 P.M. as a mixer. The plant manager met me at the plant entrance and said, "Mullins, I've been watching you. I need a third shift supervisor for the mixing area, and I'd like to offer you that position. What do you say?"

I knew in my gut that this was the answer from God. "When do you want me to start?" I replied.

He said, "Well, I need you to work your second shift mixing job today, and then just work a double and start tonight."

"That works for me!" I said.

Soon after becoming a supervisor, I had the opportunity to take some management courses through the company's training department. It was there that I was introduced to the concept of creating a **personal mission statement**. I quickly realized that a personal mission statement helps answer the question, "Who am I going to be?"

Writing my personal mission statement helped me understand that I can have a passion for studying and teaching the Bible without being a pastor. I began to realize that my true calling is to be a person who has a positive influence on the lives of my family and others.

Crisis Generates Clarity

In my own life, I have found that when I experience a major crisis, that is when I truly find clarity. It has been said that a crisis generates clarity. Most people need to go through the loss of a loved one, receive a bad diagnosis, or lose a job to gain clarity about what is truly important in their lives.

Taking proactive initiative to engage your creative brain when there is no crisis is essential. I understand that it may feel overwhelming right now. However, you have already completed a significant amount of pre-work in order to craft your personal mission statement.

What Is A Personal Mission Statement?

Writing your personal mission statement involves integrating your beliefs, attitudes, needs, behaviors, and how you define success into a simple statement. I wrote my personal mission statement for the first time in 1981. Every year, I review it to ensure it remains relevant to the way I think, believe, feel, need, and behave. Here is my 2023 personal mission statement:

My Personal Mission:

1. To create thought habits that align with the Creator of this universe.

    - I will sow thoughts of gratitude, hope, faith, love, trust, honesty, optimism, enthusiasm, confidence, and excellence.

2. To believe:

    - Everything happens for a reason. There are no coincidences.

    - Everything that happens to me and my loved ones is divinely filtered.

    - Decisions bring consequences, some good and some bad.

    - My behavior is a result of my decisions, not my conditions.

    - Nothing that has happened or will happen to me will define me.

3. To be a person of:

    - Integrity - Adherence to moral and ethical principles.

    - Wisdom - The application of experience, knowledge, and good judgment.

    - Influence - The capacity to have a positive effect on others' character, development, or behavior.

    - Excellence - To surpass others or do extremely well.

    - Competence - The ability to successfully and effectively accomplish tasks.

4. To be motivated by:

    - My need to live in accordance with moral and ethical principles.

    - My need for the application of knowledge and skill.

    - My need to positively impact someone's life.

    - My need to do better than anyone else.

- My need to perform successfully and effectively.

5. To demonstrate the following behaviors:

    - Acting in a manner that reflects adherence to moral and ethical principles.

    - Acting in a manner that demonstrates the application of knowledge and skill.

    - Acting in a manner that produces a positive influence in the lives of my family and others.

    - Acting in a manner that reflects excellence.

    - Acting in a manner that demonstrates competence.

Writing your personal mission statement is a critical step in taking control of your life and choosing your personal character. It requires introspection, time, and effort. Your personal mission statement will provide boundaries that make decision-making easier. It will assist you in making decisions about education, career, relationships, finances, and family. It will help you stay focused on what is most important to you and guide you in spending your time effectively.

Remember, the secret of getting ahead is getting started. The assessment below asks you to rank responses to the following five questions in order of priority:

1. What kind of **thought habits** do you want to create? (Rank a 30-item list)

2. What are your primary **core beliefs** - the way you choose to think? (Rank a 25-item list)

3. What are your primary **attitudes/values** - the way you feel? (Rank a 24-item list)

4. What are your primary **needs** - the way you are motivated? (Rank a 24-item list)

5. What are your primary **behaviors** - the way you act? (Rank a 24-item list)

The output of this assessment will resemble my personal mission statement, but it will reflect your own content. Crafting your personal mission statement may take multiple attempts before achieving a concise expression of your personal character and values. Remember, there is no one in the world like you, and your personal mission statement should reflect that uniqueness. The most important thing is that it reflects the type of thoughts you want to cultivate, what you believe, the kind of person you want to be, how you want to be motivated, and the behaviors you want to demonstrate.

Chapter 18 Assignment:

Go to **SaltYourThoughts.com** and complete the **Writing My Personal Mission Statement** assessment.

SALT Summaries:
Chapter 18: Who Am I?

- What is a **personal mission statement**?

- Writing your personal mission statement involves integrating:

    - Your beliefs: The way you choose to think.

    - Your attitudes: The way you choose to feel.

    - Your needs: The way you are motivated.

    - Your behaviors: The way you choose to act.

    - How you define success into a simple statement.

- Crisis generates clarity

    - Most people never really find clarity until they experience a major crisis.

    - Most people must experience losing a loved one, receiving a bad diagnosis, or losing a job to gain clarity about what is most important in their life.

    - It takes proactive initiative to engage your creative brain when there is no crisis.

- Writing your personal mission statement involves integrating your beliefs, attitudes, needs, behaviors, and how you define success into a simple statement.

    - Your Personal Mission Statement will provide the boundaries that make decision-making easier.

    - It will assist you in making decisions about education, career, relationships, finances, and family.

    - It will help you stay focused on what is most important to you and guide you in how to spend your time effectively.

VISUALIZE THAT!

Chapter 19

VISUALIZE THAT!

"For assuredly, I say to you, whoever says to this mountain, 'Be removed and be cast into the sea,' and does not doubt in his heart, but believes that those things he says will be done, he will have whatever he says. Therefore, I say to you, whatever things you ask when you pray, believe that you receive them, and you will have them."
Mark 11:23-24 NKJV

The End Goal

I HAVE LEARNED THAT it is critical to visualize your end goal! Allow me to share a story of how I learned to visualize my end goal. What I'm about to share with you happened after I secured a big sale to keep my doors open in 1996. Like any business, I needed additional sales to sustain my operations.

I spent many hours preparing, practicing, and visualizing the sales presentation of my software. I wanted the presentation to be clear and precise. I visualized the prospects nodding their heads in agreement with all my critical points. However, what I failed to do was visualize the close of the sale. As a result, when I reached the point of trying to close the sale, the prospects started giving me excuses and expressing their doubts. They thought it looked great but were afraid it wouldn't work for them. Remember, computers were still a new concept at that time.

Then I met a man named Steve. He was selling temporary services to the same customers I was selling my software selection system. One day, we coincidentally met at a prospect's office. This was the third time I had seen him during my sales meetings. He had the appointment before mine with the same person. When I finished my appointment, he was waiting for me. He asked if we could grab a quick bite to eat so he could understand what I was selling. We had a great meeting and quickly became friends. That day, we decided to create a joint product and sell it to prospects as a team.

After creating our joint product, Steve and I went to our first sales meeting together. He graciously allowed me to present the joint product. Throughout the sales presentation, their heads nodded in agreement. They agreed that turnover was a problem and that they needed a solution. Just as I was about to transition to the close, Steve stood up and said, "Billy, get your things together. I don't think these people get it. I don't think they see the value that we see and what we can bring to them. Come on, our next meeting is 30 minutes away. Maybe they will understand it there."

I was confused and didn't understand what had just happened. I simply started packing up my projector and computer. The CFO said, "I don't know why you said that. We completely understand it!" Steve replied, "Well, I'm just not convinced. I don't believe you understand the value of reducing your turnover. I don't think you realize how much turnover costs you every year. Our price is only a fraction of your cost, and I just don't think you truly comprehend it."

The CFO asked about the cost of our product, and when Steve told him our price, the CFO said, "You're right. That is only a fraction of our turnover cost. How soon can we get started?" Steve looked at me and said, "Billy, I guess he does want it. You take it from here."

The CFO signed the contract that day, and we began working on the implementation the next day.

When we got into our car to leave, I asked Steve, "What in the heck happened? Why did you tell the CFO he didn't get it? I thought he was understanding nicely."

Steve replied, "People are funny. If they think you're desperate to make a sale, they don't want to buy from you even if you have a great product. So, you tell them they don't understand it or they can't have it, and they will start trying to convince you they understand it and almost beg you for it! You started to look like you were losing your confidence. I could tell you had not visualized the close of the sale, so I stopped you. You know our price is just a fraction of their turnover cost and we will save them hundreds of thousands if not millions of dollars! **Visualize That!**"

Steve taught me so much that day. I learned how important it is to visualize all the way to the end goal. Not just the close of the sale, but the client using the product and loving it! And that is exactly what I did from that day forward! Steve and I owned this segment of the market until he sold his company several years later!

What Is Visualization?

Visualization is the **habit** of thinking and imagining what you want to accomplish and achieve in the future as if it were true today. Mark 11:24 says, "Whatever things you ask when you pray, believe that you receive them, and you will have them." Asking, believing, and receiving in the future as if it were today is visualization.

Visualization intensifies your thoughts and requires you to utilize the unique human characteristic of imagination. **It is the practice of imagining what you want to achieve or have in the future as if it were true today.** Visualization transfers your thoughts into active pictures, where you see yourself having what you want. The more you involve all five senses of sight, smell, touch, taste, and hearing in your visualization, the more intense the feeling becomes.

When the frequencies of your thoughts are intensified, they attract more of the same back to you through your Reticular Activation System (RAS). The process of visualization directs your RAS to be aware of the end goal. Visualization is the picture of your thoughts, your first narrative.

There was a 4-minute interview by Oprah Winfrey with Jim Carrey on February 17, 1997 that is well worth watching. I will do my best to briefly describe it:

During the interview, Oprah tells Jim Carrey that she has heard about this visualization thing that he did, and she wants him to share it with the audience. Jim then provides the following explanation:

"In 1987, I had nothing. Every night, I would drive up the mountain on Mulholland Drive. I would get to the top and look out over the city and visualize having a director interested in me and people that I respected saying, 'I really like your work!' Then I would visualize things coming to me that I wanted. Again, I had nothing at this point in my life, but visualizing made me feel better. I would drive home and think, 'Well, I do have these things, they are out there, I just don't have a hold of them yet.'

"So, one day in 1992, I wrote myself a check for $10,000,000 for 'acting services rendered' and dated it for Thanksgiving 3 years later in 1995. I put it in my wallet and kept it there. It deteriorated and deteriorated and deteriorated. Then, just before Thanksgiving in 1995, I was given a check for $10,000,000 for the movie I made, 'Dumb and Dumber.' Visualization works if you work hard. You can't visualize and then just go eat a sandwich!"

I totally agree with Jim Carrey. "Visualization works if you work hard."

Visualization is the habit of thinking/imagining what you want to accomplish and achieve in the future as if it were true today. So, let's break this habit down into useable steps:

The Habit of Visualization

1. Clearly articulate the **end goal for each role** in your life.

2. Sit down. Take 5 minutes and visualize the end goal:

    - Identify the **emotions** you feel having achieved your goal

    - What does the end goal **look** like?

    - What does the end goal **smell** like?

    - What does the end goal **sound** like?

    - What does the end goal **taste** like?

3. **Focus:** Zero in on the next five actions that need to be accomplished.

4. **Prioritize:** Ask Yourself "What can I do today to make this happen?"

5. **Persevere:** Never Give Up, Never Give In!

Chapter 19 Assignment:

In Chapter 17, you completed nine assessments (How Do You Define Success, Parts 1-9). Go to **SaltYourThoughts.com** and review the output of each assessment, and then engage the **Habit of Visualization**.

SALT Summaries:
Chapter 19: Visualize That!

- I have learned that it is critical to visualize your end goal!

- Visualization is the habit of thinking and imagining what you want to accomplish and achieve in the future as if it were true today.

  - **Visualization is a method you can use to Turbo-Charge Your Thoughts!**

- Visualization intensifies your thoughts.

  - It requires you to utilize the unique human characteristic of imagination.

  - Visualization involves imagining what you want to achieve or have in the future as if it were true today.

  - It transfers your thoughts into active pictures, where you see yourself having what you want.

- The more your visualization involves using all five senses of sight, smell, touch, taste, and hearing, the more intense the feeling becomes.

- When the frequencies of our thoughts are intensified, they attract more of the same back to you through your Reticular Activation System (RAS).

- The process of visualization directs your RAS to be aware of the end goal.

- Visualization is the picture of our thoughts, the first narrative.

- Actor Jim Carrey on visualization: "Visualization works if you work hard. You can't visualize and then just go eat a sandwich!"

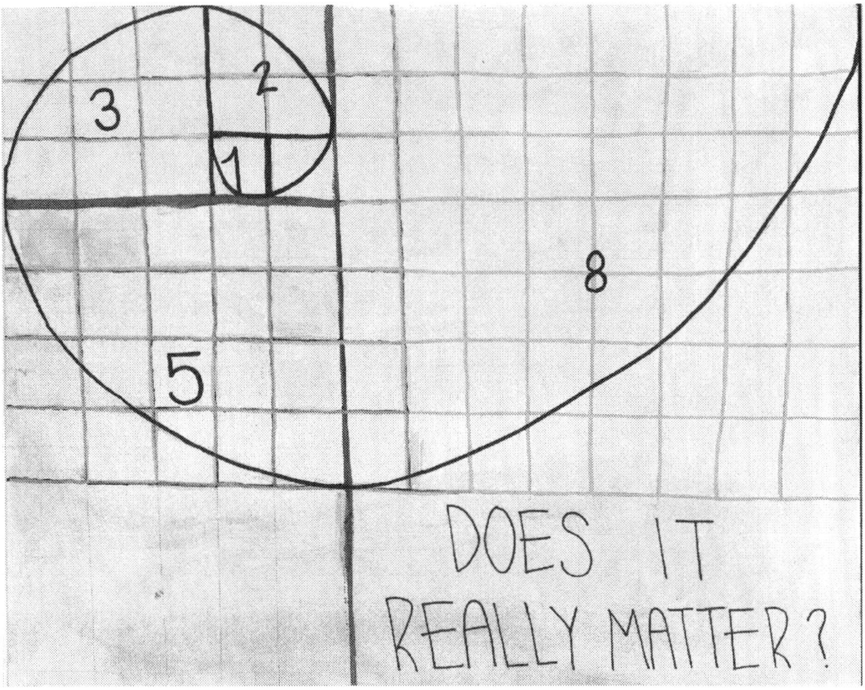
3
2
1
8
5
DOES IT
REALLY MATTER?

Chapter 20

DOES IT REALLY MATTER?

"In matters of style, swim with the current; in matters of principle, stand like a rock."
Thomas Jefferson

Performance

WHEN MY SON TREY was 5 years old, he wanted to play Little League baseball. We signed up, and he was placed on a team. We went to practice three times a week for four weeks, and then the season began.

We were the home team for our very first game. I was 31 years old at the time. I had played softball in college, so I knew the rules. The first three batters came to the plate, and our little team got three outs in a row. Imagine my confusion when the other team continued to bat their complete lineup. It was then that I found out they didn't keep score either, and at the end of the season, everyone got a trophy.

I learned that this league's purpose was training, not performance. But since when does "training" not include individual performance? Our kids go to school for training, and yet they receive grades. Someone ends up with the highest grade, and someone ends up with the lowest grade. Life includes individual performance, and you control yours!

Does It Really Matter?

One of the best questions you can ever ask yourself is, "Does it really matter?"

It is very easy to get caught up in things — things that keep you busy, things that take your mind off your problems, things that waste time, things that are easy to do, things that pressure you to get them done.

Does it really matter if your daughter loses that high school volleyball game? Does it really matter if the car isn't washed? Does it really matter if the floor isn't mopped?

I'm not saying these things aren't important in the moment, but it is imperative to ask yourself the question to put life into perspective: "Does it really matter?"

Learning to Prioritize

My 15-year-old daughter, Isabella, is a fantastic volleyball player. It is her sport!

She began playing volleyball in the 4th grade at her school when she was 9 years old. She fell in love with the sport and decided she wanted to play club volleyball, so she has been playing year-round since she was 10.

When she was younger, she played the libero position, which is a defensive specialist. The libero is the primary person to receive the ball from the opponent and pass it to the setter.

This year, she is a sophomore in high school and primarily plays as a hitter, both on the outside and the right side.

Isabella is not the tallest girl on the team. She is about 5'6" and weighs about 110 pounds (sorry for sharing this, Isabella, but I need to make a point).

She looks more like a libero than a hitter, but her hitting technique generates as much power as the tallest and strongest person on the team. She simply doesn't look like a hitter. (She is actually dainty.)

Now, if you have gathered any impression about me through the writing of this book, I hope you have deduced that I love to gather and review data. So, it should not surprise you that I keep the stats for Isabella's volleyball team.

What has astonished me is how differently people view the data.

The school videos each game and then sends the video to a company called HUDL that reviews the footage. Specifically regarding "hitting," HUDL records kill attempts, kills, and kill attempt errors (errors that cost a point for the team) for each hitter.

At this point in the season, we have an athlete in the hitter position (let's call her Hitter #1) who has 185 kill attempts, 54 kills, and 32 errors, resulting in a total of 22 points earned for the team (54 - 32 = 22).

A different athlete (let's call her Hitter #2) has 143 kill attempts, 39 kills, and 17 errors, resulting in a total of 22 points earned for the team (39 - 17 = 22).

How would you compare and prioritize the data between Hitter #1 and Hitter #2?

If you value kills above everything else, Hitter #1 has 54 and Hitter #2 only has 39, so Hitter #1 is the better hitter.

If you value total points earned over kills, both of them have 22 points, which would make them equal.

But if you also consider and value the number of errors made (how many points were given to the other team), you come to a different conclusion.

Hitter #1 gave away 32 points while only earning 22 points, which puts her at -10 points for the season, whereas Hitter #2 gave away 17 points while earning 22 points, which puts her at +5 points for the season.

The point I am making is this: *What you value most will determine how you prioritize the data.*

I have come to realize that most people struggle with identifying *what matters most* which results in failing to prioritize appropriately.

The most important question to ask yourself is: **Is this a crisis?**

IS THIS A CRISIS?

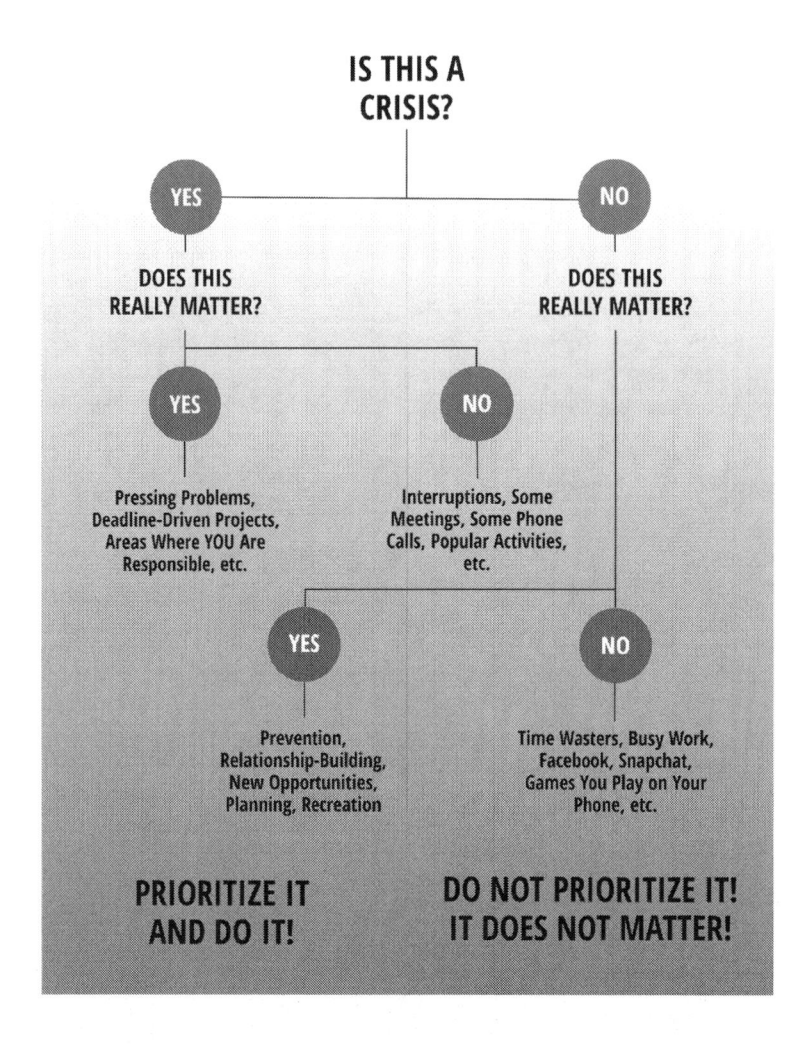

- **YES** → **DOES THIS REALLY MATTER?**
  - **YES**: Pressing Problems, Deadline-Driven Projects, Areas Where YOU Are Responsible, etc. → **PRIORITIZE IT AND DO IT!**
- **NO** → **DOES THIS REALLY MATTER?**
  - **NO**: Interruptions, Some Meetings, Some Phone Calls, Popular Activities, etc.
    - **YES**: Prevention, Relationship-Building, New Opportunities, Planning, Recreation → **PRIORITIZE IT AND DO IT!**
    - **NO**: Time Wasters, Busy Work, Facebook, Snapchat, Games You Play on Your Phone, etc. → **DO NOT PRIORITIZE IT! IT DOES NOT MATTER!**

Consider the "Decision Tree" above: The first question to ask yourself is, **"Is this a crisis?"** Crises find a way to get in your face. They insist on your action. Often, they are pleasant, easy, and fun to do. But so often they don't really matter. If the answer to the first question, "Is this a Crisis?" is "YES," then you need to ask yourself the second question.

The second question to ask yourself is, "Does this really matter?" Things that really matter have to do with results. If something really matters, it has an impact on the way you think, the way you feel, the way you are motivated, and the way you act, or a desired outcome.

If the answer to the second question, "Does this really matter?" is "YES," then it is most likely a pressing problem, deadline-driven project, or an area where you are responsible. That means this item should be **prioritized immediately**.

We all have crises in our lives, but crises consume many people. You have already learned that whatever you tell your Reticular Activation System is important is what you will see more of. So, if you focus your thoughts on problems, guess what you get? More problems. This will cause you to spend so much of your time on "problems" that they totally dominate you. It results in stress, burnout, crisis management, and a general feeling of unfulfillment.

If the answer to the second question, "Does this really matter?" is "NO," then it could be grouped with interruptions, some meetings, some phone calls, or popular activities. That means this item **should not be prioritized**.

If the answer to the first question, "Is this a Crisis?" is "NO," then you need to ask yourself the second question: "Does this really matter?"

If the answer to the second question, "Does this really matter?" is "YES," then it most likely deals with matters such as prevention, relationship building, new opportunities, planning, exercise, and recreation. These matters do not act on you because they are not a crisis. That means you must think and then choose to make these matters a priority. You want to **schedule these matters when you can think and concentrate the best**. I prioritize these matters in the morning when I am fresh and full of energy. My wife, Sandra, prefers the evening. Just pick the time of day that works best for you. The more time you spend planning and preparing, the less time you will spend having to deal with crises that really matter.

If the answer to the second question, "Does this really matter?" is "NO," then it could be grouped as time wasters, busy work, Facebook, Snapchat, or games you play on your phone. That means this item **should not be prioritized**.

Becoming Proactive

As I mentioned before, we live in a society that is rushed, stressed, uncertain, indifferent, distracted, and fatigued. This results in people tending to allow the environment, other people, and circumstances to act on them, and they settle into habitual reactive behavior. They simply lack the time, energy, or cognitive resources to choose to become proactive.

When you SALT Your Thoughts, you become a proactive person. You push the reset button and leave yesterday in the past. You align your thoughts with the positive energy of God every morning. You allow yourself to be filled with gratitude. Because you have identified your own set of beliefs, you can make decisions that you know are congruent with your beliefs. When new situations arise, you can utilize your self-awareness, imagination, conscience, and independent will to evaluate the situation and make decisions based on your own defined values. That means you have already chosen the needs that you desire to motivate you. Someone else's "need" doesn't take precedence over your own. That results in you being in control of your own behavior because you are not reacting to situations, you are acting on situations! You are creating or controlling a situation by causing something to happen rather than responding to it after it has happened, which is the definition of being proactive!

Chapter 20: Assignment

Go to SaltYourThoughts.com. Utilize the **Does This Really Matter** decision tree to evaluate your current day or week and identify how much time you are spending in the areas below.

1. **Crises that really matter** (most likely a pressing problem, deadline-driven project, or an area where you are responsible)

2. **Crises that don't matter** (most likely interruptions, some meetings, some phone calls, popular activities)

3. **Things that are not a crisis but really matter** (such as prevention, relationship building, new opportunities, planning, exercise, and recreation)

4. **Things that are not a crisis and don't matter** (things that could be grouped as time wasters, busy work, Facebook, Snapchat, games you play on your phone)

The more you SALT Your Thoughts, the more time you have for #3, which includes matters such as prevention, relationship building, new opportunities, planning, exercise, and recreation.

Spending more time on matters such as prevention, relationship building, new opportunities, planning, exercise, and recreation reduces the time you need for #1, which are crises that really matter.

We all have crises that really matter (#1). However, we don't want to live in constant crisis.

#2 and #4 don't matter! Try to spend as little time as possible in these two areas.

SALT Summaries:
Chapter 20: Does It Really Matter?

- Performance:
  - Since when does "training" not include individual performance?
  - Our kids go to school for "training," and yet they receive grades. Someone ends up with the highest grade, and someone ends up with the lowest grade.
  - Life includes individual performance — and you control yours!
- One of the best questions you can ever ask yourself is, "**Does it really matter?**"
- Learn to prioritize:
  - When it comes to your life, what you value most will determine how you prioritize the data.
  - I have come to realize that most people do not know how to prioritize.
- Utilize the "Does This Really Matter" decision tree.
  - The more you SALT Your Thoughts, the more time you have for #3 above, which includes matters such as prevention, relationship building, new opportunities, planning, exercise, and recreation.
  - Spending more time on matters such as prevention, relationship building, new opportunities, planning, exercise, and recreation reduces the time you need for #1 - crises that really matter.
  - We all have crises that really matter (#1), but we just do not want to live in crisis!
  - #2 and #4 above don't matter! Spend as little time as possible in these two areas!

My Vision Board...

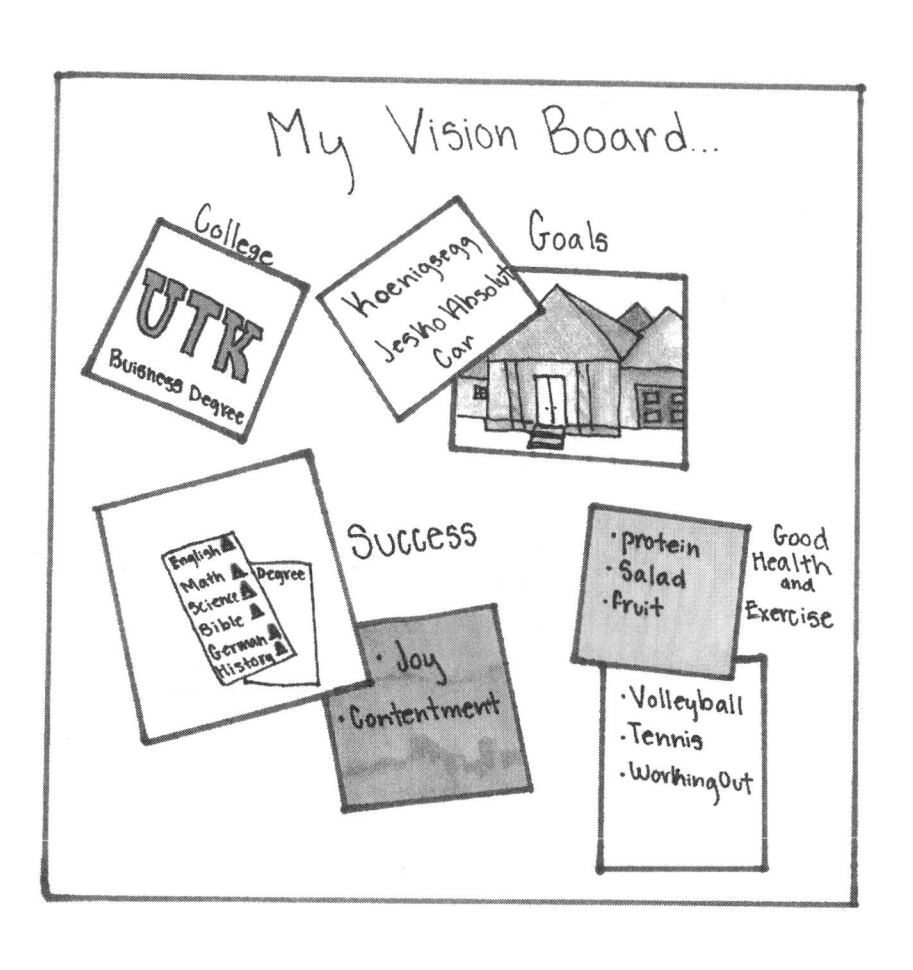

College
UTK — Buisness Degree

Goals
Koenigsegg Jesko Absolut Car

Success
- English, Math, Science, Bible, German, History — Degree
- Joy
- Contentment

Good Health and Exercise
- protein
- Salad
- Fruit

- Volleyball
- Tennis
- Working Out

Chapter 21

Your Vision Board

"The only thing worse than being blind is having sight but no vision."
Helen Keller

What Is a Vision Board?

IN 2019, SANDRA AND I were enjoying a brisk spring evening on the small patio in our backyard. We started visualizing what we would like our backyard to look like. Our backyard was a steep hill, but we began envisioning it as level ground. Once we had leveled the yard in our minds' eye, we started discussing the possibilities for a level backyard. Sandra imagined a nice volleyball court, and I envisioned a beautiful pool. Sandra liked the idea of a waterfall gently falling into the pool, and I suggested adding fire torches at the top of the waterfall. We had so much fun discussing our ideas that we decided to bring them to life.

I created an Excel spreadsheet and had a land survey done. I meticulously mapped our property by the foot in the spreadsheet. I printed out several sheets of 8.5 x 11 paper until we had a complete map of our property. This paper map became our vision board.

We researched different types of pools and looked at pictures until we found the one we wanted. I printed a picture of the pool and pasted it on our vision board. Isabella wanted a volleyball court, so we found a picture of a volleyball court and added it to our vision board. I desired a putting green, so I found a picture of one and included it on our vision board. We visualized and included everything we desired on our vision board.

A **vision board** summarizes your thinking around a subject. It can be for a backyard, a new house, a business, or even your life. A vision board should provide you with clear direction for your thoughts, beliefs, attitudes, needs, and actions. It allows you to visualize your goals and serves as a constant reminder of your priorities.

How Do You Create a Vision Board?

When Sandra and I renovated our house, Sandra had a vision board for each little project, and we also had a master vision board.

You can create a vision board for almost anything. For example, you could create a vision board featuring all your positive mood triggers. Another idea is to create a vision board that represents how you define success.

Any subject that you desire to focus your thoughts on is a great candidate for a vision board. Always keep your vision board aligned with your end goal. Keep your vision boards in a place where you see them every day.

Stages of Life

Let's discuss how the content of a vision board might change based on the stage of life you are currently in.

If you are a teenager (13 to 19 years old), you might create a vision board for the sports team you are trying to join or the college you want to attend. It could include pictures of the ACT or SAT scores you aim to achieve, the campus you desire to be on, and the clubs you want to join.

If you are an adult (20 to 39 years old), you might create a vision board for the spouse you are looking for, the job you want to acquire, the house you want to purchase, or the child you want to have. You can imagine the types of pictures you could include on your vision board.

If you are a middle-aged adult (40 to 59 years old), you might create a vision board for the type of "empty nest" you envision, including pictures of activities or travel that you can enjoy now that you have more discretionary time.

If you are a senior adult (60 years and older), you might create a vision board for the activities you want to engage in now that you no longer have to work every day, or for the location and style of your retirement life.

You can create a vision board for anything that will provide you with focus and clarity of mind.

Your Life's Vision Board

If you have completed each assigned task along the way, the components of your life's vision board have already been created.

Chapter 21 Assignment:

Now it's time to go to **SaltYourThoughts.com** and view and print **Your Life's Vision Board**.

SALT Summaries:
Chapter 21: Your Vision Board

- A **vision board**:

    - summarizes your thinking around a subject.

    - should provide you clear direction for your thoughts, beliefs, attitudes, needs, and actions

    - allows you to visualize your goals. A vision board is a constant reminder of your priorities.

- How do you create a vision board?

    - You can create a vision board for almost anything.

    - Always focus your vision board on your end goal.

- You can create a vision board for anything that will give you focus and clarity of mind!

- If you have completed each assigned task along the way, you have completed your life's vision board

PART 6

The System: Execute Your Plan

WEEK

SUN	MON	TUE	WED	THU	FRI	SAT

Chapter 22

Execution

"By failing to prepare, you are preparing to fail."
Benjamin Franklin

Preparation

ABRAHAM LINCOLN ONCE SAID, "If I only had an hour to chop down a tree, I would spend the first 45 minutes sharpening my ax." This quote has been used in business seminars for years, illustrating the importance of preparation, planning, practice, and strategy. Once you have clearly articulated your desired results (the end goal), a dull ax will not facilitate working effectively or efficiently.

I have always been an entrepreneur. In my 20s, a friend and I purchased a machine that could hold up to 10 hardwood trees on a conveyor table. The table conveyed a single tree into a trough. Once a single tree was in the trough, the operator could clamp onto the tree and pull it forward to be cut into a specific length determined by the operator. Then, the operator could initiate a 54-inch chainsaw mechanism to cut the wood into the specified length. Once the log was cut, it was pushed into a splitter. After the log was split, it dropped onto a conveyor belt that loaded the truck. It was a wonderful machine, and it was fun to operate. That is, until the blade was dull!

We found that if the blade was dull, we could only produce about 8 ricks of wood in 8 hours. But if we prepared and kept a sharp blade on the saw, we could produce 40 ricks of wood in 8 hours. I learned firsthand what Abraham Lincoln was talking about!

The key learning is: Preparation and planning are critical components of effective execution.

The Concept of a Seven-Day Week

I believe the concept of a seven-day week originated from the Biblical account of God creating the earth and everything on it in six days and then resting on the seventh. Some would say that it originated with the Babylonians.

Regardless of the origin, the concept of a seven-day week permeates our entire lives. Business, education, and many other aspects of our world function within the framework of a seven-day week.

Planning and organizing your time around the natural concept of a seven-day week makes much more sense to me than daily planning. Daily planning implies a reaction to what is happening to you, as opposed to planning what you will act on.

Chapter 22 Assignment:

Go to **SaltYourThoughts.com** and plan and organize your week according to the steps below:

Step #1 – Review Your Roles
Pick a day of the week that is most convenient to set aside 15-30 minutes each week to plan your week. Most people choose Saturday or Sunday. The most important thing is to set aside the same time each week to plan the next week. In Chapter 12, you identified your roles. You used your self-awareness to identify the different roles in which you function on a day-to-day basis. Now let's use your roles as a framework for planning your week. Step #1 is to review your roles.

Step #2 – Set Goals for Each Role
Now look at your roles and identify two or three goals you would like to accomplish for each of your roles in the coming week. Some people fear the word "goal" as if setting a goal and not achieving it makes them feel like a failure. Not setting any goal is the real failure! In Chapter 20, you learned that things that are not a crisis, but really matter — such as prevention, relationship building, new opportunities, planning, exercise, and recreation — are things that you must plan in order to do. Because these things are not a crisis, they do not "act on you;" you must "act on them." Have you ever wondered why you can't find time for exercise? It is because you haven't planned it! Just be sure you are setting goals around those activities that are most important to you. The most important thing about setting your goals for the coming week is to "advance the ball forward" as they say in golf. It is better to take small steps forward than to leap in the wrong direction! My point is, don't obsess over these weekly goals. You are simply taking control of your life!

Step #3 – Schedule the Time to Accomplish Your Goals for the Coming Week
Now that you have some goals set for each of your roles, you can look at the coming 7-day week and schedule time to accomplish those goals. Let's say you took my advice and set a goal to set aside an hour three times over the next seven days for exercise. After reviewing the calendar, you decide to set aside from 6:30 a.m. to 7:30 a.m. Monday, Wednesday, and Friday for your exercise. There are some goals that you can only accomplish while you are at work. Others may only be accomplished when you are not at work. You need to consider your own personal preferences when you schedule your time. For example, I do my best writing in the mornings. So, I set aside 5:00 a.m. to 9:00 a.m. every morning to write. If I try to write in the afternoons, my mind is already fatigued, and it is just not as fruitful.

Now, look at things that are scheduled by someone else but important for you to attend. For example, you may have a child like I do that is involved in a sport. The games are scheduled, and you may desire to attend those games, like I do. So, put them on the schedule!

So, using all your goals and what you know about yourself, schedule your goals for the coming week. Now, you are in control, and you are not reacting to what comes your way! By your own definition, your goals are the most important things for you to accomplish in the next seven days. Have you ever made that happen before?

Key Point: Always schedule the most important things first!

Let the less important "things" fill in around the most important "things"!

Now, evaluate every appointment or priority item for the day in the context of your weekly goals. Transfer or reschedule items that are less important for this week to a time in the future. You may look at some items on your schedule and simply eliminate them.

Now that you have time set aside for the things you feel are most important, look at the remaining unscheduled time on your calendar. This unscheduled time will provide you the flexibility on your calendar to spontaneously handle unanticipated situations. We will call that daily planning.

Step #4 – Daily Planning

Chapter 23 shares your new morning ritual. Step #8 of your new morning ritual has you look at that day's schedule, and based on the latest information you have, you can adjust that day's schedule as needed. Having this flexibility is imperative for a schedule to work. Having set aside time on the week's schedule to accomplish the activities most important to you gives context to the daily planning.

Each morning as you review the schedule for the day, you can see the natural framework that your roles and goals provide for the week. You can feel the balance it provides as you handle the requests or demands for time on your schedule.

Now you are the one in control. It is your schedule! You choose what gets on your schedule and what does not.

SALT Summaries:
Chapter 22: Execution

- Preparation and planning are critical components of effective execution.

- Planning and organizing your time around the natural concept of a week makes much more sense than daily planning.

- Daily planning implies a reaction to what is happening to you, as opposed to planning what you will act on.

- Preparation and planning your seven-day week:

  - Step #1 – Review your roles.

  - Step #2 – Set goals for each role.

  - Step #3 – Schedule the time to accomplish your goals for the coming week.

  - Step #4 – Daily planning.

- Now you are the one in control. It is your schedule! You choose what gets on your schedule and what does not.

MY MORNING SALT RITUAL

▷ This is the day the Lord has made; I will rejoice and be glad in it!

STEP #1 - Push the reset button: Align my thoughts (the source of my beliefs) with the positive energy of God every morning.

STEP #2 - Choose to engage MY FOUR HUMAN ATTRIBUTES.

STEP #3 - Review MY CORE THOUGHTS: Engage reticular activation system - I will find what I seek.

STEP #4 - Review MY CORE BELIEFS (the way I think), so that my decisions are congruent with my beliefs.

STEP #5 - Review MY CORE VALUES (the way I choose to feel) that define my home base for which I make decisions.

STEP #6 - Review MY CORE NEEDS (the way I am motivated) because my needs drive my behaviors.

STEP #7 - Align MY CORE BEHAVIORS (the way I choose to act) with their source - the thought.

STEP #8 - Visualize today's end goal: Ask, believe, and receive.

Chapter 23

YOUR NEW MORNING SALT RITUAL

"God's mercy is fresh and new every morning."
Joyce Meyer

SALT Your Thoughts!

I LOVE SALT ON watermelon! In fact, I love salt on just about anything. Salt has been used to preserve food for thousands of years. It is the most common seasoning, providing flavor, texture, and enhancing the color of the food we eat. In small amounts, salt can intensify sweetness, which is why it is sometimes sprinkled on fresh fruit or added to candies like caramel. It can also counteract bitter flavors in food. If you like to eat like I do, salt is simply amazing!

I started SALTing My Thoughts at 14 years old, when I went to boarding school for the 9th grade. I really didn't call it SALTing My Thoughts back then, but that is exactly what I did.

As soon as I would wake up, while I was getting ready for my day, I would thank the Lord for another day of life. Then I would remind myself of five things for which I was grateful.

Then I would remind myself of five beliefs that my mother had taught me. Then, I would take a couple of minutes and think about the tasks I had to do that day, and visualize my desired outcomes for that day. Finally, I would say to myself ten times, "I am ready, I am ready, I am ready..." Then I would say a short prayer to God, asking Him to guide my steps throughout the day. Once I completed this little ritual, I knew I was ready for whatever the day would bring.

I was blessed that my mother had taught me about God, and that I should connect with Him every morning, because we live in a world that is at war between good and evil. This war certainly has an impact on our physical lives, but the primary battle is in our mind. What we think about, we eventually do.

At 14, my little morning ritual was my way to ground myself, to connect with God, remember my mother and the principles that she taught me to live by, and get focused for the day. As I grew older, it was simply my way to stay connected to who I wanted to become. **I started each day by setting up my brain to look for the right things!** If my mother had not died tragically in a car accident, I doubt I would have even had a morning ritual. So in many ways, her death — and my response to it — has made me who I am today.

Until I wrote this book, I thought everyone started their morning in a similar way. When I realized that most people start their morning reacting to the world around them instead of thinking intentionally, I began to understand the significance of the difference in my morning ritual. I finally comprehended that the *real difference* began as soon as I woke up. The real difference was my connection to the ultimate power of the universe every morning.

The Bible says in 2 Corinthians chapter 10 that we walk in this world, but our battle is really against spiritual forces of evil that desire to control our minds with negative thinking and lies about God. But we have been given the gift of The Divine Power Of God to overcome ANYTHING — including any negative thoughts that try to control our mind. The Bible says the way to conquer and overcome is to **renew your mind daily**.

> "Finally, brothers and sisters, whatever is true, whatever is honorable, whatever is right, whatever is pure, whatever is lovely, whatever is com-

mendable, if there is any excellence, and if anything worthy of praise, think about these things." Philippians 4:8 (NASB20)

I don't think I have ever really shared with anyone (except for Sandra) how I start my mornings. When I realized the *secret power* I was unleashing on my life every morning, I became compelled to share it with Isabella. And now I am sharing it with you! I challenge you to embrace this new movement and new way of thinking: **SALT Your Thoughts every morning!**

If you SALT Your Thoughts, I believe it will have the same effect on you. When you focus your thoughts on those things for which you are grateful, those things that give you joy, and those positive triggers, you are in fact aligning yourself with the only positive power in this universe: God.

It is critically important for you to develop your morning ritual. I can bore you with psychological research, but I don't need to; it just makes common sense. Help me make the world a better place and join the MOVEMENT that has already begun! I am getting positive feedback from family and friends, readers and reviewers. Because they are SALTing Their Thoughts, they are happier, more intentional, more productive, more purposeful, and more effective. These effects don't just happen. You cause them to happen with focused thoughts. So, it makes sense to start each day with the correct thoughts. The best morning ritual I know is to SALT Your Thoughts. When you subscribe to SaltYourThoughts.com, you will receive a daily email utilizing your completed assignments making it even easier to SALT Your Thoughts daily.

Here is how to SALT Your Thoughts in eight easy steps. (I love how Isabella took notes when I taught it to her, so here they are in her writing):

This is the day the Lord has made; I will rejoice and be glad in it!

Step #1 - Push my reset button: Align my thoughts (the source of my beliefs) with the positive energy of God every morning. (Chapter 4-5)

    1. Let go of the past! Choose to control my state of mind!

    2. Focus on my gratitude list.

3. Focus on my joy list.

4. Focus on my positive mood triggers.

Step #2 - Choose to engage my four human attributes (Chapter 3):

1. Self-awareness: My awareness of my own thoughts, feelings, and actions

2. Imagination: My ability to visualize a new reality

3. Conscience: My awareness of what is morally right or wrong

4. Independent will: My ability to choose to act based on self-awareness

Step #3 - Review my core thoughts; engage my reticular activation system; I will find what I seek. (Chapter 6)

Step #4 - Review my core beliefs (the way I think), so that my decisions are congruent with my beliefs. (Chapter 7)

1. Review my mission - my core beliefs. (Chapter 18)

Step #5 - Review my core values (the way I choose to feel) that define my home base for which I make decisions. (Chapter 13-14)

1. Review my mission - my core values. (Chapter 18)

Step #6 - Review my core needs (the way I am motivated) because my needs drive my behaviors. (Chapter 15)

1. Review my mission - my core needs. (Chapter 18)

Step #7 - Align my core behaviors (the way I choose to act) with their source - my thoughts. (Chapter 17)

1. Review my mission - my core behaviors. (Chapter 18)

Step #8 - Visualize today's end goal: Ask, believe, and receive. (Chapter 18)

1. Look at my weekly plan, then look at my schedule for today.

2. Respond to any unanticipated events, relationships, prioritizing activities as needed.

Chapter 23 Assignment:

Read through the explanation and expansion of the eight steps below, checking that you have completed the accompanying assessments as you go.

Expanding on the Eight Steps to SALT Your Thoughts

Let's break down each step into smaller pieces of information. But before you feel overwhelmed, let me quickly explain that if you have completed all the chapter assignments, the SALT Your Thoughts website will provide you with your information in these eight steps.

Step #1 — Push My Reset Button: Focus My Thoughts on Positive Energy
Pushing the reset button is a simple tool that provides a physiological, tactile, and tangible method to stop and take a breath. Yesterday is behind you; it's time to let it go. The past only has power if you focus on it today. Remember it, learn from it, and let it go. You are most effective when you focus on today and plan for tomorrow.

Focus on the things for which you are grateful. The assignment for Chapter 9 is to identify your gratitude list. When you think grateful thoughts, you are aligning your thoughts with positive energy.

Focus on the things that bring you joy. The assignment for Chapter 10 is to identify your joy list. When you think joyful thoughts, you are aligning your thoughts with positive energy.

Focus your thoughts on your positive mood triggers. The assignment for Chapter 11 is to identify your list of positive mood triggers. Your positive mood triggers provide an immediate boost of positive energy.

Focus Your Thoughts on Positive Energy. Now, let's break this sentence into two components. The first component is to understand the value of Positive Thinking. In 1952, Norman Vincent Peale wrote a book entitled *The Power of Positive Thinking*. He believed that the roots of success lie in the mind.[17] The purpose of the book was to teach you how to believe in yourself and how to break the habit of worrying. It also taught how to take control of your life by taking control of your thoughts and changing your attitude.

The concept of choosing to concentrate on positive thoughts has been around for at least 70 years. Unfortunately, many authors have written about this "power" without ever identifying its source. Norman Vincent Peale was a minister. He knew that the origin of this power was, is, and always will be, God. And that leads us to the second part of the sentence.

Who or what is the source of positive energy? I have already shared the powerful influence my mother had on me as a child. I believe I was truly blessed. My mother introduced me to God when I was a young boy. However, many of you may have never had the opportunity to "know" God. For some of you, the concept of "God" is foreign to the five primary senses of seeing, touching, hearing, tasting, or smelling, which makes God difficult to grasp. Many of you may feel like my son Trey did when he was about four years old. He had a bad dream and woke up crying. I came in to comfort him, and he told me about his dream and how afraid he was. In an effort to comfort him, I said, "Trey, God is always with you, so you don't ever need to be afraid." He responded, "Daddy, you don't understand. I need something with skin on it!"

So, let's put some skin on God. In Chapter 4 of this book, we discussed that the human brain is composed of about 100 billion nerve cells (neurons) interconnected by trillions of connections called synapses. Thoughts emit measurable frequencies. These frequencies emit brainwaves. Our thoughts are the cause, and the brainwave is the effect. Brainwaves are electrical impulses in the brain. All brainwaves are produced by thoughts, which are synchronized electrical pulses from masses of neurons communicating with each other. Our brainwaves occur at various frequencies, some fast and some slow. The classic names of these EEG bands are delta, theta, alpha, beta, and gamma. They are measured in cycles per second or hertz (Hz).

The point I am making here is that your thoughts emit a frequency. You are just like a television station's transmission tower. You broadcast the frequency of your thoughts into the air. It is critical to understand that God also broadcasts the frequency of His thoughts into the air.[18] Remember, "Like Attracts Like", so when you are thinking positive thoughts your thoughts are aligning with the positive (Goodness) of God.

At this point in our history, virtually all disciplines — religion, sciences, philosophy, quantum physics, etc. — agree that this universe is completely made of "energy" and that this energy is "somehow all connected." For those with a Naturalism worldview, the "somehow all connected" is that there was nothing at first, then it randomly exploded, and now there is energy that connects everything in the universe. Now, how much faith does it take to believe that? The consequence for those with a Naturalism worldview is most tragic because, by denying the existence of the Creator God, they choose to spend eternity separated from Him.

For those with a Christian/Theism worldview, the "somehow all connected" is that there is a Creator God who created this universe and everything in it with order and precision. God authored the Natural Law of Perpetual Transmutation of Energy, which asserts that energy can neither be created nor destroyed (except by God). God also authored the Law of Vibration, which states that everything moves and nothing rests. Vibrations of the same frequency resonate with each other, so like energy attracts like energy. Furthermore, He authored the Law of Attraction, which states that "like attracts like." This means that people attract energy similar to the energy they project. Positive people attract other positive people, while negative people attract other negative people. The fact is that you attract people, ideas, and resources that are in harmony with your dominant thoughts. You, and only you, have the independent will to choose your own dominant thoughts. In other words, you have the responsibility and the power to be the author of your own narrative. **What you think about is what you become!**

When God created humans (Adam and Eve), He gave humans the **power of choice — independent will**. God loves us and desires us to love Him back **of our own free will**. In the Garden of Eden, Adam and Eve were given the keys to this world and dominion over everything in it. They had a choice between good and evil. They could tune their frequencies to God's Channel or Satan's Channel. Naturally, they were tuned into God's Channel, but they had the freedom to choose. Unfortunately, Adam and Eve were deceived and chose evil. They handed over the keys and dominion of this world to Satan. The Bible says they gave Satan the keys to the air where all the frequencies are emitted, both positive and negative. Their disobedience brought sin and death into this world, separating Adam, Eve, and all their descendants (us) from God. But, because of His complete love for Adam and Eve (and us), God shared His plan of redemption with them. He would pay the penalty for their sin, and Adam and Eve, and all of their descendants (us) would have a choice to accept His provision for us.

God never stopped broadcasting on His Channel. Due to our lineage from Adam, our natural tendency now is to tune into Satan's Channel. This is a problem that only God could fix. So, God, being the very definition of love, sent His Son (Jesus) to earth as a second Adam. Jesus was born naturally tuned into God's Channel, just like Adam. Despite facing temptations in every manner that Adam did, Jesus chose to remain tuned into God's channel. Romans 6:23 says, "The wages of sin is death, but the gift of God is eternal life in Christ Jesus our Lord." Jesus took on human form to pay the penalty of sin, which is death. He lived a perfectly sinless life and then gave His life as the complete payment for all the sins ever committed in this world. However, He did not remain in the grave; He rose again on the third day. He took your place on the cross and paid your entire debt for sin. His life, death, and resurrection redeemed both the title deed and dominion of this world. The war has been won. All that is left for evil to do is to battle for your mind! **I believe it won't be long before He returns to claim what He has purchased!**

In Chapter 9 of this book, you made a list of the things in your life for which you are grateful. If you are grateful for it, there must be something about it that is good or positive. So, I must ask you a simple question: Where do good or positive things come from?

Luke 18:19 NKJV says, "No one is good but One, that is, God." That means that anything that is good or positive comes from God. Good cannot come from anyone but God. If you have ever had good in your life, it came from God. So, when you focus your thoughts and concentrate on those things for which you are grateful, you are aligning yourself with the only One/Thing in this universe that is good and positive, and that is God!

James 1:17 NKJV says, "Every good gift and every perfect gift is from above and comes down from the Father." If you have received any good gifts, those gifts are from God. There is nothing that is positive in this world that doesn't come from God. Positive energy emanates from God.

Jesus gave His life for YOU!

So, if you want some good positive energy, where do you find it? God. When you are grateful, it is good, positive energy, and it comes from God. In Chapter 10 you made a list of what gives you joy. Guess what? Those things that give you joy are good, positive energy, so they also come from God.

I must warn you, however. When you understand and acknowledge that God has been involved in your life and authored everything that ever happened to you or for you that was good, God's plan is to draw you into a relationship with Him. He desires to have a relationship with you.

You can focus your thoughts on positive energy and *not* be a born-again Christian. God still likes to share His good, positive energy with you. But if you desire to go a little deeper and accept the gift of salvation, it is very simple. I can walk you through it right here, right now. All you have to do is pray this prayer:

"God, I know You are the Creator God of this universe. I know You sent Jesus to this world to live, die, and be resurrected so that He could reconcile us to You. I believe Jesus became a human, lived a perfect life, and died a sinner's death for me. I believe Jesus paid the penalty for my sin. I believe He conquered death and rose from the grave on the third day. I believe He ascended to heaven, but He is coming back to get me, and I am looking forward to that day! So, I ask You to be the Lord and Savior of my life. In the name of Jesus, Amen."

If you prayed that prayer, all heaven is rejoicing at this moment, and I can't wait to see you there!

Step #2 — Engage My Four Human Attributes
In his 2008 book *Outliers*, Malcolm Gladwell wrote that "ten thousand hours is the magic number of greatness."[19] According to Gladwell, to be considered elite and truly experienced within a certain craft, you must practice it for 10,000 hours.

I totally agree with Gladwell! It takes 10,000 hours of practice to become an expert at anything. That means at 40 hours per week, and 50 of the 52 weeks a year (which equals 2,000 hours) it takes five years to reach the expert level of anything. Let's take professional sports for a moment. Most professional athletes start out with a natural "gift" and passion for the sport, and then they put in the 10,000 hours to become an expert in that sport. But unfortunately, just like your closet, if you don't continue to practice even after you are an expert, you lose those expert skills.

In Chapter 3, I explained that we humans have been given a gift. We have been given four human attributes that make us uniquely human.[20] Taking just a moment each morning to remind yourself of your four human attributes can enhance your ability to utilize them more effectively.

   1. Self-Awareness: Awareness of your own thoughts, feelings, and actions

   2. Imagination: The ability to visualize a new reality

3. Conscience: Awareness of what is morally right or wrong

4. Independent Will: The ability to choose to act based on self-awareness

Step #3 — Review My Core Thoughts; Engage Your Reticular Activation System (I Find What I Seek)

Your Reticular Activation System is the feedback loop between your conscious mind and your subconscious mind. Your subconscious mind determines what it thinks is important to you based on the intensity of your thoughts and feelings. Now that you know about the Reticular Activation System, you can cause your conscious mind to focus and plainly state to your subconscious mind EXACTLY what to think, be, need, and do.

Remember, like attracts like. Positive thoughts attract positive thoughts. Remember in Step #1, you just connected yourself to the positive energy of God. Step #4 helps you utilize it all day long! **Think about what you seek, and you will find it.** Tell your Reticular Activation System to make you aware of the "energy" of those around you. If the people around you are positive, your radio tower is sending out positive thoughts. If you find yourself surrounded by people who are complaining about everything, *it might be time to change your own thoughts.*

The critical lesson: Concentrating your THOUGHTS on a definite purpose becomes POWER![21]

If you need a quick check on what kind of thought seeds you are planting, go to SaltYourThoughts.com and complete the Reticular Activation System survey again.

Step #4 — Review My Core Beliefs (The Way I Think)

Have you ever organized your closet? Clothes color-coordinated on hangers, and all drawers with their contents neatly folded? I like everything neat and tidy and in exactly the right place. How long will your closet stay that way? Will it stay that way for a whole week? The point I want to make is this: We live in a world where we can get "things" organized and they naturally move to a state of chaos if you are not SALTing Your Thoughts daily. Wouldn't it be nice if you could organize your closet one time, and it would never get disorganized again for the rest of your life? But it doesn't work that way. Instead, it takes diligence and constant effort to keep anything organized.

Our thoughts and beliefs can be a little like our closet. The principles that we believe in can get a little cluttered, and we can lose touch with what we really believe is most important. That is why it is so important to write down and review your beliefs every day. Reviewing your beliefs helps you remember those things that are most important to you. It helps you put a stake in the ground so that you can manage new information and process it effectively. You become 42% more likely to achieve your goals and dreams simply by writing them down and reviewing them on a regular basis.

Have you ever made a knee-jerk decision and then realized it was not congruent with who you really are? You are not the only one! It happens to all of us. But it happens less frequently when we review our beliefs daily.

There are two components for Step #4. First, simply review the Seven Principles of the Farm. You will be surprised how they affect and explain much of life:

1. We reap only what has been sown.

2. We reap the same in kind as we sow.

3. We reap in a different season than we sow.

4. We reap more than we sow.

5. We reap in proportion to what we sow.

6. We reap the full harvest only if we hoe out the weeds.

7. We can't do anything about last year's harvest.

Second, you were given an assignment for Chapter 7 to go to SaltYourThoughts.com and complete the following four surveys. The reports for these surveys are a quick reference guide for Step #4.

If you have not completed these 4 surveys, please go to SaltYourThoughts.com to complete:

- The Habits of Your Mind: Your Beliefs (Rank 25 Items)

- The Habits of Your Mind: Beliefs About Your Attitudes (Rank 15 Items)

- The Habits of Your Mind: Beliefs About Your Needs (Rank 10 Items)

- The Habits of Your Mind: Beliefs About Your Actions (Rank 25 Items)

Step #5 — Review My Core Personal Values (The Way I Choose to Feel)
There are two components for Step #5. First, review the results of your SALT Type Indicator and Temperament from your assignment for Chapter 13. These reports provide a tangible reminder of your attitudes. If you have not taken the SALT Type Indicator, go to SaltYourThoughts.com to complete it.

Second, review the results of the two assessments provided in Chapter 14. Remember, your Personal Value is an attitude of personal quality that causes a need that you move toward. *Your Personal Values define your home base for which you make decisions.* It is just like picking up a stick. When you pick up one end of the stick, you pick up the other. The "other" end of the stick for every value is a need. As a result, your personal values define your attitudes (the way you feel). Your personal values are on the inside — they are *how you measure yourself*.

If you have not taken the assessments, complete them at SaltYourThoughts.com.

Step #6 — Review My Core Needs (The Way I Am Motivated)
Your needs drive your behaviors. The other end of the personal value stick is the need. Your needs come from inside you — the desire to become or be the best you can be. What is fascinating to me is that your motivation increases as your needs are met. In other words, the more you grow, the more you want to grow. *You are designed to become, and you become what you think about.*

However, if your needs are not met, it is a source of stress or even dysfunctional behavior. This cause-and-effect relationship between your personal values and your needs sets up the opportunity for chronic stress. Unmet needs are a source of chronic stress.

Stress is a normal psychological and physical reaction to the demands of life. A small amount of stress can be good, motivating you to perform well. But multiple challenges daily can push you beyond your ability to cope. Remember, your brain comes hard-wired with an alarm system for your protection — your subconscious mind. It depends on your conscious mind to be its gatekeeper. Your subconscious mind perceives information through intuition as a function of survival, thus "fight-or-flight."

During conditions of stress, panic, fear, and excitement, the subconscious mind is unguarded and open to the suggestion of self-depreciation, fear, selfishness, hatred, greed, and other negative forces. These false suggestions (lies) embedded in the subconscious mind become the cause of stress, fear, worry, disease, and poverty. The subconscious mind left unguarded leaves it susceptible to error and misinformation. When your subconscious mind perceives a threat, it signals your body to release a burst of hormones that increase your heart rate and raise your blood pressure. This "fight-or-flight" response fuels you to deal with the threat.

Once the threat is gone, your body is meant to return to a normal, relaxed state. Unfortunately, the nonstop complications of modern life mean that some people's alarm systems rarely shut off. Understanding your temperament, your core needs, your stressors enables you to choose the antidote for stress — to SALT Your Thoughts and choose to change your state of mind!

For this reason, it is imperative to review your needs daily. You are responsible. Your needs drive your behaviors. But you and only you define your needs. If you did not complete the assessment for Chapter 15, go to SaltYourThoughts.com to complete it.

Step #7 — Align My Core Behaviors (the Way I Choose to Act) with the Source: My Thoughts
Sometimes there is a disconnect between what we say is important to us and how much time we spend doing the things that are most important to us. Life often seems to get in the way of what we have determined to be important as it relates to our roles, goals, and how we have defined success. Sometimes we realize there is a disconnect, and sometimes we don't.

Step #7 provides you with a quick health check. Review your Personal Mission Statement. It is like your report card in high school. Does your behavior get an A, B, C, D, or F? When you grade your behaviors with an A or B, your thoughts, beliefs, attitudes/values, and needs/motivators are most likely all in alignment.

But what about the times when you would grade your own behavior as a C, D, or F? While there can be many causes, let's discuss the three most common ones.

I introduced the roles, the customer of the role, the positive affirmation statement for each role, and the goals for each role in Chapter 12. I also shared that when you profess a strong, positive affirmation statement in the form of a belief and commitment statement about each of your roles, it enables you to identify and visualize what your desired actions are as an end goal for each role. This positive affirmation statement is the definition of what your "acceptable" behavior should look like.

One common problem is when your positive affirmation statement is vague or unclear. If your end goal for a role is unclear, it causes your desired actions to be unclear.

Another common problem is when you have two very clearly stated positive affirmation statements, but the goals for each role conflict. For example, I have a stated health goal to walk 5 miles five times each week. It takes me an hour and 15 minutes to walk five miles. This is one of those goals that really matter, but it is not critical. These take extra planning to execute because it is easy to let something that really matters and is also critical take its place. The days I run out of time are typically a result of poor planning or poor prioritization.

A third common problem can result when there is a driving need that exposes itself in a behavior we didn't intend.

Remember Amy in Chapter 14? As an ISFJ (Protector), she found it stressful trying to manage her six team members and ensure that they complete their semester-long project. Though she believed that managing her time effectively would improve her GPA and give her peace of mind, she ended up spending hours on social media to calm her nerves.

That is why Step #7 is so important. It provides the process for you to look for incongruences.

Step #7 is where you review your roles, positive affirmation statements, and goals and conduct a reality check. The areas that you have done well, take a moment and pat yourself on the back. Let's say you realize you were impatient with someone the day before. Instead of telling yourself you will not be impatient again, speak out loud to yourself and say, "Today I will demonstrate patience to everyone I interact with." There is nothing gained by engaging in self-deprecation (belittling or undervaluing yourself). The past is behind you, let it go!

If for some reason you have not completed your roles and goals, go to SaltYourThoughts.com to complete them.

Step #8 — Visualize Your End Goal: Ask, Believe, Receive

Step #8 is my favorite step! Visualizing is the habit of thinking/imagining what you want to accomplish and achieve in the future as if it were true today. Visualization intensifies your thoughts. Visualization transfers your thoughts into active pictures.

Your active pictures are where you see yourself having what you want. The more your visualization involves using all five senses of sight, smell, touch, taste, and hearing, the more intense the feeling. When the frequencies of our thoughts are intensified, they attract more of the same back to you through your Reticular Activation System. The process of visualization directs your Reticular Activation System to be aware of the end goal. Visualization is the picture of our thoughts; your first narrative.

Step #8 concludes with the following:

- **Ask** the Creator God for His help and guidance for your day.

- **Believe** He will provide you His help and guidance for your day.

- **Receive** His help and guidance for your day, immediately!

Review your goals as well as how you have defined success. In Chapter 17, you were assigned nine separate assessments that help you define success. If you have not completed them, please go to **SaltYourThoughts.com** to do so.

SALT Summaries:
Chapter 23: Your New Morning SALT Ritual

- It is critically important for you to develop a "Morning Ritual."
    - "Effects" don't just happen. You cause them to happen with your thoughts.
    - You should be able to accomplish this new Morning Ritual in less than 15 minutes.
    - It will set your mind on the correct thoughts and shield you from distractions.
- Every morning wake up and say:

"This is the day the Lord has made; I will rejoice and be glad in it!"

- Then, SALT Your Thoughts:
    - Step 1: Push My Reset Button: Focus my thoughts on positive energy.
        - Reset: Yesterday is behind me; Focus on Today & Tomorrow.
        - Focus on my Gratitude List.
        - Focus on my Joy List.
        - Focus on my Positive Mood Triggers.
    - Step 2: Engage My Four Human Attributes:
        - Self-Awareness: Awareness of your own thoughts, feelings, and actions.
        - Imagination: The ability to visualize a new reality.
        - Conscience: Awareness of what is morally right or wrong.
        - Independent Will: The ability to choose to act based on self-awareness.
    - Step 3: Review My Core Thoughts – Engage my Reticular Activation Sys-

tem (I Will Find What I Seek).

- Step 4: Review My Core Beliefs (The Way I Think).

- Step 5: Review My Core Values (The Way I Choose to Feel).

- Step 6: Review My Core Needs (The Way I Am Motivated).

- Step 7: Align My Core Behaviors (the Way I Act) with the Source: My Thoughts.

- Step 8: Visualize My End Goal: Ask, Believe, and Receive.

PART 7

Tools for Measuring Your Progress

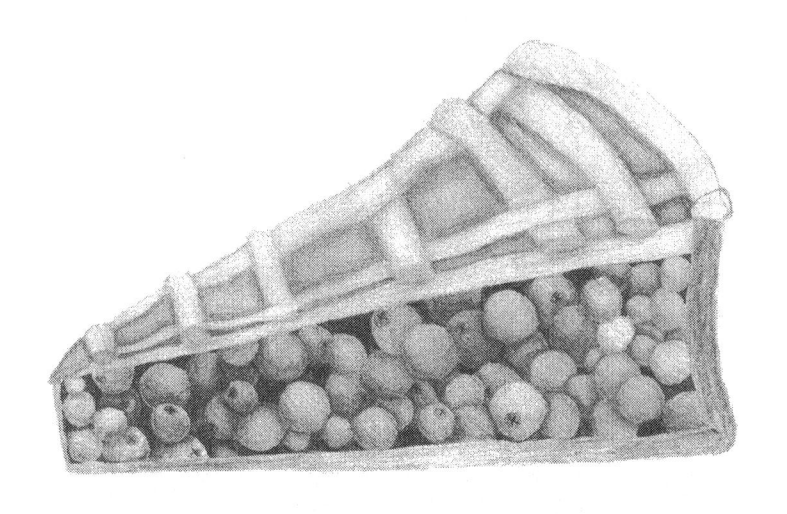

PIECE OF THE PIE

Chapter 24

WHAT GETS MEASURED GETS DONE!

"Drag your thoughts away from your troubles... by the ears, by the heels, or any other way you can manage it."
Mark Twain

Piece of the Pie

WHEN I WAS ABOUT 10 years old, I remember a particular holiday meal at my grandmother's house. I remember it well because my mother made two blueberry pies. My mother made the best pie in the world! I love pie. I would rather have pie than any other dessert. But my mother's blueberry pie was the best ever!

My grandmother was a great cook, and her specialty was the main course! This particular meal included both roast beef and turkey. It was piping hot and ready to eat. I don't know if my mother or my grandmother made the gravy, but I love gravy too and it smelled wonderful.

Normally, I would position myself smack dab in front of the meat. But, on this day, what I wanted most was that blueberry pie! My "job" in the kitchen at 10 years old was "taster." I would stand right beside my mother when she cooked, and she would let me taste everything. It was a wonderful job! I had already licked the spoon for the pie, and I knew it was particularly good on this day. The problem was they put one pie on one end of the table and the other pie on the other end of the table. So, I picked my seat right in front of one of the pies.

I was really hungry for that pie, so it seemed like forever before we finally said the blessing and started to eat. I passed my plate for the meat and gravy. I had to watch carefully to be sure I got plenty of gravy but not too much food. I had to save room for the pie. When my plate came back to me, I sat it down in front of me. Suddenly, I realized the pie was gone. I don't mean moved, I mean gone!

I panicked. I looked at my mother and said, "Where is my pie?" She smiled a beautiful motherly smile and said, "It's in the kitchen. Don't worry son, I'll be sure you get a piece." Then, the whole family made fun of me asking about the pie and broke into the old nursery rhyme, "Can she bake a cherry pie, Billy boy, Billy boy. Can she bake a cherry pie charming Billy..." This was a common practice because my whole family knew how much I loved pie. I found out later that my mother moved the pie so she could ensure everyone got a piece. She knew my plan.

I wanted a whole pie! At 10 years old I wasn't thinking about the limited amount of pie left for the rest of the family. In my 10-year-old mind, I thought my mother had made one of the pies just for me!

Some people think there is a limited amount of "pie" in the universe. They have what is called the "Scarcity Mentality." Someone who has the Scarcity Mentality believes there is a limited amount of resources for the whole universe, and there is not enough for everyone. The Scarcity Mentality is characterized as the belief that there is a limited amount of "pie" in life. Which means, if someone gets a big piece of the pie, because there is a limited amount, it directly limits the size of the piece available to everyone else. This unhealthy mentality can lead to intense feelings of anxiety and even a sense of loss when others do well. It also alerts your Reticular Activation System to see what is wrong with everything, which results in a very unhappy and unsatisfied life.

As an adult, I believe "God's Universal Pie" has more than enough "resources" for everyone. THANK GOODNESS! The size of your piece of pie does not impact the size of my piece of pie.

Knowledge, Skills, and Abilities

As a psychologist, one of my most enjoyable tasks is identifying the knowledge, skills, or abilities that differentiate top performers from low performers in a specific job. I define a skill as a learned ability to use one's knowledge effectively and readily in execution or performance. I define an ability as a natural ability to use one's knowledge effectively and readily in execution or performance. This process involves job analysis, which is the process of identifying all the knowledge, skills, and abilities required to perform a specific job. It also involves interviewing top performers and low performers about their thoughts about their jobs. It is critical to interview the direct supervisors of each of the employees involved in the process to acquire management's perspective on the employees. Finally, it involves correlating the performance scores of both groups with specific knowledge, skills, and abilities. (Sorry if this is boring to you.)

I engaged in this process for every client of my company. Every company I work with has someone involved in quality control. The common skill or ability for all quality control technicians that differentiates top performers from low performers is the ability to see the glass half empty. These individuals have either the learned ability or natural ability to identify what is wrong with something before they can see what is right with it. This ability or trait is called "negative affectivity," and it significantly affects the performance of quality control technicians statistically.

However, if an individual views all of life through the lens of negative affectivity, it activates their reticular activation system and directs their thinking toward what's wrong rather than what's right. This way of thinking can have some very negative consequences. Have you ever known someone with high negative affectivity?

What Is Negative Affectivity?

Negative Affectivity is a psychometric scale intended to demonstrate the relationship between positive and negative affect within specific personality traits.

The term "Negative Affectivity" is the academic way of discussing emotions and expressions. It refers to the emotions or feelings that you might experience and display, influencing your actions and decision-making. Positive Affectivity, on the other hand, pertains to positive emotions and expressions such as joy, alertness, and determination. Negative Affectivity, on the contrary, encompasses negative emotions and expressions like guilt, anger, or sadness. The challenge is that as humans, we can experience both positive and negative effects simultaneously. For instance, when your best friend gets a new car, you can feel happy for them (positive effect) and a little jealous (negative effect) at the same time. The real question for you is, "Which side of your nature do you want to nourish and cultivate?"

Negative Affectivity (NA) is a broad personality trait that refers to a stable tendency to experience negative emotions. Individuals high in NA are more likely to consistently report negative mood states regardless of the situation.[22] They also report more somatic symptoms and demonstrate an attention bias toward adverse stimuli or potentially threatening situations. From a cognitive perspective, individuals with high NA tend to have pessimistic thoughts, leading to a propensity for worry.[23]

Positive Affectivity (PA) pertains to positive emotions and expressions. I describe someone with Positive Affectivity as a person who possesses an abundance mentality. The Abundance Mentality is the belief that there are enough resources in the world for everyone. In other words, a person with the Abundance Mentality sees the universe as an enormous pie where everyone can have as big a piece as they desire, without diminishing the size of the piece available to others.

Go to SaltYourThoughts.com and you'll find the assessment for measuring your Reticular Activation System. It is my recommendation to take this assessment once per month to keep you aware of your dominant thoughts. SALTing Your Thoughts will help you keep your dominant thoughts positive.

Measuring Your Reticular Activation System

Remember, your reticular activation system (RAS) plays a very important role: It's the gatekeeper of information that is allowed into the conscious mind. Your RAS determines what is important and what can be safely ignored. It serves as the tool your brain uses to handle the overwhelming amount of information your senses send to the brain. It is uniquely designed to differentiate between relevant and irrelevant pieces of information. Your RAS acts as the feedback loop between your conscious mind and your subconscious mind.

Measuring your RAS is a simple assessment that helps you determine whether you are training your RAS to focus on the positive or the negative effects of life. When you have subscribed to SaltYourThoughts.com you will be able to take this assessment monthly for the next twelve months and monitor your progress.

Chapter 24 Assignment:

Go to **SaltYourThoughts.com** and complete the **Measuring Your Reticular Activation System** assessment.

SALT Summaries:
Chapter 24: What Gets Measured, Gets Done!

- Knowledge, Skills, and Abilities

    - A **skill** is a learned ability to use one's knowledge effectively and readily in execution or performance.

    - An **ability** is a natural ability to use one's knowledge effectively and readily in execution or performance.

- What is Negative Affectivity (NA)?

    - Negative Affectivity is a psychometric scale that intends to show the relationship between positive and negative affect within certain personality traits.

    - Individuals who are high in NA are more likely to report negative affective mood states across time regardless of the situation.

    - From a cognitive point of view, individuals who are high in NA tend to think gloomy thoughts, which causes an inclination to worry.

    - However, if an individual views all of life through the Negative Affectivity lens, it turns on their Reticular Activation System and focuses their thinking on what's wrong instead of what's right.

        - This way of thinking can have some very negative consequences.

- What is Positive Affectivity (PA)?

    - Someone with Positive Affectivity has the abundance mentality.

        - The abundance mentality is the belief that there are enough resources in the world for everyone.

- Measuring Your Reticular Activation System

- Measuring your RAS will let you know if you are training your RAS to look for the positive or the negative in life.

- When you have subscribed to SaltYourThoughts.com you will be able to take this assessment monthly for the next twelve months and monitor your progress.

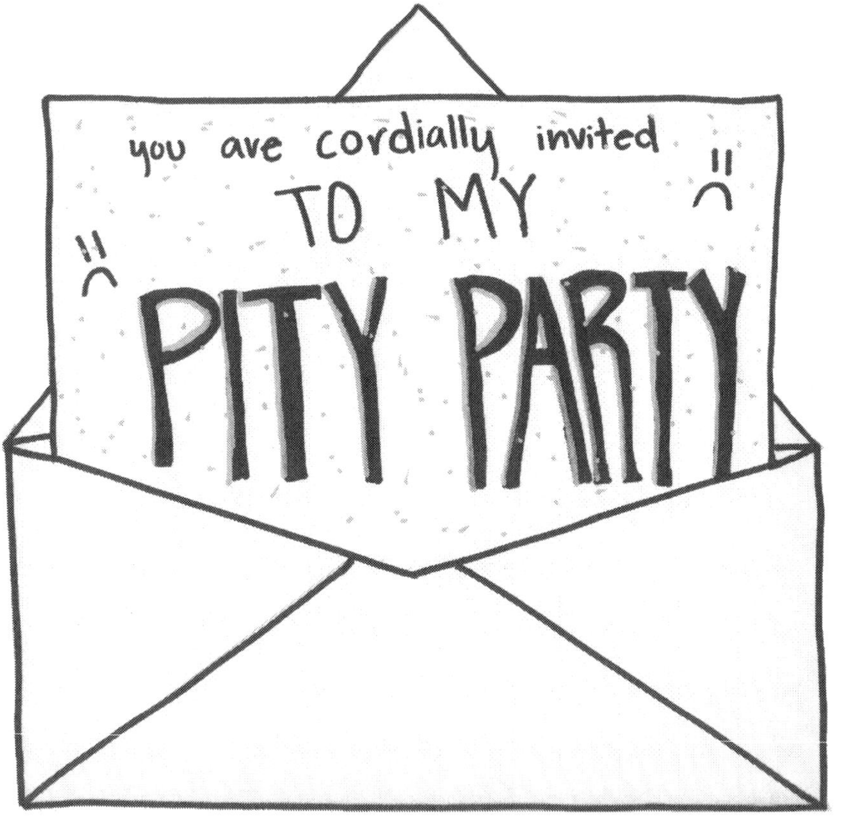
you are cordially invited
TO MY
PITY PARTY

Chapter 25

YOU ARE NOT A VICTIM!

"You can't play the role of a victim all your life without becoming one in the end."
Danilo Kis

The Victim Mentality

HUMANS IN EVERY CULTURE seem to be drawn to the "virus" that they are a victim of fate. Something "out there" is believed to control their destiny. Consequently, they find pleasure in hosting "pity parties" where they share their "victim" stories.

Pity parties signal your Reticular Activation System (RAS) to focus on and reveal all the "negative effects" around you. This mindset contradicts our goal. It convinces you that you are not responsible and shifts blame onto someone or something else. The two dominant indicators that an individual has succumbed to the *victim mentality* is when they are unwilling to take personal responsibility and they continue to place blame on others.

Several years ago I counseled a couple that had been married for 20 years. The husband was an ESTP (The Promoter), SP (Artisan). He was friendly, adaptable, and action-oriented. He was a "doer" who focused on immediate results. He lived in the here-and-now, a risk-taker living a fast-paced lifestyle. He was very impatient with long explanations. He was extremely loyal to his peers, but not usually respectful of laws and rules if they got in the way of getting things done. Overall, he had great people skills.

The wife was an ISFJ (The Protector), SJ (Guardian). She was quiet, kind, and conscientious. She could be depended on to follow through. She usually put the needs of others above her own needs. She was stable and practical, and valued security and tradition. Normally, she was extremely perceptive of others' needs.

The only trait they shared was S (Sensing). Their first 10 years of marriage was fantastic. They enjoyed each other's differences and celebrated them discussing them in detail in their common dominant language of Sensing. But then the "honeymoon" wore off. Jobs, kids, and life happened.

He began to perceive her "follow through" as nagging. Her need for security and tradition poured cold water on his fast-paced risk taking opportunities. To him, she appeared to want to help everyone but him. He began to blame her for his perceived loss of adventure and loss of financial advancement.

She began to perceive his extroversion as an excuse to get away from her. His continual push for "new and different" caused her to dig in her heels and demand stability. Now extremely insecure, she became overly demanding and demeaning in an effort to hide it. She began to blame him for her insecurity and her unhappiness.

By the time we started meeting together, both of them had spent years stacking little "hate" rocks of blame and lack of responsibility between them. This created a wall blocking their true feelings and communication. Both of them had lived for years with the victim mentality unwilling to take personal responsibility and placing the blame for their failing relationship on each other.

But, with counseling, their true feelings of love for each other were revived. They were able to throw off the victim mentality and take personal responsibility for their own actions and their own feelings of happiness. They have been married now for 40 years!

I personally believe that marriage (the ultimate human relationship) is always in a state of flux. It takes daily effort to water, fertilize, and cultivate a rich and thriving marriage.

I firmly believe that God is in control of everything in this universe except your independent will. God granted you a free, independent will because He desires you to choose to reciprocate His love through your own volition. While you may not have control over what happens to you, you do have the choice of how you respond to what happens to you!

Remember Viktor Frankl?

You learned in Chapter 3 about Viktor Frankl, who identified that humans have four unique attributes:

1. Self-Awareness – The awareness of your own thoughts, feelings, and actions

2. Imagination – The ability to visualize a new reality

3. Conscience – The deep inner awareness of what is morally right or wrong

4. Independent Will – The ability to choose to act based on our self-awareness

These four unique attributes of humans make us fundamentally different from any creature on this earth! Humans possess the power and responsibility to choose!

And that choice, like everything else in life, begins with your SALTed Thoughts!

How Do You Measure Your Proactivity?

Locus of Control (LOC) is a psychometric scale that measures the degree to which individuals believe they have control over the outcomes of events in their lives. The concept was developed by Julian B. Rotter in 1954 and has since become a significant aspect of personality psychology. A person's "locus" (plural "loci," derived from Latin for "place" or "location") is conceptualized as internal (believing in one's ability to control one's own life) or external (believing that life is governed by external factors beyond personal influence, or that chance or fate determines one's life).[24]

Individuals with a strong *internal* LOC attribute events in their lives primarily to their own actions. For instance, when receiving exam results, individuals with an internal LOC tend to credit or blame themselves and their abilities. Conversely, individuals with a strong *external* locus of control tend to attribute outcomes to external factors such as the teacher or the exam.

The Rotter LOC Scale is a simple assessment that determines whether you tend to believe you are in control of your life or if you believe you have no control. When you have subscribed to SaltYourThoughts.com, you will be able to take this assessment monthly for the next twelve months and monitor your progress. It will reveal whether you are being proactive or reactive, and it will identify if you are SALTing Your Thoughts!

Chapter 25 Assignment:

Go to **SaltYourThoughts.com** and complete the **Locus of Control** assessment.

SALT Summaries:
Chapter 25: You Are Not A Victim!

- "The Victim Mentality"

  - Humans in every culture seem to be drawn to the "virus" that they are a victim of fate.

  - Something "out there" is believed to be controlling their destiny.

- Humans have the power and responsibility to choose!

- That choice, like everything else in life, begins with your thoughts!

- How Do You Measure Your Proactivity?

  - Locus Of Control (LOC)

    - Internal LOC: A belief that one can control one's own life.

      - Individuals with a strong internal LOC believe events in their life are primarily a result of their own actions. They tend to praise or blame themselves and their abilities.

    - External LOC: A belief that life is controlled by outside factors which the person cannot influence.

      - Individuals with a strong external LOC tend to praise or blame external factors beyond themselves.

- The Rotter LOC Scale is a simple assessment that determines if you tend to believe you are in control of your life or if you tend to believe you have no control.

- When you have subscribed to SaltYourThoughts.com, you will be able to take this assessment monthly for the next twelve months and monitor your progress.

- LOC will identify if you are SALTing Your Thoughts.

EVERYTHING

- PREPARATION
- CONCIENTIOUSNESS
- ATTENTION TO DETAIL
- ORDER
- STICK TO PLAN
- DO IT RIGHT

IN ITS PLACE

Chapter 26

EVERYTHING IN ITS PLACE

"Good thoughts are no better than good dreams if you don't follow through."
Ralph Waldo Emerson

Getting It Done!

I LOVE STARTING NEW projects. It's fun for me to map out a new project. It is exciting to create a new concept and bring all the pieces together to make something functional.

But it is difficult to finish the project. It takes perseverance, grit, and follow-through to complete a project. But nothing worth having comes easy! My greatest accomplishments in life have come after overcoming obstacles, challenges, and discouragements. I've already shared many of my life experiences. There have been times when I wondered if I should quit, but I've learned that if I can "press on" when almost everyone else would give up, I'm at the tipping point for success! I have learned to "Never Give Up, and Never Give In!" After all, if getting it done were easy, everyone would do it. **Execution and follow-through differentiate success from failure.**

Start living by the principle **"What Gets Measured, Gets Done."** *Measuring* your progress as well as *measuring* the desired outcomes is the best method I know for ensuring success. Measuring engages your Reticular Activation System. It tells your brain exactly what you believe is important, so your brain allows more information to get to your conscious mind. The more information you have the better the decisions you will make. Measuring also gives you another advantage. It causes your brain to develop a strong sense of *Prioritization, Organization,* and *Follow-Through,* which are all attributes of a psychometric scale called **conscientiousness**.

For example, I have a personal exercise goal to average 70,000 steps per week or 10,000 steps per day. My phone keeps up with my steps. I live a very busy life, just like you. I desire to walk 5 miles, five times per week, but I know if I walk 5 miles three times per week it is easy to meet the 70,000 step goal. I check the app on my phone daily to see how I am doing. Each Saturday I look back at the last seven days and see if I met my goal of 70,000 steps for the week. But, some weeks I am just not able to make the goal. I have learned that "Making My Goal" isn't necessarily the most important thing. **The most important thing is to develop the habit of conscientiousness**. Developing the **habit of conscientiousness** (*Prioritization, Organization,* and *Follow-Through)* causes your goals to leap off the screen and become livable, tangible traits of your life.

I have read many books in my life and attended many management courses on how to set goals. I am sure that the concept of setting goals is also familiar to you. I believe setting goals for each important role of your life is an extremely important task to accomplish, if you desire to live a more productive, effective and fulfilled life. However, **if you do not measure it, it will never get done!** Measuring your progress is just as important as setting the goal. If you don't measure it, you will never know if you accomplished it. I believe **consistent execution** will never happen without developing the habit of conscientiousness.

For most people, the *pain* of finding out a goal was not met causes them to not want to measure their outcomes. The fear of failure and the pain associated with it can overshadow the pleasure of acknowledging their accomplishments. In fact, in my experience the primary reason people avoid setting goals is their fear that they will not accomplish them.

You have already learned that you can't do anything to change yesterday! You *must* let yesterday, last week, last month, and last year GO! Instead, focus on today and tomorrow. There is no value in beating yourself up about something you can do nothing about. The more important life lesson is developing the habit of conscientiousness which will help you control your impulses and, therefore, better control your life. The better you control your life, the more productive, effective, and fulfilled you will feel about "doing" your life.

"Doing" is an action, a behavior: The Way You Act. The way you "live" your life. Doing is the result of an effort to fulfill your needs. Your needs are The Way You Are Motivated. Your motivational need is a result of your Attitude. Your Attitude is The Way You Feel. The way you feel is influenced by your Beliefs. Your Beliefs are a result of The Way You Think. And the way you think is a result of your thoughts.

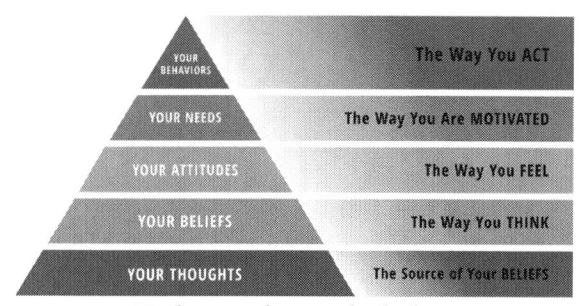

YOUR BEHAVIORS	The Way You ACT
YOUR NEEDS	The Way You Are MOTIVATED
YOUR ATTITUDES	The Way You FEEL
YOUR BELIEFS	The Way You THINK
YOUR THOUGHTS	The Source of Your BELIEFS

You become what you think about.

SALTing Your Thoughts Helps You "Do" Life Better?

Developing the habit of conscientiousness will positively enhance your life! You have already learned that by simply writing down your goals, you are 42% more likely to achieve them. That statistic assumes you are following up or measuring whether or not you have met the goal you have written down.

Conscientiousness is a personality trait found in the Five Factor Personality Model, which examines impulse control. Individuals who are more conscientious are better able to control their impulses. They are the classmates who organize their class assignments by color or the co-worker who utilizes a computer calendar synced to their phone and maintains a desk calendar. These individuals possess a strong sense of prioritization and organization. They excel in analysis, knowing what to analyze and how much time to allocate. Others often describe them as "detail-oriented," "prudent," or "reliable."

While some people naturally exhibit higher levels of conscientiousness, it is also a skill that can be developed with the desire to improve. The Five Factor Personality Model has long been used by employers as an indicator of "fit" and "performance." Notably, conscientiousness is the only scale that significantly correlates with performance, which aligns with common sense. The more meticulous, precise, and careful you are in "doing the job right," the better your job performance.

Developing conscientiousness is a valuable skill that can benefit every aspect of your life: physically, mentally, socially, and spiritually. Go to SaltYourThoughts.com and complete the assessment titled **Conscientiousness.** When you have subscribed to SaltYourThoughts.com, you will be able to take this assessment monthly for the next 12 months and monitor your progress.

Chapter 26 Assignment:

Go to **SaltYourThoughts.com** and complete the **Conscientiousness** assessment.

SALT Summaries:
Chapter 26: Everything In Its Place

- Nothing worth having comes easy!

- My best accomplishments in life came after I was able to overcome obstacles, challenges, and discouragements.

- I have learned that if I can "press on" when almost everyone else would quit, I am at the tipping point for success!

- I believe execution and follow-through are what differentiate between success and failure.

- What Is Conscientiousness?

  - Conscientiousness is a personality trait characterized by being meticulous and careful.

  - It examines impulse control.

    - Individuals who are more conscientious are better able to control their impulses.

    - They tend to have a great sense of prioritization and organization.

    - They excel at analysis, knowing exactly what to analyze and how much time it should take.

    - Others typically describe them as "detail-oriented," "prudent," or "reliable."

- Conscientiousness can be a learned skill.

  - You simply need to desire to develop it.

- I believe conscientiousness is a skill you should desire to develop.

  - It will help you in every aspect of your life: physically, mentally, socially, and spiritually.

- My recommendation is to take the assessment each month for the next 12 months.

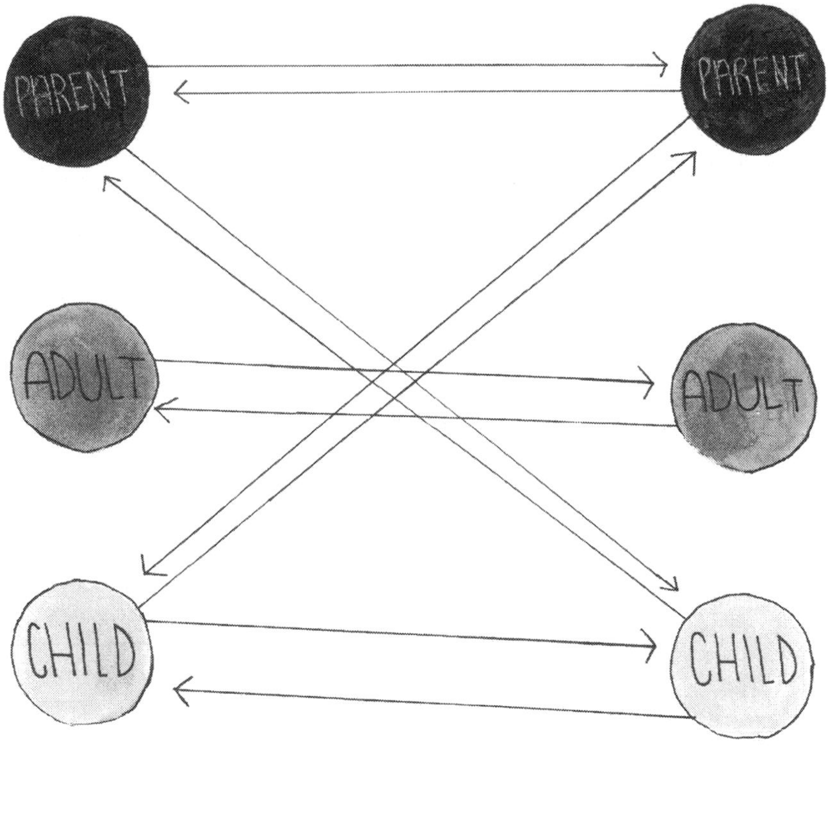
PARENT
PARENT
ADULT
ADULT
CHILD
CHILD

Chapter 27

ARE YOU EVEN SPEAKING THE SAME LANGUAGE?

"The key to successful leadership today is influence, not authority."
Ken Blanchard

Parenting

IT IS TOUGH TO be a parent! You want the best for your children and you want them to grow up to positively contribute to the communities in which they live. And most importantly, you want them to love and appreciate you.

At its best, communication from a parent to a child is nurturing, instructing, and supporting. At its worst, it is controlling, critical, and patronizing. At its best, communication from a child to a parent is curious, playful, creative, and spontaneous. At its worst, it is rebellious, full of temper tantrums, being obstinate, and displaying insecurity. Sometimes it doesn't even seem like you are speaking the same language!

Ultimately, as a parent you know you want your relationship with your child to grow and actually move through stages as they develop through their own stages of growth. If you are talking to your 22-year-old as if he were 2, that isn't what I would call a healthy relationship. Instead, you want to gradually increase your child's responsibilities so that when they become a young adult and are ready to go to college, they are also ready for the responsibilities. This means your communication and your parenting style must change from Parent-to-Child to Adult-to-Adult.

Situational Leadership

From the time I was 20 years old, I have held various management positions, ranging from low-level to executive roles. "Management" involves coordinating people, processes, and resources to achieve a specific goal. It encompasses training, controlling, supervising, coaching, leading, and mentoring individuals and teams.

I have delivered numerous hours of leadership and management training, both in person and through learning management software. It is crucial to understand that leadership is not management, and management is not leadership. Warren Bennis, a renowned business author, encapsulates it best: "Leadership is doing the right things, management is doing things right."

In business, leadership must take precedence. You need to make choices that define your product or service, identify the target market, devise marketing and sales plans to reach consumers, analyze the competition, establish operational plans, and recruit a team with the necessary knowledge, skills, ability, and determination to execute the strategy. Once you are confident you are doing the right things (leadership), you can then focus on doing things right (management). Now, it's time to apply this business awareness to your personal life.

In your personal life and your family life, leadership (doing the right things) must also come first. You must determine what the "right things" are, which is why this book is organized as it is. You must complete the Personal Leadership steps initially. Personal Leadership begins with your thoughts and entails understanding the underlying principles (the Seven Principles of the Farm). It involves choosing to be a responsible person, identifying and clarifying your beliefs, determining the type of person you aspire to become, and defining your own version of success.

In your personal life and family life, management (doing things right) follows Personal Leadership. After defining what the "right things" are for yourself, Personal Management gets things done. Management executes the plan established by leadership, both in business and in your personal life. It's easy to get caught up in "Personal Management" and forget that "Personal Leadership" must come first.

We often find ourselves running from one task to another, striving to "manage" our time effectively. Somehow, we confuse busyness with effectiveness. We live reactionary lives, focusing on activities and tasks, even if they don't lead to the desired outcome. We become so busy that we forget to take the time to ensure we are doing the right things.

One of the best classes I teach on leadership is called "Situational Leadership." Let me explain.

In his 1965 paper titled "Developmental Sequence in Small Groups," psychologist Bruce Tuckman defined four stages of team development: 1) Forming, 2) Storming, 3) Norming, and 4) Performing. These stages represent the path that teams follow to achieve high performance.[25] Tuckman later added a fifth stage, but for our discussion, we will focus on his original four.

Situational Leadership

Team Development Stage	Forming	Storming	Norming	Performing
Team Feeling	High Expectation	Frustration, Anger	Inclusion	Satisfaction
Team Role Definitions	Role Ambiguity	Competition	Resolution	Trust
Team Motivation	High	Low	Medium	High
Team Skill Level	Below Standard	Moving Toward Standard	Meets Standard	Exceeds Standard
Situational Leadership Style Required	Supervisor	Coach	Leader	Mentor
Situational Leadership Method	Role Definition, Control	Role Identification	Goal Identification	Self-Directed Work Team
Leadership Power Required	Expert Power; Reward Power; Coercive Power	Expert Power; Referent Power	Referent Power; Information Power	Referent Power; Information Power
Communication Mode	Adult	Adult	Adult	Adult

These four stages of team development occur not only in the workplace but also in your home, with your friends, in your class, in your church group, or any peer group. Whenever three or more people decide to form a team to accomplish a shared goal, they will inevitably go through these four stages of team development.

Team Development Stage 1: Forming

When a new team is formed, the individuals involved tend to be excited about the opportunity, and there is a sense of high expectations. Team roles are not yet fully defined, which means anything is possible. The motivation level of a new team is high due to the potential opportunities, but the skill level is below standard.

The leader of a new team must possess "Expert Job Knowledge," which grants them Expert Power. This Expert Power empowers the Situational Leader to directly supervise the team, define roles, and assign tasks to each team member. The leader, equipped with extensive knowledge, cannot be deceived and is capable of overseeing team members who attempt to take on roles they lack competence in. Additionally, the leader must have the authority to reward or discipline based on performance, utilizing Reward Power and Coercive Power. Simultaneously, the leader must assign team members to roles in which they possess the necessary competence.

Even though the leader in this stage needs to directly supervise the team, the leader needs to resist the desire to communicate in Parent/Child Mode and focus their communication on the Adult/Adult Mode.

Team Development Stage 2: Storming

The initial excitement of the team has now faded. Competition arises for the different roles within the team, leading to frustration for those who did not secure their desired positions and anger directed towards those who did. At this stage of Team Development, the motivation level of the team is at its lowest. However, the team's skill level is improving as members succeed in obtaining their roles.

The Situational Leader of the team must continue to demonstrate Expert Power as roles are still being identified. However, the leader now needs to have earned the respect and admiration of the team (Referent Power). The Situational Leadership Style should transition from being a supervisor to being a coach. Players perform their best for coaches they respect and admire. During "game time," the coach determines who gets to "play" and who remains on the sidelines, and the players comply because of their respect and admiration for the coach.

Even though the leader in this stage needs to coach the team, the leader needs to resist the desire to communicate in Child/Child Mode and focus their communication on the Adult/Adult Mode.

Team Development Stage 3: Norming

This stage builds upon the "wins/victories" achieved during the Storming phase. The roles that have been defined, identified, and clarified in the first two stages have now been resolved. The team experiences a newfound sense of inclusion and takes pride in being members of the team. Both team motivation and skill level are improving. The team is meeting performance standards, which fosters pride and motivation.

The Situational Leader can now shift to a leadership style focused on goal identification and goal attainment. While still maintaining respect and admiration (Referent Power), the leader should also display Information Power. With Information Power, the leader can guide the team through the maze of information required to identify and achieve the team goals.

The natural mode of communication for Information Power is the Adult/Adult Mode.

Team Development Stage 4: Performing

In the Performing Stage, the team is operating at its peak. The team members feel satisfied, trust each other, and exhibit high motivation. They are surpassing performance expectations and functioning as a self-directed unit.

In this stage, the Situational Leader assumes the role of a mentor. The most effective mode of communication is the **Adult Ego State**, where *influence* occurs. When you have a highly motivated and skilled team, the last thing you need is a leader who wants to micromanage. The Situational Leader continues to leverage Referent Power and Information Power to influence the team.

Effective communication throughout each stage of team development is undoubtedly crucial. In fact, I would argue that mastering effective communication is one of the most important skills to acquire. This is because every communication exchange between individuals carries the potential of going awry. The best model for communication exchange, in my opinion, is Transactional Analysis.

What Is Transactional Analysis?

Transactional Analysis is a psychoanalytic theory and therapeutic method developed by Eric Berne during the 1960s.[26] Transactions refer to the communication exchanges between individuals. In a conversation, the person initiating the communication provides the "transaction stimulus," and the person receiving it responds with a "transaction response." Transactional Analysis analyzes this process of communication exchanges with others, requiring us to be conscious of our thoughts, emotions, and behaviors during interactions. It also acknowledges that the human personality consists of three "ego states," each representing a complete system of thought, feeling, and behavior through which we engage with others.

These are the **Three Ego States:**

1. The Parent Ego State:

    a. The positive side of the Parent Ego State includes these thoughts, feelings, and behaviors:

    i. Nurturing Your Child

    ii. Supporting Your Child

    iii. Keeping Your Child Calm

    iv. Ensuring the Safety of Your Child

    b. The negative side of the Parent Ego State includes these thoughts, feelings, and behaviors:

SALT YOUR THOUGHTS

      i. Controlling Your Child

      ii. Being Critical of Your Child

      iii. Patronizing Your Child

      iv. Pointing Fingers at Your Child

2. The Adult Ego State:

    a. The Adult Ego State is the most effective mode of communication.

    b. The Adult Ego State is the method of communication you should desire to develop.

    c. The Adult Ego State includes these thoughts, feelings, and behaviors:

      i. Applying Reasonable Logic in Communication

      ii. Engaging in Rational Communication

      iii. Practicing Non-Threatening Communication

      iv. Being Open to Others' Opinions without Feeling Threatened

3. The Child Ego State:

    a. The positive side of the Child Ego State includes these thoughts, feelings, and behaviors:

      i. Being Curious

      ii. Being Playful

      iii. Being Creative

      iv. Being Spontaneous

    b. The negative side of the Child Ego State includes these thoughts, feelings, and behaviors:

      i. Being Rebellious

ii. Throwing Temper Tantrums

   iii. Being Difficult

   iv. Displaying Insecurity

[Diagram: Three circles labeled P, A, C representing ego states, with + (positive) traits on the left and − (negative) traits on the right.

P (+): keep safe, calming, nurturing, supportive
P (−): controlling, critical, patronizing, finger-pointing

A (+): reasonable, logical, rational, non-threatening, non-threatened

C (+): curious, creative, playful, spontaneous
C (−): rebellious, tantrums, difficult, insecurity]

The following chart provides a flowchart of the possible communication exchanges between people. By utilizing the Three Ego States, there are only five possible communication exchanges between two individuals. During a conversation, the person initiating the communication provides the "Transaction Stimulus," and the person receiving it responds with the "Transaction Response." The figure below illustrates the communication flow between Ego States:

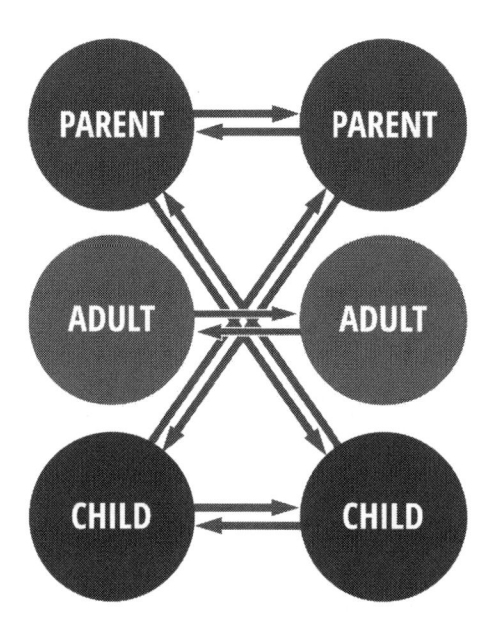

Parent "Transaction Stimulus" to Child "Transaction Response"

- There are two possible Parent Ego State Transaction Stimuli: the "Nurturing Parent" and the "Controlling Parent."

- There are two possible Child Ego State Transaction Responses: the "Compliant Child" and the "Rebellious Child."

- Typically, if the Parent Transaction Stimulus is the "Nurturing Parent," the Child Transaction Response is the "Compliant Child." If the Parent Transaction Stimulus is the "Controlling Parent," the Child Transaction Response is the "Rebellious Child." However, this depends on the relationship between the individuals involved.

It is important to note that the Parent "Transaction Stimulus" to Child "Transaction Response" can occur between two adults, between two children, and even when the child assumes the parent role and the parent takes on the child role. It simply labels the type of communication happening between two people. However, this method of communication ceases to be effective once a child reaches the age of accountability (around 10-12 years old) and does not have long-term effectiveness outside the home.

Child "Transaction Stimulus" to Parent "Transaction Response"

- There are two possible Child Ego State Transaction Stimuli: the "Compliant Child" and the "Rebellious Child."

- There are two possible Parent Ego State Transaction Responses: the "Nurturing Parent" and the "Controlling Parent."

- Typically, if the Child Transaction Stimulus is the "Compliant Child," the Parent Transaction Response is the "Nurturing Parent." If the Child Transaction Stimulus is the "Rebellious Child," the Parent Transaction Response is the "Controlling Parent." However, this depends on the relationship between the individuals involved.

Similar to the previous case, the Child "Transaction Stimulus" to Parent "Transaction Response" can occur between adults or children, and roles can be reversed. It is merely a label for the type of communication happening between two people. However, this method of communication is not effective and lacks long-term effectiveness outside the home.

Parent "Transaction Stimulus" to Parent "Transaction Response"

- This label for communication does not categorize two parents talking about a child. Instead, it refers to two people both attempting to parent each other.

- It is fascinating to observe that one of the individuals involved will eventually engage the other individual's Child Ego State, turning the conversation into Parent "Transaction Stimulus" to Child "Transaction Response."

The Parent "Transaction Stimulus" to Parent "Transaction Response" always results in a conversion to the Parent "Transaction Stimulus" to Child "Transaction Response." As mentioned earlier, this method of communication is not effective.

Child "Transaction Stimulus" to Child "Transaction Response"

- There are two possible Child Ego State Transaction Stimuli: the "Compliant Child" and the "Rebellious Child."

- There are also two possible Child Ego State Transaction Responses: the "Compliant Child" and the "Rebellious Child."

These conversations can be lighthearted and fun, serving as a desired result. If the goal is to have fun, this method of communication can be effective. However, there is a more effective method of communication that can also result in "fun."

Adult "Transaction Stimulus" to Adult "Transaction Response"

- Adult "Transaction Stimulus" to Adult "Transaction Response" is the most effective method of communication between humans.

- It is logical, reasonable, rational, and non-threatening.

Initially, the Adult "Transaction Stimulus" may elicit a Parent or Child "Transaction Response." However, if the "Transaction Stimulus" remains Adult and avoids getting "hooked," the "Transaction Response" will eventually shift to the Adult Ego State. Therefore, if you are the "Transaction Stimulus," practice communication in the Adult Ego State. As long as you continue to stimulate communication in the Adult Ego State, you will eventually "hook" the Adult "Transaction Response."

The same principle applies to the Adult "Transaction Response." Regardless of the "Transaction Stimulus" (whether Parent or Child), if you respond from your Adult Ego State consistently, you will eventually "hook" the other individual's Adult Ego State.

This little tip on communication can change your life! If you are the Transaction Stimulus (the person stimulating the conversation), stay in Adult Mode even if the person responding to you responds in either parent or child mode. You will ultimately move the conversation to Adult to Adult. And, if you are the Transaction Response (the person responding to someone who is stimulating the conversation), stay in Adult Response Mode even if the person stimulating the conversation is in the parent or child mode. You will ultimately move the conversation to Adult to Adult.

The ultimate thing to understand from the chart above is the Adult/Adult communication mode is the most effective method of communication between humans. It is logical, responsible, rational, and non-threatening.

Situational Leadership and Transactional Analysis Combined

For a team in the **Forming Stage**, Situational Leadership suggests that the best leadership style is to function as a *supervisor*. The natural ego state for a supervisor is Parent. However, the most effective mode of communication as a supervisor is Adult to Adult.

For a team in the **Storming Stage**, Situational Leadership suggests that the best leadership style is to function as a *coach*. The natural ego state for a coach is Parent. However, the most effective mode of communication as a coach is Adult to Adult.

For a team in the **Norming Stage**, Situational Leadership suggests that the best leadership style is to function as a *leader*. The natural ego state for a leader is Adult, and the most effective mode of communication is Adult to Adult.

For a team in the **Performing Stage**, Situational Leadership suggests that the best leadership style is to function as a *mentor*. The natural ego state for a mentor is Adult, and the most effective mode of communication is Adult to Adult.

Temperament and Transactional Analysis

Understanding your temperament (Chapter 13), the natural ego state of your temperament, and your preferred communication mode is imperative if you desire to become more effective in your communication efforts.

Please refer to the following chart:

TEMPERAMENT AND TRANSACTIONAL ANALYSIS

TEMPERAMENT	POINT OF REFERENCE	DRIVING PERSONAL VALUE	NATURAL EGO STATE	PREFERRED COMMUNICATION MODE
SJ	Past	Responsibility	Parent	Parent / Child
SP	The Here & Now	Fun / Excitement	Child	Child / Child
NT	The Interval & the Intersection	Competence / Excellence	Adult	Adult / Adult
NF	The Future & the Pathway	Relationships / Meaning / Possibilities	Adult / Child	Adult / Adult Child / Child

SJs and Transactional Analysis

The SJ's point of reference is the past. Present and future opportunities are "filtered" by what has happened in the past. Therefore, "remembering" the past is crucial, respectful, and responsible for an SJ.

For an SJ, responsibility is the driving personal value. The need for the SJ to be responsible is as strong as their need to "make" others responsible. The natural ego state of Parent facilitates their need in defining responsibilities. So, their preferred communication mode is Parent "Transaction Stimulus" to Child "Transaction Response".

If an SJ desires to communicate more effectively, the SJ needs to develop the skill of the Adult "Transaction Stimulus" to Adult "Transaction Response" mode of communication.

SPs and Transactional Analysis

The SP's point of reference is the here and now. The SP spends very little time considering the past or the future. The SP reasons that they can't do anything about the past, so there is no need to spend valuable time worrying about it. The SP knows the future will come tomorrow, and when tomorrow becomes today, they will deal with it.

For an SP, the here and now defines reality. Fun and excitement are the driving personal values. The need for the SP is the need for adrenaline. Skillfully handling the spontaneous events of "today" provides the fun and excitement that is so fulfilling for the SP. The natural ego state of Child facilitates their need for fun and excitement. So, their preferred communication mode is Child "Transaction Stimulus" to Child "Transaction Response."

If an SP desires to communicate more effectively, the SP needs to develop the skill of the Adult "Transaction Stimulus" to Adult "Transaction Response" mode of communication.

NTs and Transactional Analysis

The NT's point of reference is the pattern and the intersection. The NT looks for patterns in the past, present, and future. The NT reasons that looking at patterns will lead to learning and effectiveness.

For an NT, competence and excellence define reality. Competence and excellence are the driving personal values. The need for the NT is the need to be excellent in all things or not to do them. The natural ego state of Adult facilitates their need for competence and excellence. So, their preferred communication mode is Adult "Transaction Stimulus" to Adult "Transaction Response."

NFs and Transactional Analysis

The NF's point of reference is the future and the pathway. The NF looks to the future and desires everyone to become the best they can be. The NF reasons that if everyone desires to improve, the future will be full of harmony and meaningfulness.

For an NF, relationships, meaning, and possibilities are the driving personal values. The need for the NF to be unique and make a difference (have meaning) causes the NF to look for possibilities in everything. The dual natural ego states of Adult and Child facilitate their need for possibilities and fun. So, their preferred communication mode is Adult "Transaction Stimulus" to Adult "Transaction Response" and/or Child "Transaction Stimulus" to Child "Transaction Response."

If an NF desires to communicate more effectively, the NF needs to discipline themselves to stay in the Adult "Transaction Stimulus" to Adult "Transaction Response" mode of communication.

Chapter 27 Assignment:

Go to **SaltYourThoughts.com** and complete the **Measuring Your Mode of Communication** assessment.

SALT Summaries:
Chapter 27: Are You Even Speaking The Same Language?

- Situational Leadership
  - Team Development Stage 1 - Forming
    - When a new team is formed, the people involved in the new team tend to be excited about the opportunity.
    - The motivation level of a new team is high.
    - The skill level is below standard.
    - The leader of a new team must have "Expert Job Knowledge," which equates to Expert Power.
    - The leader should function as a supervisor and reward and punish based on performance.
  - Team Development Stage 2 - Storming
    - Now there is competition for the different roles played by each team member.
    - There is frustration for not "winning" a certain position and anger directed at those who did.
    - The motivation level of the team is at its lowest.
    - The team skill level is improving.
    - The situational leader of the team must display Expert Power and Referent Power.
    - The situational leadership style needs to move to a coach.

- Team Development Stage 3 - Norming

    - Team motivation and skill level are both improving.

    - The team is now meeting performance standards.

    - The situational leader needs to display Referent Power and Information Power.

    - Situational leadership style needs to move to a leader.

- Team Development Stage 4 - Performing

    - Motivation is high.

    - The team is exceeding performance standards.

    - The situational leader needs to function as a mentor.

    - The situational leader continues to use Referent Power and Information Power.

- What Is Transactional Analysis?

    - The Three Ego States:

        - The Parent Ego State

        - The Adult Ego State

        - The Child Ego State

- Situational Leadership and TA

- Temperament and TA

MAKING GOOD DECISIONS

Chapter 28

How To Make Good Decisions

"If your only tool is a hammer, then every problem looks like a nail."
Abraham Maslow

Problems Cause Problems

THINK ABOUT IT. IF you go to your general practitioner for a health problem, your general practitioner's "nail" is medication. If you go to a surgeon for your problem, the surgeon's "nail" is an operation or surgery. Maslow had it right: "If your only tool is a hammer, then every problem looks like a nail."

But how does this principle impact communication? In 2005, my company was growing and we certainly had our share of growing pains. I was still wearing many hats. So, when a problem was identified based on my nature (ENTJ), there were only two things to do:

    1. Analyze the problem using objective data.

    2. Make a decision using logically proven criteria.

And I wanted it done as fast as possible! But, at this time, I had a team of people. One of my new management team members would say, "To what extent does the team agree with the decision?" A different management team member would say, "What similar problems have we had in the past?" Then a third management team member would say, "How can we approach this problem differently?"

Fortunately for me and the team, I knew that — as driven as I was to fix the problem — these other questions were questions that needed to be asked and answered. But many people in charge fail to value other perspectives, believing their questions are the only ones that need answered.

Listening to the other voices (which, in the sections that follow, I am going to call languages) means you can make a more complete solution to the problem. Failing to listen to the other voices will cause other problems!

The Four Languages of Type

The primary reason I became so intrigued with Myers/Briggs is that it can be such a powerful communication tool. Within MBTI, there are four (4) languages, and each of the four languages provides four different perspectives.

If you are solving a problem, all four of the perspectives need to be considered in order to have a complete solution. But if you are just talking with a friend who is speaking a different language (i.e. coming from a different perspective) simple communication can become difficult.

The *Perceiving* Function contains two (2) of the languages:

    1. **Sensing**: The perception of details and current realities.

    2. **Intuition**: The perception of patterns and future possibilities.

The *Judging* Function contains two (2) of the languages:

    1. **Thinking**: Decisions are made based on principles and logical consequences.

    2. **Feeling**: Decisions are made based on values and consequences for people.

How Does Your Language Impact Communication?

The following chart will help you identify the primary and secondary language of each personality type. It is important to note that relationships tend to communicate more effectively if both individuals are using their primary or secondary language. This is why you may feel more in alignment with certain friends than others.

This chart will assist you in any relationship, especially marriage. Many times, people marry their opposites and then struggle to communicate at home because they are literally speaking different languages!

TEMPERAMENT AND TRANSACTIONAL ANALYSIS

MBTI TYPE	TEMPERAMENT	1ST PREFERRED LANGUAGE	2ND PREFERRED LANGUAGE	3RD PREFERRED LANGUAGE	4TH PREFERRED LANGUAGE
ISTJ	SJ	T-Thinking	S-Sensing	N-iNtuition	F-Feeling
ESTJ	SJ	T-Thinking	S-Sensing	N-iNtuition	F-Feeling
ISTP	SP	S-Sensing	T-Thinking	F-Feeling	N-iNtuition
ESTP	SP	S-Sensing	T-Thinking	F-Feeling	N-iNtuition
ISFJ	SJ	F-Feeling	S-Sensing	N-iNtuition	T-Thinking
ESFJ	SJ	F-Feeling	S-Sensing	N-iNtuition	T-Thinking
ISFP	SP	S-Sensing	F-Feeling	T-Thinking	N-iNtuition
ESFP	SP	S-Sensing	F-Feeling	T-Thinking	N-iNtuition
INFJ	NF	F-Feeling	N-iNtuition	S-Sensing	T-Thinking
ENFJ	NF	F-Feeling	N-iNtuition	S-Sensing	T-Thinking
INFP	NF	N-iNtuition	F-Feeling	T-Thinking	S-Sensing
ENFP	NF	N-iNtuition	F-Feeling	T-Thinking	S-Sensing
INTJ	NT	T-Thinking	N-iNtuition	S-Sensing	F-Feeling
ENTJ	NT	T-Thinking	N-iNtuition	S-Sensing	F-Feeling
INTP	NT	N-iNtuition	T-Thinking	F-Feeling	S-Sensing
ENTP	NT	N-iNtuition	T-Thinking	F-Feeling	S-Sensing

Information modified from Henry L. (Dick) Thompson's CommunicationWheel®

Patterns of Interest:

- STs are clustered together.
    - STJs 1st Preferred Language is T and 2nd Preferred Language is S.
    - STPs' 1st Preferred Language is S and 2nd Preferred Language is T.
    - STJs and STPs tend to communicate well with each other.
- SFs are clustered together.
    - SFJs 1st Preferred Language is F and 2nd Preferred Language is S.
    - SFPs' 1st Preferred Language is S and 2nd Preferred Language is F.
    - SFJs and SFPs tend to communicate well with each other.
- NFs are clustered together.
    - NFJs 1st Preferred Language is F and 2nd Preferred Language is N.
    - NFPs' 1st Preferred Language is N and 2nd Preferred Language is P.
    - NFJs and NFPs tend to communicate well with each other.
- NTs are clustered together.
    - NTJs 1st Preferred Language is T and 2nd Preferred Language is N.
    - NTPs' 1st Preferred Language is N and 2nd Preferred Language is T.
    - NTJs and NTPs tend to communicate well with each other.
- When the 1st Preferred Language is the same, the Types tend to communicate well with each other.
    - Perceiving Function
        - 1st Preferred Language - S-Sensing

- ISTP, ESTP, ISFP, and ESFP

- Perceiving Function

  - 1st Preferred Language - N-iNtuition

    - INFP, ENFP, INTP, and ENTP

- Judging Function

  - 1st Preferred Language - T-Thinking

    - ISTJ, ESTJ, INTJ, and ENTJ

- Judging Function

  - 1st Preferred Language - F-Feeling

    - ISFJ, ESFJ, INFJ, and ENFJ

- When you are trying to communicate with someone who is using your 4th Preferred Language to communicate with you, effective communication can only happen if you shift to their 1st or 2nd Preferred Language. However, this chart and the following 8-Step Process for solving problems will assist you in this endeavor.

- Notice on the *Perceiving* Function (How you take in or perceive information):

  - If your 1st Preferred Language is S-Sensing, then your 4th Preferred Language is N-iNtuition! This means you prefer to gather information through details and current realities. The last thing you want to do is gather information about patterns and future possibilities. Sensing is NOT better than iNtuition.

  - If your 1st Preferred Language is N-iNtuition, then your 4th Preferred Language is S-Sensing! This means you prefer to gather information through viewing patterns and future possibilities. The last thing you want to do is have to gather information about details and current realities. iNtuition is NOT better than Sensing.

- Notice on the *Judging* Function (How you make decisions):

    - If your 1st Preferred Language is T-Thinking, then your 4th Preferred Language is F-Feeling! This means you prefer to make decisions based on principles and logical consequences. You have no interest in making decisions based on values and consequences for people. Thinking is NOT better than Feeling.

    - If your 1st Preferred Language is F-Feeling, then your 4th Preferred Language is T-Thinking! This means you prefer to make decisions based on values and consequences for people. You have no interest in making decisions based on principles and logical consequences. Feeling is NOT better than Thinking.

Understanding your own language and the language of others is critically important for effective communication, which is required for effective problem solving.

How To Make Good Decisions

You now understand the four (4) languages of MBTI type. The perceiving function (how you take in or perceive information) contains two (2) languages: Sensing and Intuition. And the judging function (how you make decisions) contains two (2) of the languages: Thinking and Feeling. Now you can understand the need for a problem-solving solution that covers all types.

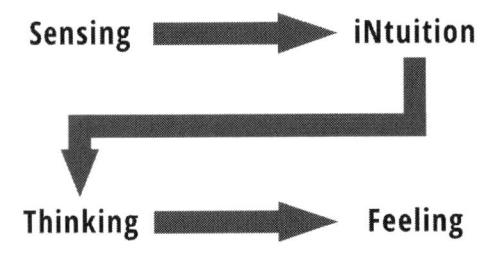

```
Sensing ──────▶ iNtuition
   ▲               │
   │               ▼
Thinking ◀────── Feeling
```

The 8-Step Process to Solve Problems With a Complete Solution

The *Perceiving* Function (how you take in or perceive information):

1. Define the problem as completely as possible (Sensing).

2. Define known causes for the problem to exist. This is done to help ignite possible solutions, not to dwell on negatives (Sensing).

3. Define known results of the problem as it exists or if it continues to exist (Sensing).

4. Examine all relevant details about the problem (Sensing).

5. Come up with all possible solutions to the existing problem. Brainstorm, do not edit at this point. Be creative with your thinking (Intuition).

The *Judging* Function (how you make decisions):

1. Determine what might be a logical solution or solutions. Define the level of authority and empowerment needed to implement the solution. Do you have the authority and empowerment? (Thinking).

2. Determine how this solution will impact the people involved. If the impact will be positive, go forward with implementation. If not, recycle (Feeling).

3. Recycle through this process as many times as needed to create the best solution to be implemented (Thinking & Feeling).

Chapter 28 Assignment:

Go to **SaltYourThoughts.com** and utilize the **8 Step Process To Solve Problems With a Complete Solution** the next time you are solving a problem.

SALT Summaries:
Chapter 28: How To Make Good Decisions

- The Four Languages Of Type:

  - The perceiving function (how you take in or perceive information) contains two (2) of the languages:

    - Sensing – The perception of details and current realities.

    - Intuition – The perception of patterns and future possibilities.

  - The judging function (how you make decisions) contains two (2) of the languages:

    - Thinking – Decisions are made based on principles and logical consequences.

    - Feeling – Decisions are made based on values and consequences for people.

- How does your language impact communication?

  - It is important to note that relationships tend to communicate more effectively if both individuals are communicating in their primary or secondary language.

  - This is why you have friends that you feel more in alignment with than other friends.

  - This chart will assist you in any relationship, especially marriage.

  - Many times people marry their opposites, then get home and they have trouble communicating because they literally are talking a different language!

- The 8-step process to solve problems:

- The *Perceiving* Function (how you take in or perceive information):

  - Define the cause of the problem as completely as possible (Sensing).

  - Measure the current impact of the problem (Sensing).

  - Analyze the continuing impact on the future (Sensing).

  - Analyze all relevant details about the problem (Sensing).

  - Improve - Discuss all possible solutions to the existing problem. Brainstorm, do not edit at this point. Be creative with your thinking (Intuition).

- The *Judging* Function (how you make decisions):

  - Control - Determine the most logical solution or solutions. Define the level of authority and empowerment needed to implement the solution. Do you have the authority and empowerment? (Thinking).

  - Control - Determine how this solution will impact the people who will be involved. If the impact will be positive, go forward with implementation. If not, recycle (Feeling).

  - Control - Recycle through this process as many times as needed to create the best solution to be implemented (Thinking & Feeling).

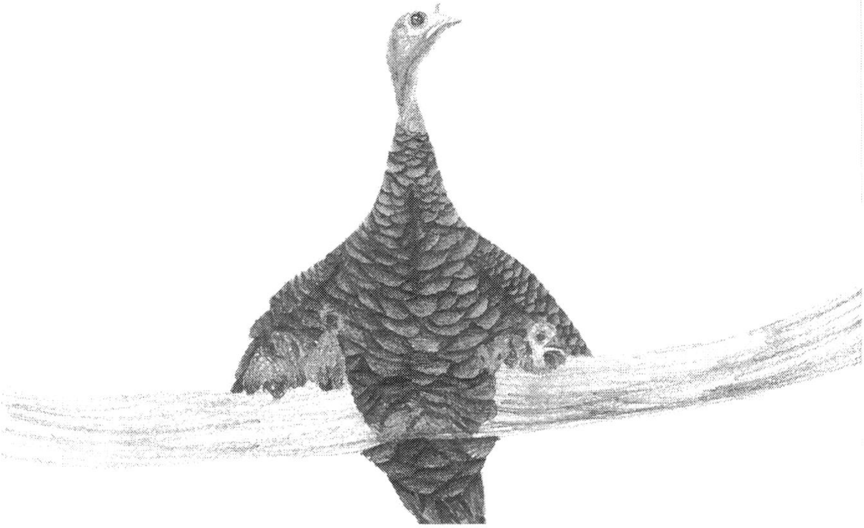

Chapter 29

DON'T FORGET TO THINK!

"It is easier to resist at the beginning than at the end."
Leonardo da Vinci

My SALT Shaker Was Almost Empty!

SEVERAL YEARS AGO, I was asked to lead the Selection Process for the Middle School Principal position of my son's (Trey's) and daughter's (Jeana's) middle school. The School Board was quite aware of my software system and said they wanted to make this selection decision based on qualifications rather than their normal process of decisions based on relationships.

Please understand, I'm not saying that making decisions based on relationships is a bad thing; I just don't think it should be the ONLY thing. I believe that whoever gets hired for a job should actually possess the knowledge, skills, and abilities to do that job. So, though this apparent change coming from the Board greatly encouraged me about the School Board, I still had them sign a commitment statement saying that when the final decision was made, it would be made based primarily on qualifications.

I was in the middle of launching my new company, and I didn't have any spare time. I knew helping the school would help my own children and the community, so I was willing to set aside a significant amount of time to complete the project. My greatest concern was that I would spend all the time setting up a system, creating the assessment, setting up the selection criteria, running the process, and then the Board revert to their old process of making the decision based on relationships.

I conducted job analysis and created a very detailed job description which specified the knowledge, skills, and abilities required for this position. I also identified the fact that there were five different stakeholder groups: the School Board, the School Faculty, the Parents, the Students, and the Community. So, I set up representatives from each group, met with them and identified the role they would play in the selection process. Then walked each group through the process to identify how they would define a successful Middle School Principal. I spent over 120 hours (time I really didn't have) on this project.

What was fascinating to me was that each stakeholder group's #1 measure for success was that the new Middle School Principal should *listen* to them. So, I took the time with each group to define the *measurable* actions of listening. Here is what the five stakeholder groups agreed on:

The Four Measurable Actions of Listening:

1. The ability to accurately receive information from an individual or a group of individuals.

    a. This can be measured by observing if the listener demonstrates attention to the individual or group of individuals by looking at them, showing empathy, asking questions, and taking notes.

2. The ability to repeat the information received back to the individual or a group of individuals to clarify the issues and demonstrate that the information received accurately.

    a. This can be measured by observing if the listener repeats back what was heard and clarifies any differences until the individual or a group of individuals was convinced the message had been received accurately.

3. The ability to take action on the information received.

    a. This can be measured by observing if the listener compiles information received, logically identifies and deducts the appropriate course of action, and takes that course of action.

4. The ability to follow up with the individual or a group of individuals and communicate how the appropriate course of action was deduced, and that the appropriate action had been taken.

   a. This can be measured by observing if the listener called a follow up meeting with the individual or a group of individuals and communicated how the appropriate course of action was deduced, and that the appropriate action had been taken.

Armed with this information I created five role play scenarios (one for each stakeholder group) that would be used to evaluate and differentiate the top five candidates. Each stakeholder group provided input for their role play scenario, identified the individual(s) involved in the actual role play, and identified specifically *how* the Four Measurable Actions of Listening would be measured from their role play.

I then posted the position nationally on my company's software system. The software required each candidate to complete the online employment application, meet the education and experience requirements, and complete the assessment I had created which measured the candidate's knowledge, skills, and abilities. The software then ranked the candidates from most qualified to least qualified. We then invited the top four candidates to our school for a tour and a face-to-face interview with the five stakeholder groups. At the last minute, the Board requested we also consider a fifth candidate that really didn't meet the educational or experience requirements but was someone the Board "wanted to look at." This caused me concern that they were back to their old way of thinking.

We scheduled all five of the candidates for their onsite visit over the next two weeks. Each stakeholder group had the opportunity to meet and interact freely with each candidate during their onsite visit. At the end of the day, each candidate was invited into the auditorium for the official face-to-face interview with the representatives of each of the five stakeholder groups. This was an exciting and fun experience for the stakeholder groups. They had never been allowed to participate in such an important selection process. The whole community was excited and talking about the process. There were high expectations that the additional efforts would yield the best decision possible.

The process worked flawlessly! Each stakeholder group executed their role play scenarios professionally and consistently. All five stakeholder groups rated each candidate on all five of the role play scenarios based on the predefined measures of success for that scenario. After all the interviews were completed, I compiled all the data and created reports and graphs to communicate the compiled information to the School Board.

Finally, the day came for me to present the information to the School Board. The meeting time was set for 7:00 p.m. I have managed hundreds of these type selection processes and rarely do all of the stakeholders agree. But in this case all five stakeholder groups ranked the same candidate as their #1 pick! This candidate had over 20 years of experience as a Principal, he was also the #1 pick based on the knowledge, skill, and ability assessment of my software, and every stakeholder group measured this candidate significantly higher than any other candidates. I estimated the "Selection Decision" to take less than 30 minutes, which was roughly the time it would take me to present the data. Boy, was I ever wrong!

I was correct, it took me about 30 minutes to present the data. The data suggested the decision was simple. I opened the floor for discussion but received very little feedback. I expected to see the same enthusiasm and energy of the five stakeholder groups in the Board. Instead, I heard crickets (nothing). It became apparent to me that something or someone was stifling the energy.

Finally, the *former* Chairman of The Board spoke up (she didn't currently have the title of Chairman, but still clearly ran the show) and said, "Billy, thank you for all your hard work. I know you have put a lot of time and effort into this, and I want you to know the Board appreciates it. But, we have decided to go a different direction. We believe our best candidate is the one your process has ranked as #5 (this was the candidate they added at the last minute). I know he has never held the title of Principal, but he has been a physical education teacher for 10 years. We like him best because I have known his family for years. And, by the way, the information shared in this meeting is confidential and no one can discuss any of this outside this room."

I had to hit my reset button! Then, I SALTed My Thoughts! I quickly sorted the data and compared the #1 candidate and the #5 candidate on each of the job-related hiring criteria, which took another hour of time. There simply was no comparison, yet the former Chairman of the Board stood her ground, and no one else on the Board said a word. I could not tell if they were all in agreement or if they were simply afraid of disagreeing with the former Chairman of the Board. I knew this individual had bullied and manipulated the School Board for years, which is why I was surprised the Board wanted to use me and my software in the first place. It was very clear that the other board members did not want to tangle with her, but they were ready for a change. I knew her and her tactics well.

It took me 4 more hours to finally identify what she perceived to be the real problem. I was finally able to peel the onion and find out that she believed the ethnic culture of the country from which the #1 candidate originated to be grossly discriminatory to women, to the extent of making women walk five paces behind their husband. She presented her perception as fact and evidence. When in fact Candidate #1 had demonstrated the absolute opposite character during his onsite visit and interview.

I then provided the details of the five stakeholder groups role play scenarios. In each of the five scenarios the #1 candidate demonstrated the Four Measurable Actions of Listening. He demonstrated he could actively receive information, accurately repeat the information he had received, logically deduct the appropriate course of action, take the appropriate course of action, and then follow up on how the appropriate course of action was deduced, and that the appropriate action had been taken, all while demonstrating respect and compassion regardless of race or gender. I also reminded her that his wife had joined him on his visit to our school and he did not make her walk five steps behind him!

Candidate #5 performed the poorest of all the candidates on the five stakeholder groups role play scenarios. In fact, he failed on all of the Four Measurable Actions of Listening. Which is why the stakeholder groups rated him as the #5 candidate.

It was now 12:30 a.m. and the current Chairman of the Board said, "Billy, based on the discussion we have had, the Board wants to offer the position to candidate #5."

I came face-to-face with the fact the Board was willing to take one single piece of evidence presented by the former Chairman of the Board (she had known him for several years) and discount all the objective data that had been collected over several weeks of time.

Now, let me explain the psychology of the situation. I believe the former Chairman of the Board believed she was supporting the best decision. She simply defined the best candidate by whether or not she knew the family. But, when the definition of "best" doesn't line up, the responsible thing to do is gather more data. The best approach is to simply say with respect, you need to review more information or more data so that you can make an informed decision (Stay in Adult Mode, which is what I did).

Staying in the Adult Mode of Communication forced the former Chairman of The Board to attempt to apply peer pressure. She passive-aggressively invoked her own empathy for the candidate onto the rest of the Board by stating, "We like him best, BECAUSE I have known his family for years."

Remember, her voice is the only voice I had heard all evening. The other Board members — either out of respect, fear of conflict, or complacency — simply did not speak out. The more facts I presented, the more she attempted to bully me and the process. Bullying (physically and mentally) is the primary tactic of peer pressure. **Peer pressure** is always *an attempt to create a shortcut in your decision-making process by forcing you to comply and not to think.*

In today's information-saturated world, we all actively seek shortcuts, and when we find one that works *most of the time*, we simply no longer feel the need to think hard about the issue. **And when you don't have to think, you don't think.** The other Board members had allowed the former Chairman of the Board to think for the Board for a long time. They were willing to continue to follow her lead without thinking.

Back to the story. I started gathering up my materials. All the while asking God to help me respond in the manner that He would have me respond. I paused for a moment from gathering up my materials. (My SALT Shaker was almost empty.) I needed to find a way to engage each individual Board member and help them understand they were responsible for their own decisions. I looked up from gathering my materials and asked, "Do each of you believe you can defend your choice to the stakeholder groups?" There was a resounding "Yes!" from the former Chairman of The Board! She was still the only voice I had heard all night!

I said, "Fantastic! Before you leave tonight, you might want to select the person or group of people you choose to respond to the newspaper tomorrow. I plan to share my data and summary reports I shared with you at the beginning of the meeting with the newspaper in the morning. I am sure they will be interested in your justification." Then, I started walking toward the door with all my reports in my hands.

The current Chairman of the Board stopped me at the door and said, "I don't believe you can do that." I reminded him of the Board's agreement to make the *Selection Decision* primarily based on the objective data gathered from the selection process. I further explained that I owned the data that I had collected. I explained that the Board was reneging on their agreement to follow the process even though the whole community knew and was excited about the selection process I had put in place to hire this Middle School Principal. I further explained that my process and my software clearly identified the most qualified candidate for the position and they were choosing to ignore the data and make a choice for the community based on the former Chairman of The Board knowing the family of their chosen candidate. I explained that what was really happening was the former Chairman of The Board was attempting to make the community believe that my process had identified her candidate as the #1 candidate based on his qualifications, which was a lie. I then explained that the only way I knew to hold them **all** accountable for their decision was to list each Board member's name and to make the data public. I further explained that if the Board members were really comfortable with their decision they should each have no problem articulating the reasons for their decision to the public.

Suddenly, a Board member stood up and said, "Billy, I'm not comfortable with candidate #5. I want it known that I choose #1. I believe #1 is the most qualified. But, for years, we have made decisions based on the former Chairman of the Board's relationship with the candidate. I personally believe we will make a better decision if we make our selection based on the qualifications of each candidate, and the candidate with the best qualifications appears to be #1. Honestly, I simply didn't want to cause any conflict. But you have made me realize that I am responsible for my own recommendation. I believe this decision is so important, I want my opinion to be heard even if it causes conflict."

I responded quickly and said, "If we can simply have an open discussion with all Board members participating, there will be no reason for me to go to the press! I have confidence this group can make the best decision for the school."

Finally the room was filled with voices. Energy and excitement exploded in the room. We finally had a real discussion about all of the candidates. I went to the chalk board and we listed the strengths and weaknesses of each candidate. After thoroughly reviewing all the information and data gathered, the Board (as a whole) came to the conclusion that candidate #1 was the most qualified. When the votes were counted 17 of the 20 Board members recommended candidate #1 be offered the position because of the overwhelming evidence that he was the most qualified candidate.

We finally made the offer to the #1 candidate at 1:30 a.m. He accepted the position immediately. He said that he and his wife had been praying about his decision and agreed that if he was offered the position he would accept it. He served diligently and competently as the middle school principal for several years until he suddenly had a heart attack and passed away. At his funeral, one after another the representatives from all five of the stakeholder groups testified that he had been the best principal the school had ever had! At that moment, I sat there with tears of joy in my eyes. Tears, because I was going to miss him. Hope, because I know I will see him again. And joy, because I could see the evidence that I had taught others to SALT Their Thoughts.

Very often when we make decisions — whether they are big ones or small ones — we don't always use the relevant information available to us. Instead, we choose to use a single piece of evidence for which we have a lot of confidence and allow that single piece of evidence to blind our judgment.

A Single Piece of Good Evidence

In his book *Influence: The Psychology of Persuasion*, Robert B. Cialdini quotes from a study done by animal behaviorist M. W. Fox in 1974 where Fox shares the story of how caring turkey mothers are for their young. They spend most of their time tending, cleaning, warming, huddling, loving, watching, and protecting their young beneath their wings. But there is something odd about their method. Virtually all of this "mothering" is triggered by a "single piece of evidence," which is the "cheep-cheep" sound of young turkey chicks. The turkey ignores other identifying features of the chicks, like smell, touch, or even appearance, in the mothering process. If a chick makes the "cheep-cheep" sound, its mother will care for it. If the chick does not make the "cheep-cheep" sound, the mother will ignore or sometimes even kill the chick.[27]

The extreme reliance of maternal turkeys upon this one sound was dramatically illustrated by Fox in his description of an experiment involving a mother turkey and a stuffed polecat. For a mother turkey, a polecat is a natural and hated enemy. When a turkey mother sees a polecat, it immediately becomes enraged and begins to squawk, peck, and claw. In fact, the experimenters found that even a stuffed model of a polecat, drawn by a string toward a mother turkey, received an immediate and furious attack. However, when a small recorder was placed inside the same stuffed polecat, and that recorder played the "cheep-cheep" sound of the young turkey chick, the mother not only accepted the oncoming polecat but gathered it under her wings. When the recording was turned off, the stuffed polecat again drew the vicious attack.

Ethologists (those who study animals in their natural settings) tell us that this sort of thing is far from unique to the turkey. This blindly mechanical response to a single trigger happens in a wide variety of species, including humans. It is called a "fixed-action pattern." They can involve intricate sequences of behavior. The fundamental characteristic of these patterns is that the behaviors that compose them occur in virtually the same fashion and in the same order every time. These patterns appear to be embedded in the scripts or habits of the animals.

Before you enjoy how easy it is to fool an animal that can be tricked into a fixed action pattern, you need to realize two things. First, the automatic, fixed-action patterns of these animals work very well most of the time. For example, it makes sense for mother turkeys to respond maternally to that single "cheep-cheep" sound. By reacting to that single stimulus, the average mother turkey will nearly always behave correctly. My point here is that fixed-action patterns in and of themselves are not bad. They are simply *a shortcut to eliminate the need to think*. Most of the time, the shortcut works fine. **The problem arises when someone or something exploits the shortcut.**

The second important thing to understand is that you too have your preprogrammed scripts or habits. They may usually work to your advantage, but the trigger that activates them can be used to stimulate you into using the script or habit at the wrong time.

In an experiment conducted by Harvard social psychologist Ellan Langer, it was found that if you ask someone to do you a favor, you will be more successful if you provide a reason. People simply need to have a reason for what they do. Langer demonstrated this fact by asking a small favor of people waiting in line to use a library copy machine: "Excuse me, I have five pages. May I use the Xerox machine because I'm in a rush?" The effectiveness of the request-plus-reason method was almost total: 94% of those asked allowed her to skip ahead of them in line. Compare this success rate to the results when she made the request only: "Excuse me, I have five pages. May I use the Xerox machine?" Under those circumstances, only 60% of those asked complied with the request. It appears that the crucial difference between the two requests was the additional information provided by the words "because I'm in a rush." But a third type of request tried by Langer showed that this was not the case. It seems that it was not the whole series of words, but the first one, "because," that made the difference. Instead of including a real reason for compliance, Langer's third type of request used the word "because" and then, adding nothing new, merely stated the obvious: "Excuse me, I have five pages. May I use the Xerox machine because I have to make some copies?" Even though no real reason was provided, 93% agreed to let her skip ahead of them.

The "cheep-cheep" sound of the turkey chicks triggered an automatic mothering response (which is a fixed-action pattern) from maternal turkeys. The word "because" triggered an automatic compliance response (which is a fixed-action pattern) from Langer's subjects, even when they were given no subsequent reason to comply. Just hearing the word "because" was enough of a reason to comply. Doesn't this sound familiar? The former chairman of the board said, "We like him best BECAUSE I have known his family for years." "Knowing" his family had nothing to do with his qualifications for the job. But the BECAUSE triggered a fix-action response for the rest of the board members.

Triggers of Influence

Professional marketers are paid large sums of money to identify and exploit "fixed-action patterns." These professional marketers are measured and compensated based on their ability to influence you, the buyer. The desired outcome for these marketers is to influence you to make purchases without thinking.

I share this information in the last chapter of this book to increase your awareness and provide you with further evidence of why it is crucial to SALT Your Thoughts. You are more likely to be triggered into a fixed-action pattern response when you lack the time, energy, or cognitive resources to analyze the situation thoroughly. Factors such as being rushed, stressed, uncertain, indifferent, distracted, or fatigued can cause you to focus on less available information. Unfortunately, many of us experience these conditions on a daily basis. Making decisions under these circumstances often leads to a reliance on a primitive "single-piece-of-good-evidence" approach, similar to the behavior of turkeys.

According to Cialdini, the following six items are social norms that may appear to be a single piece of good evidence but can actually adversely influence your choices or decisions if you don't take the time to SALT Your Thoughts:

1. **Consistency:** The principle of consistency states that there is an obsessive desire to be consistent with what you have already done. Once you have made a choice or taken a stand, there are personal and interpersonal pressures that push you to behave consistently with that commitment. Consistency is associated with personal and intellectual strength, logic, rationality, stability, and honesty. It becomes a powerful motivator, allowing you to avoid thinking too hard about an issue you have already decided on. Guard yourself when consistency is used as a reason not to think!

2. **Reciprocation:** The principle of reciprocation suggests that you should repay, in kind, what another person has provided you. In human culture, there is significant social pressure surrounding the process of gift-giving. This obligation to receive reduces your ability to choose whom you want to be indebted to and gives that power to others. Uninvited gifts can create feelings of obligation, which can be used as a weapon against you. Remember, nothing is truly "free." Guard yourself when Reciprocity is used as a reason not to think!

3. **Social Proof:** The principle of social proof states that the more people who find an idea correct, the more it will be perceived as correct. Social proof leads you to believe that if many people are doing something, it must be the right thing to do. Hearing that a product is the "fastest growing" or "largest selling" can sometimes influence your decision more than the actual quality of the product. In times of uncertainty, it is natural to look at the actions of others for guidance. For example, at a formal dining event with an overwhelming number of forks at your place setting, you might observe and imitate the person next to you. I hope you have better luck than I did. I found out later that the person I was sitting next to didn't know which fork to use first either! Guard yourself when social proof is used as a reason not to think!

4. **Authority:** The principle of authority suggests that there is a deep-seated sense of duty to authority. From birth, we are taught that obedience to proper authority is right, while disobedience is wrong. Information from a true authority

figure can provide you with a valuable shortcut in decision-making. In fact, the appearance of authority alone can be influential. In today's information-saturated world, you actively seek shortcuts, and when you find one that works most of the time, you no longer feel the need to think hard about the issue. And when you don't have to think, you don't. Guard yourself when authority is used as a reason not to think!

5. **Liking:** The principle of liking states that you prefer to say yes to someone you know and like. Factors such as physical attractiveness, similarity, and compliments increase the likability of a product or service. Research shows that people automatically assign favorable traits to good-looking individuals, leading to more positive attitudes toward them. People also tend to trust those they perceive as similar to themselves in terms of opinions, personality traits, backgrounds, or lifestyle. This characteristic provides various tools to reduce your desire to think. Guard yourself when liking is used as a reason not to think!

6. **Scarcity:** The principle of scarcity states that opportunities become more valuable or desirable when their availability is limited. The idea of potential loss plays a significant role in human decision-making. When our freedom to have something is limited or when an item becomes less available, we experience an increased desire for it. In fact, if an item transitions from abundance to scarcity, it increases its perceived value even more than if it had always been scarce. The toilet paper shortage during the COVID-19 epidemic in 2020 is a prime example of this phenomenon. Guard yourself when scarcity is used as a reason not to think!

Don't Forget To Think!

Anytime you allow a single trigger to stimulate your decision, you are at risk of being "fooled." As I mentioned earlier, you are more likely to be triggered into a fixed-action pattern response when you lack the time, energy, or cognitive resources to thoroughly analyze the situation. **The real battle takes place in your mind!**

You live in a complex, fast-paced, and information-laden environment where you must take control. It is essential to choose to place a reset button between stimulus and response! Utilize your Self-Awareness, Imagination, Conscience, and Independent Will to clearly communicate to your subconscious mind what you desire to think, feel, be, need, and do!

The knowledge of the solution is simple — the execution of the solution is what is difficult!

My Personal Note To You

One of my greatest personal desires is to have a positive influence on the lives of my family and others. I truly desire to be an effective person. But I struggle personally to stay focused. I like starting projects more than I like finishing them! I am not perfect. But the struggles we each face simply means we are alive! I am convinced the best way to live is to see each obstacle as a stepping stone. And each time we step over that obstacle, we gain power over the negative forces of this world that are trying to keep us separated from what is GOOD. Each time we leave the past behind us, we empower ourselves toward a victorious life. I believe with all of my heart that when you choose to SALT Your Thoughts you will become a more effective person. This new movement is changing lives! Together we can change the world!

My desired results for you reading this book are to:

1. Teach you to SALT Your Thoughts.

2. Teach you the natural cognitive sequence that starts with a *thought* and results in *behavior*.

3. Teach you to be intentional about your thoughts.

4. Help you become more effective by harnessing the power of your thoughts.

5. Provide you SaltYourThoughts.com to enable you to execute your Morning SALT Ritual every day.

6. Teach you how to push the Reset Button.

7. Help you in developing your Habit of Gratitude.

8. Teach you that Joy is a choice.

9. Help you identify your Positive Mood Triggers.

10. Teach you that Like Attracts Like.

11. Help you identify your Beliefs.

12. Teach you the four Human Attributes.

13. Help you intentionally engage your Reticular Activation System.

14. Help you identify your Attitudes and Personal Values.

15. Help you identify your Needs.

16. Help you to align your Behaviors with your Thoughts.

17. Teach you the power of Visualization.

18. Point you to and connect you to the only true source of energy in the universe: the Creator God.

19. Teach you that the only source of "good" in the universe is God!

20. Teach you the Seven Principles of the Farm.

21. Teach you that what matters most is how you *respond* to what you experience in life.

22. Help you define what success is to you.

23. Help you identify your 4-Letter MBTI Type and Temperament.

24. Help you understand yourself and others better.

25. Help you be a better communicator.

26. Teach you how to Visualize.

27. Teach you that what gets measured gets done.

28. Teach you that anything you measure will improve.

29. Help you become more effective by harnessing the power of your thoughts.

30. Teach you the secret for living a Productive, Effective, and Fulfilled Life.

When I say "SALT Your Thoughts," I am suggesting that you *preserve, enhance,* and *intensify* your thoughts. Salt can intensify the sweetness and minimize the bitterness of your thoughts. I am convinced that if you utilize the **S**ystem to **A**lter your **L**ife **T**houghts (SALT), you will indeed live a much more effective, productive, fruitful, and fulfilled life. I hope SALT will positively influence you for the rest of your life!

The Source of All Energy and Life

The Creator God of this universe, the source of all energy and life, longs for you to desire to connect your thoughts to Him. He is waiting for you. If you ask, He will help you control your thoughts and align them with Him. Not only will you be more effective, productive, fruitful, and fulfilled, but you will have peace!

Ask For Help

"Ask, and it will be given to you; seek, and you will find; knock, and it will be opened to you." - Matthew 7:7

"If you ask anything in My name, I will do it." - John 14:14

"Therefore I say to you, whatever things you ask when you pray, believe that you receive them, and you will have them." - Mark 11:24

All My Best,
Billy

P.S. Matthew 5:13 says, "You are the salt of the earth..."

Now, GO MAKE IT HAPPEN!

Assignments By Chapter

Chapter 1

1. WORLDVIEW – PART 1 – ORIGINS
2. WORLDVIEW – PART 2 – THE NATURE OF MAN
3. WORLDVIEW – PART 3 – THE NATURE OF THE EARTH
4. WORLDVIEW – PART 4 – TRUTH
5. WORLDVIEW – PART 5 – HOPE
6. WORLDVIEW – PART 6 – WHAT IF?

Chapter 2

7. THE RETICULAR ACTIVATION SYSTEM
8. LIFE TOOL #1 – THE SEVEN PRINCIPLES OF THE FARM

Chapter 3

9. LOCUS OF CONTROL

Chapter 4

10. THE RETICULAR ACTIVATION SYSTEM
11. LIFE TOOL #2 – SALT: THE NATURAL COGNITIVE SEQUENCE

Chapter 5

12. WHAT DOES YOUR TONGUE TALK ABOUT?

Chapter 6

13. THE RETICULAR ACTIVATION SYSTEM

Chapter 7

14. HABITS OF YOUR MIND – 1 – YOUR BELIEFS
15. HABITS OF YOUR MIND – 2 – BELIEFS ABOUT YOUR ATTITUDES
16. HABITS OF YOUR MIND – 3 – BELIEFS ABOUT YOUR NEEDS
17. HABITS OF YOUR MIND – 4 – BELIEFS ABOUT YOUR ACTIONS

Chapter 8

18. LIFE TOOL #3 – YOUR LIFE'S TIMELINE

Chapter 9

19. YOUR GRATITUDE LIST

Chapter 10

20. WHAT IS JOY TO YOU?

Chapter 11

21. WHAT ARE YOUR POSITIVE MOOD TRIGGERS?

Chapter 12

22. LIFE TOOL #4 – YOUR ROLES & GOALS

Chapter 13

23. THE SALT TYPE INDICATOR

Chapter 14

24. PERSONAL VALUES I MOVE TOWARD
25. CHARACTER TRAITS I MOVE AWAY FROM

Chapter 15

26. CORE NEEDS/MOTIVATORS

Chapter 16

27. LIFE TOOL #5 – PUSH THE RESET BUTTON

Chapter 17

28. HOW DO YOU DEFINE SUCCESS – PART 1: CHARACTER TRAITS?
29. HOW DO YOU DEFINE SUCCESS – PART 2: YOUR FAMILY?
30. HOW DO YOU DEFINE SUCCESS – PART 3: YOUR WORK?
31. HOW DO YOU DEFINE SUCCESS – PART 4: YOUR NEEDS?
32. HOW DO YOU DEFINE SUCCESS – PART 5: AS A SPOUSE?
33. HOW DO YOU DEFINE SUCCESS – PART 6: AS A PARENT?
34. HOW DO YOU DEFINE SUCCESS – PART 7: HEALTH?
35. HOW DO YOU DEFINE SUCCESS – PART 8: AS A FRIEND?
36. HOW DO YOU DEFINE SUCCESS – PART 9: YOUR LEGACY?

Chapter 18

37. WRITING MY OWN PERSONAL MISSION STATEMENT – THOUGHT HABITS
38. WRITING MY OWN PERSONAL MISSION STATEMENT – CORE BELIEFS
39. WRITING MY OWN PERSONAL MISSION STATEMENT – CORE VALUES
40. WRITING MY OWN PERSONAL MISSION STATEMENT – CORE NEEDS
41. WRITING MY OWN PERSONAL MISSION STATEMENT – CORE BEHAVIORS
42. DRAFT OF MY PERSONAL MISSION STATEMENT

Chapter 19

43. LIFE TOOL #6 – THE HABIT OF VISUALIZATION

Chapter 20

44. LIFE TOOL #7 – DOES IT REALLY MATTER?

Chapter 21

45. LIFE TOOL #8 – YOUR VISION BOARD

Chapter 22

46. LIFE TOOL #9 – PLANNING YOUR WEEK

Chapter 23

47. LIFE TOOL #10 – 8 EASY STEPS TO SALT YOUR THOUGHTS

Chapter 24

48. THE RETICULAR ACTIVATION SYSTEM

Chapter 25

49. LOCUS OF CONTROL

Chapter 26

50. CONSCIENTIOUSNESS

Chapter 27

51. MEASURING YOUR MODE OF COMMUNICATION

Chapter 28

52. LIFE TOOL #11 – THE 8-STEP PROCESS TO SOLVE PROBLEMS

Chapter 29

53. LIFE ASSIGNMENT – GO MAKE IT HAPPEN!

Billy C. Mullins II is a self-made millionaire raised on a farm in Crossville, Alabama. His first business at the age of 8 was selling watermelons he had grown on the farm on the side of the road. At an early age, Billy became a believer in the Natural Law, "You reap what you sow." When he was only 12 years old, his mother was killed in a car accident, leading him to adopt her belief that God is in control, and, therefore, everything happens for a reason. He made the decision to let go of the past and live for today and tomorrow. He believes that your *thoughts* can transform life's adversities from stumbling blocks to stepping stones — something he has done his whole life.

Billy is an organizational psychologist and a pioneer in selection software development, creating a computer-aided interview that predicted performance and tenure better than humans in the 1990s. His business, Vikus Corporation, became the leader for selection software for the senior care industry from 2013-2017. Through his software and consulting, he has helped hundreds of companies increase applicant flow, evaluate and assess millions of applicants, provide individualized interview guides for face-to-face interviews, and predict both performance and tenure, decreasing his client's new hire turnover by more than 40%. In 2017, Vikus Corporation was sold for eight figures.

Billy is an entrepreneur, software engineer, leader, trainer, influencer, and now author who believes that you become what you think. This book will teach you how to become intentional about your thoughts.

This book and the online platform were born from his desire to help his 15-year-old daughter, Isabella, identify her career path. As he pondered his daughter's future, he became compelled to teach her about human effectiveness and provide her with tools she could use for the rest of her life to stay connected with who she intends to be. He realized he needed to create a System to Alter her Life Thoughts (SALT). So, he did.

SALT Your Thoughts is the secret for Isabella — and YOU — to live a productive, effective, and fulfilled life.

1. William Walker Atkinson. *The Kybalion* (The Yoga Publication Society, 1908), 26-35.

2. Victor Frankl. *Man's Search for Meaning* (Beacon Press, 1946).

3. Stephen Covey. *The 7 Habits of Highly Effective People* (Free Press, 1989), 68-71.

4. Charles F. Haanel. *The Master Key System* (Psychology Publishing, 1916), 10.

5. Ralph Lewis, M.D. "What Actually Is a Thought? And How Is Information Physical?" *Psychology Today*, 24 Feb 2019, https://www.psychologytoday.com/us/blog/finding-purpose/201902/what-actually-is-a-thought-and-how-is-information-physical. Accessed 2023.

6. Rhonda Byrne. *The Secret* (Atri Books/Beyond Words Publishing, 2006), 11.

7. William Walker Atkinson. *The Kybalion* (The Yoga Publication Society, 1908), 30.

8. William Walker Atkinson. *The Kybalion* (The Yoga Publication Society, 1908), 30.

9. William Walker Atkinson. *The Kybalion* (The Yoga Publication Society, 1908), 30.

10. Charles F. Haanel. *The Master Key System* (Psychology Publishing, 1916), 11.

11. Charles F. Haanel. *The Master Key System* (Psychology Publishing, 1916), 11.

12. Charles F. Haanel. *The Master Key System* (Psychology Publishing, 1916), 8.

13. A.H. Eagly and S. Chaiken. "Attitude structure and function." *The Handbook of Social Psychology*, 4th ed. (McGraw-Hill, 1998), 269-322.

14. Abraham Maslow. "A Theory of Human Motivation." *Psychological Review*, no. 50 (1943), 370-396.

15. Charles F. Haanel. *The Master Key System* (Psychology Publishing, 1916), 7.

16. Charles F. Haanel. *The Master Key System* (Psychology Publishing, 1916), 11.

17. Norman Vincent Peale. *The Power of Positive Thinking* (Prentice Hall, 1952).

18. Rhonda Byrne. *The Secret* (Atri Books/Beyond Words Publishing, 2006), 11.

19. Malcolm Gladwell. *Outliers* (Little, Brown and Company, 2008).

20. Viktor Frankl. *Man's Search for Meaning* (Beacon Press, 1946).

21. Charles F. Haanel. *The Master Key System* (Psychology Publishing, 1916), 11.

22. D. Watson and L.A. Clark. "Negative Affectivity: The Disposition to Experience Aversive Emotional States." *Psychological Bulletin*, no. 96(3) (1984), 465-490.

23. D. Watson and J. Pennebaker. "Health Complaints, Stress, and Distress: Exploring the Central Role of Negative Affectivity." *Psychological Review*, no. 96(2) (PubMed 1989), 234-254.

24. Julian B. Rotter. "Generalized Expectancies for Internal Versus External Control of Reinforcement." *Psychological Monographs: General and Applied*, no. 80(1) (1966), 1-28.

25. B.W. Tuckman. "Developmental Sequence in Small Groups." *Psychological Bulletin*, no. 63(6) (1965), 384-399.

26. Eric Berne. *Transactional Analysis in Psychotherapy* (Castle Books, 1961).

27. Robert B. Cialdini. *Influence: The Psychology of Persuasion* (William Morrow and Company, 1984), 2-4.

Made in the USA
Columbia, SC
24 June 2025